Jax Epoch and the Quicken Forbidden

Separation Anxiety

YGN
Rom

Jax Epoch and the Quicken Forbidden: Separation Anxiety

Also available from AiT/Planet Lar:
Jax Epoch and the Quicken Forbidden: Borrowed Magic

Published by Larry Young and Mimi Rosenheim
Originally published by Cryptic Press as *Quicken Forbidden* #'s 6-10

For more information about *Quicken Forbidden* write to:
Cryptic Press
365 Smith Street
Freeport, NY 11520
crypticpress@aol.com
www.quickenforbidden.com

For more information about AiT/Planet Lar write to:
AiT/Planet Lar
2034 47th Avenue
San Francisco, CA 94116
www.ait-planetlar.com

ISBN: 1-932051-24-4

Printed in Canada

DAVE ROMAN
writer

JOHN GREEN
artist

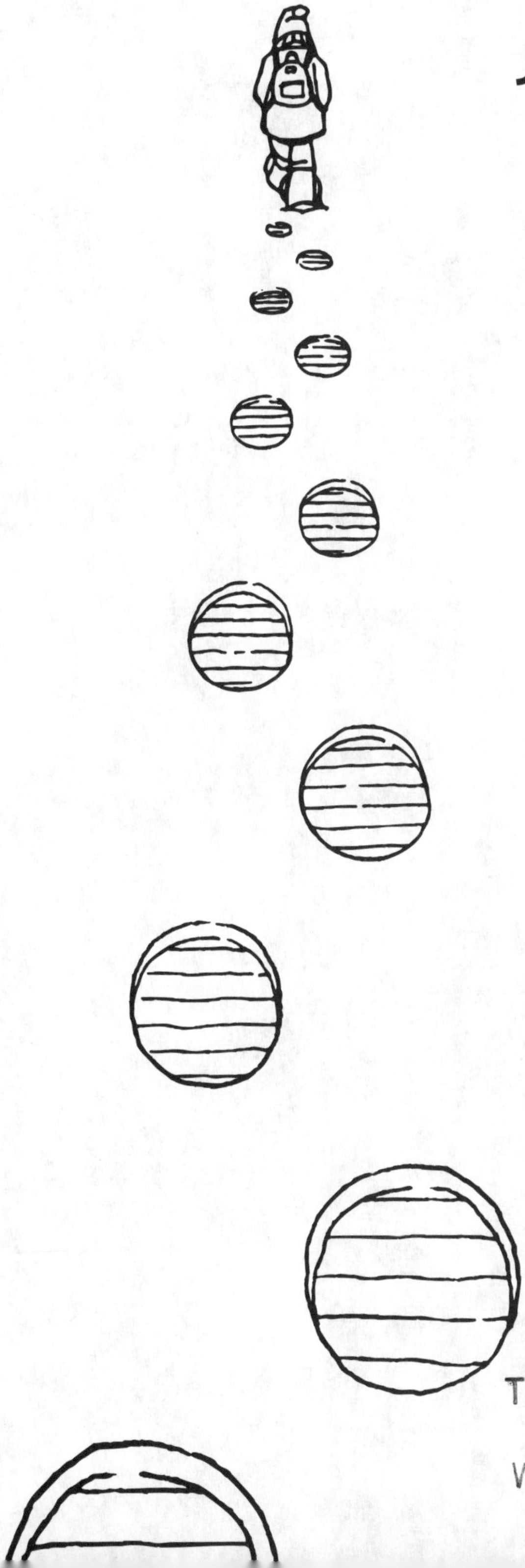

ADAM DEKRAKER
inker
pages 5-24

CHRIS YAMBAR
co-writer
pages 31-33

DAVE ROMAN
dream sequence
pages 71-75

JOHN GREEN
cover, letters and design

TRIAL SEPARATION

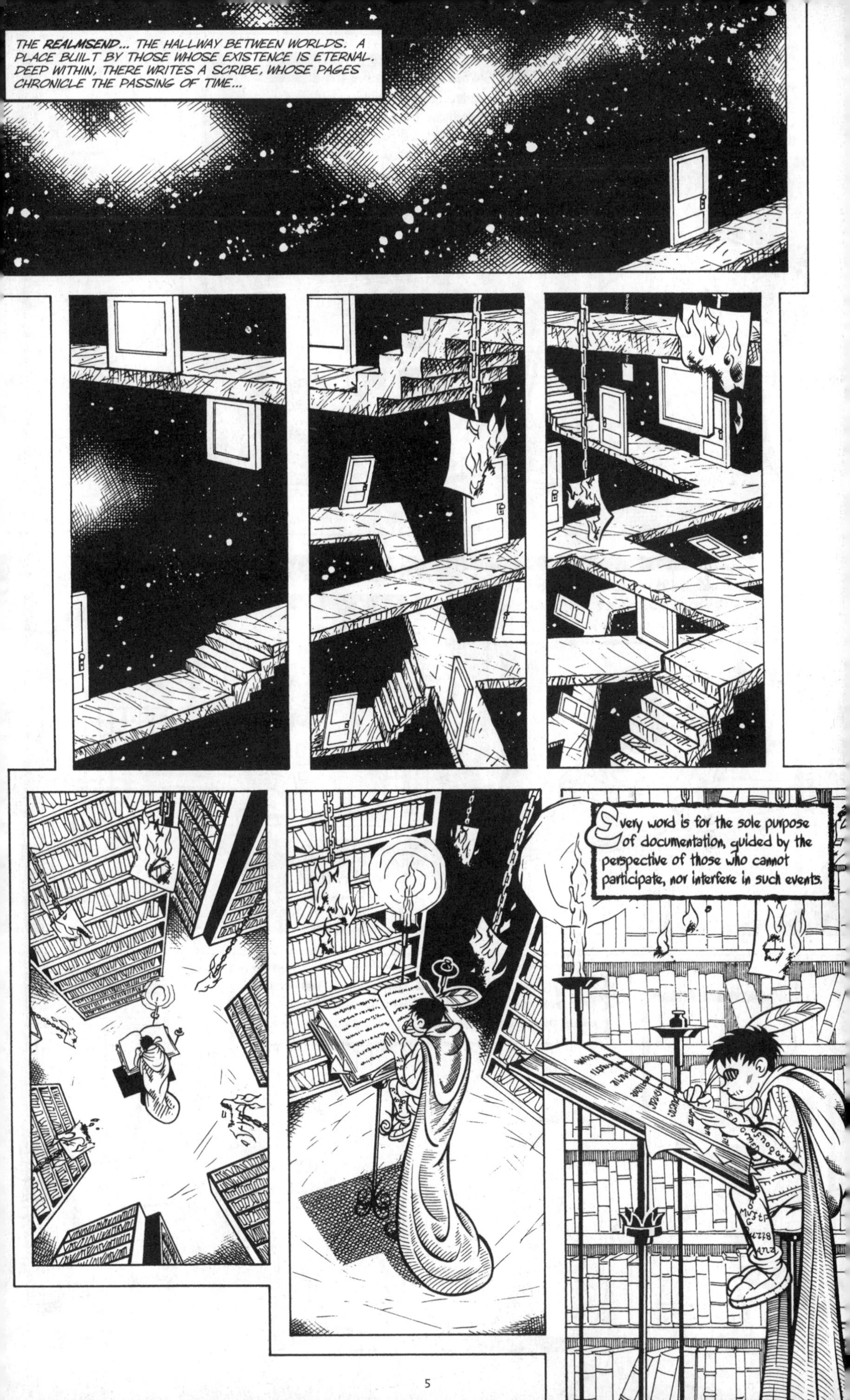
THE REALMSEND... THE HALLWAY BETWEEN WORLDS. A PLACE BUILT BY THOSE WHOSE EXISTENCE IS ETERNAL. DEEP WITHIN, THERE WRITES A SCRIBE, WHOSE PAGES CHRONICLE THE PASSING OF TIME...
Every word is for the sole purpose of documentation, guided by the perspective of those who cannot participate, nor interfere in such events.

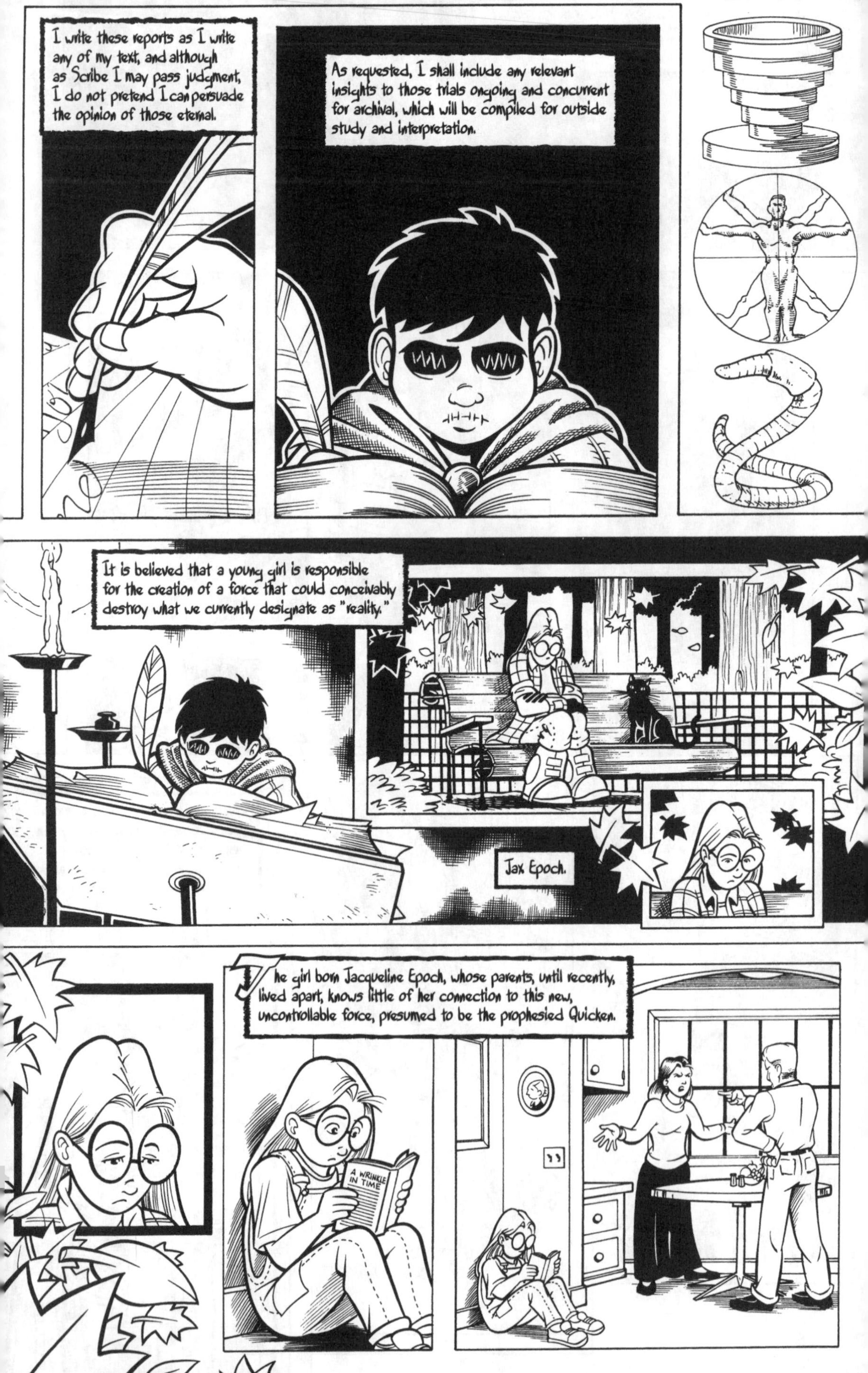
I write these reports as I write any of my text, and although as Scribe I may pass judgment, I do not pretend I can persuade the opinion of those eternal.
As requested, I shall include any relevant insights to those trials ongoing and concurrent for archival, which will be compiled for outside study and interpretation.
It is believed that a young girl is responsible for the creation of a force that could conceivably destroy what we currently designate as "reality."
Jax Epoch.
The girl born Jacqueline Epoch, whose parents, until recently, lived apart, knows little of her connection to this new, uncontrollable force, presumed to be the prophesied Quicken.
A WRINKLE IN TIME

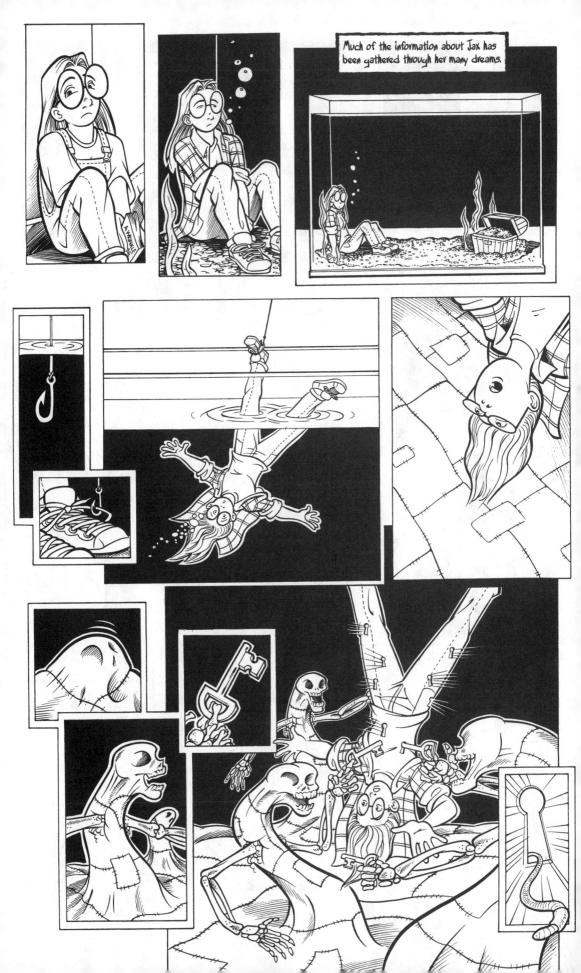

Much of the information about Jax has been gathered through her many dreams.

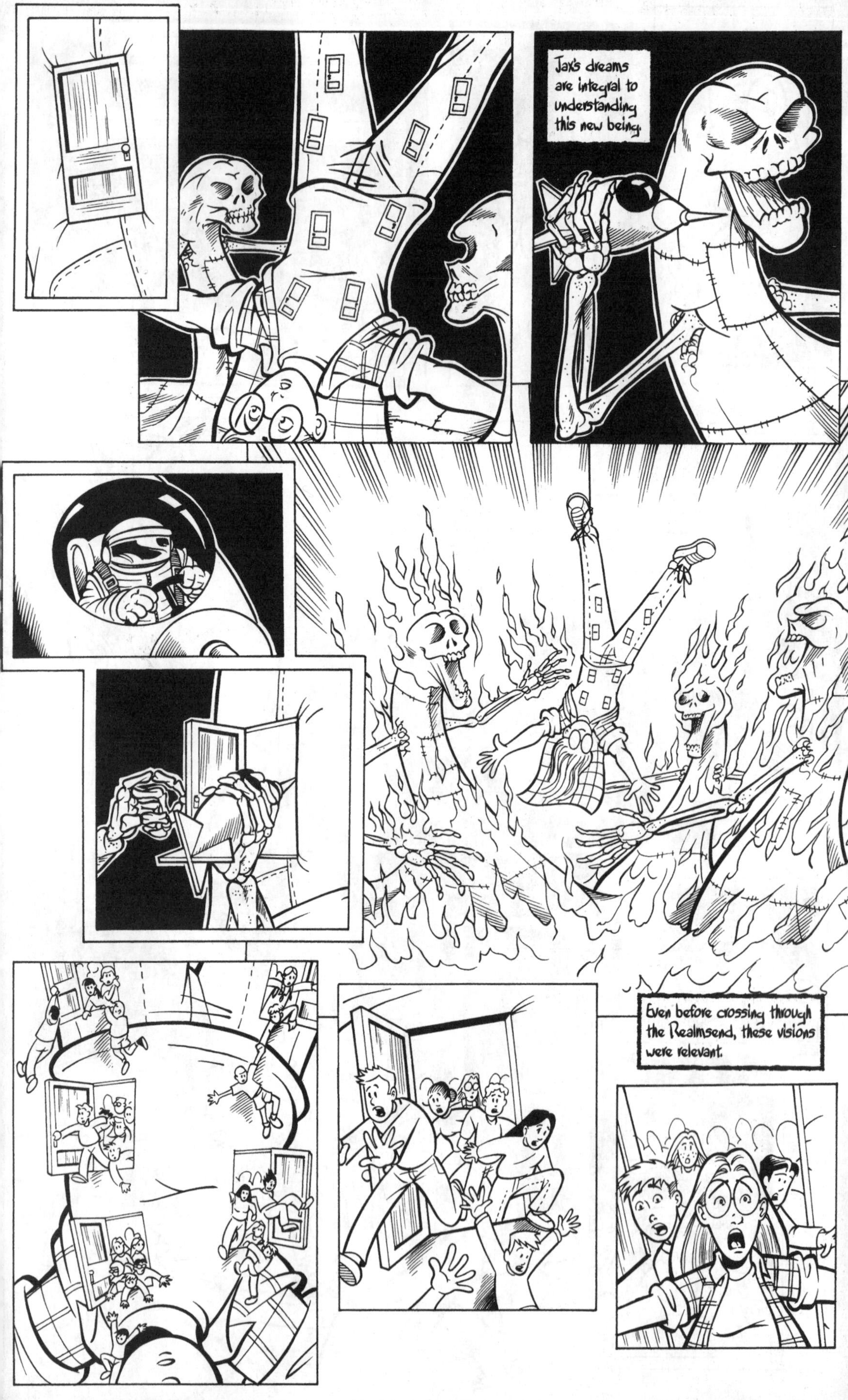
Jax's dreams are integral to understanding this new being.
Even before crossing through the Realmsend, these visions were relevant.

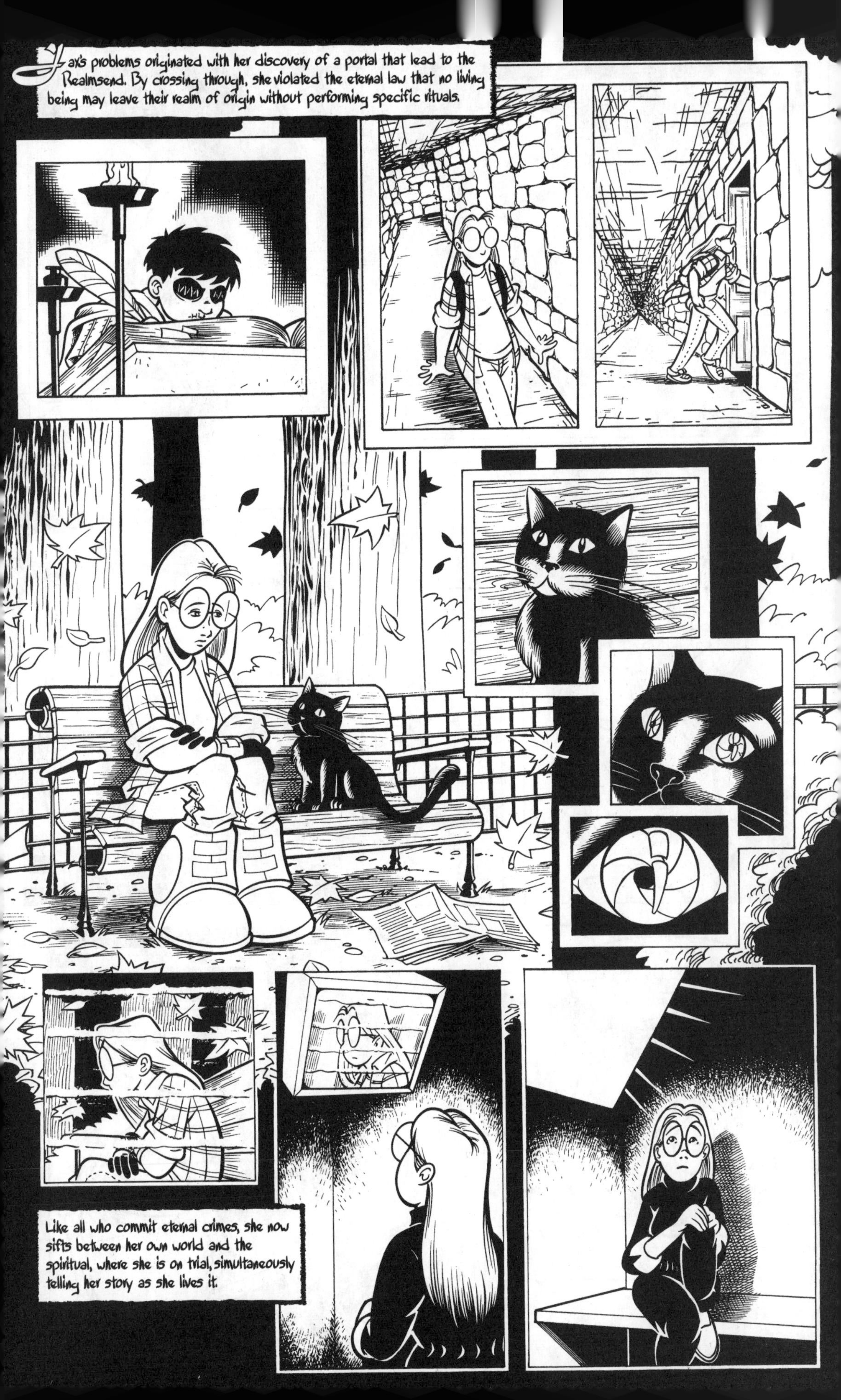
Jax's problems originated with her discovery of a portal that lead to the Realmsend. By crossing through, she violated the eternal law that no living being may leave their realm of origin without performing specific rituals.
Like all who commit eternal crimes, she now sifts between her own world and the spiritual, where she is on trial, simultaneously telling her story as she lives it.

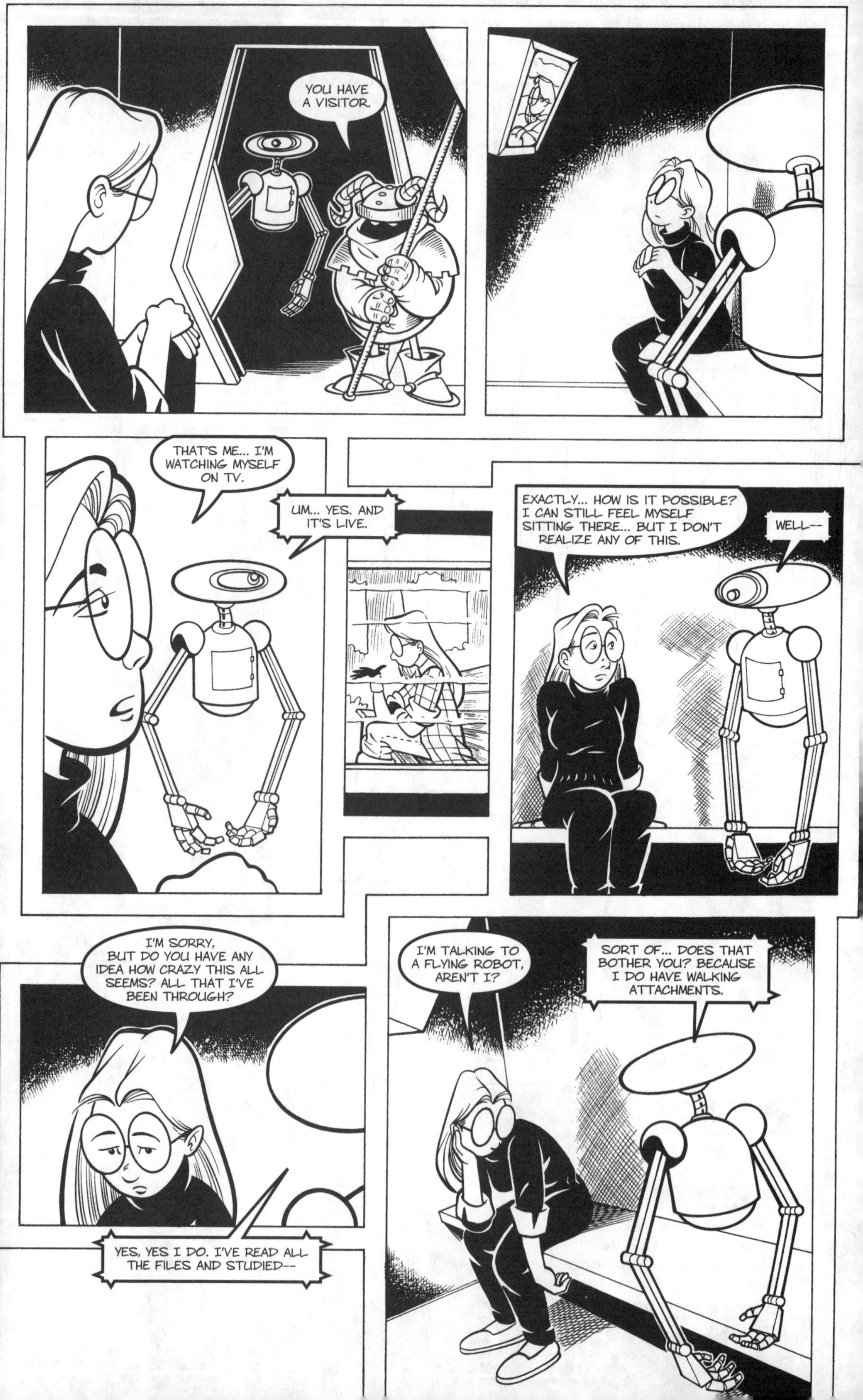
YOU HAVE A VISITOR.
THAT'S ME... I'M WATCHING MYSELF ON TV.
UM... YES. AND IT'S LIVE.
EXACTLY... HOW IS IT POSSIBLE? I CAN STILL FEEL MYSELF SITTING THERE... BUT I DON'T REALIZE ANY OF THIS.
WELL--
I'M SORRY, BUT DO YOU HAVE ANY IDEA HOW CRAZY THIS ALL SEEMS? ALL THAT I'VE BEEN THROUGH?
YES, YES I DO. I'VE READ ALL THE FILES AND STUDIED--
I'M TALKING TO A FLYING ROBOT, AREN'T I?
SORT OF... DOES THAT BOTHER YOU? BECAUSE I DO HAVE WALKING ATTACHMENTS.

UM, YES... VERY WELL, LET'S GET STRAIGHT TO BUSINESS THEN. WE'RE EXPECTED TO REPORT TO THE COURTROOM. DEPOSITIONS WILL BE BEGINNING SHORTLY.

DEPOSITIONS? BUT I STILL HAVEN'T FINISHED GIVING MY RECORD!

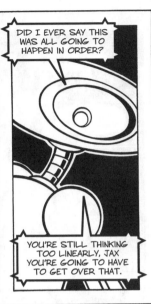

DID I EVER SAY THIS WAS ALL GOING TO HAPPEN IN ORDER?

YOU'RE STILL THINKING TOO LINEARLY, JAX YOU'RE GOING TO HAVE TO GET OVER THAT.

I MEAN... WELL, THAT IS...

...SORRY.

YOUR HONORS, WE INTEND TO PROVE THAT *INARGUABLY*, *UNDENIABLY*, JAX EPOCH IS NOTHING BUT... *GUILTY*.

GUILTY AS CHARGED.

GUILTY BY ASSOCIATION.

GUILTY BY--

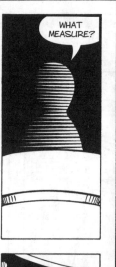

WHAT MEASURE?

WE INTEND TO SHOW THAT *THIS* GIRL...

...STOP TRYING TO LOOK INNOCENT...

...IS RESPONSIBLE FOR...

...THE DESTRUCTION OF...

...THE WORLD!!

WHICH WORLD?

ALL OF THEM!

WHAT?! HOW DOES *THAT* WORK?

THE PROOF IS ALL THERE-- AN OPEN AND SHUT CASE, I ASSURE YOU.

≷SIGH≷

LET'S BEGIN, SHALL WE?

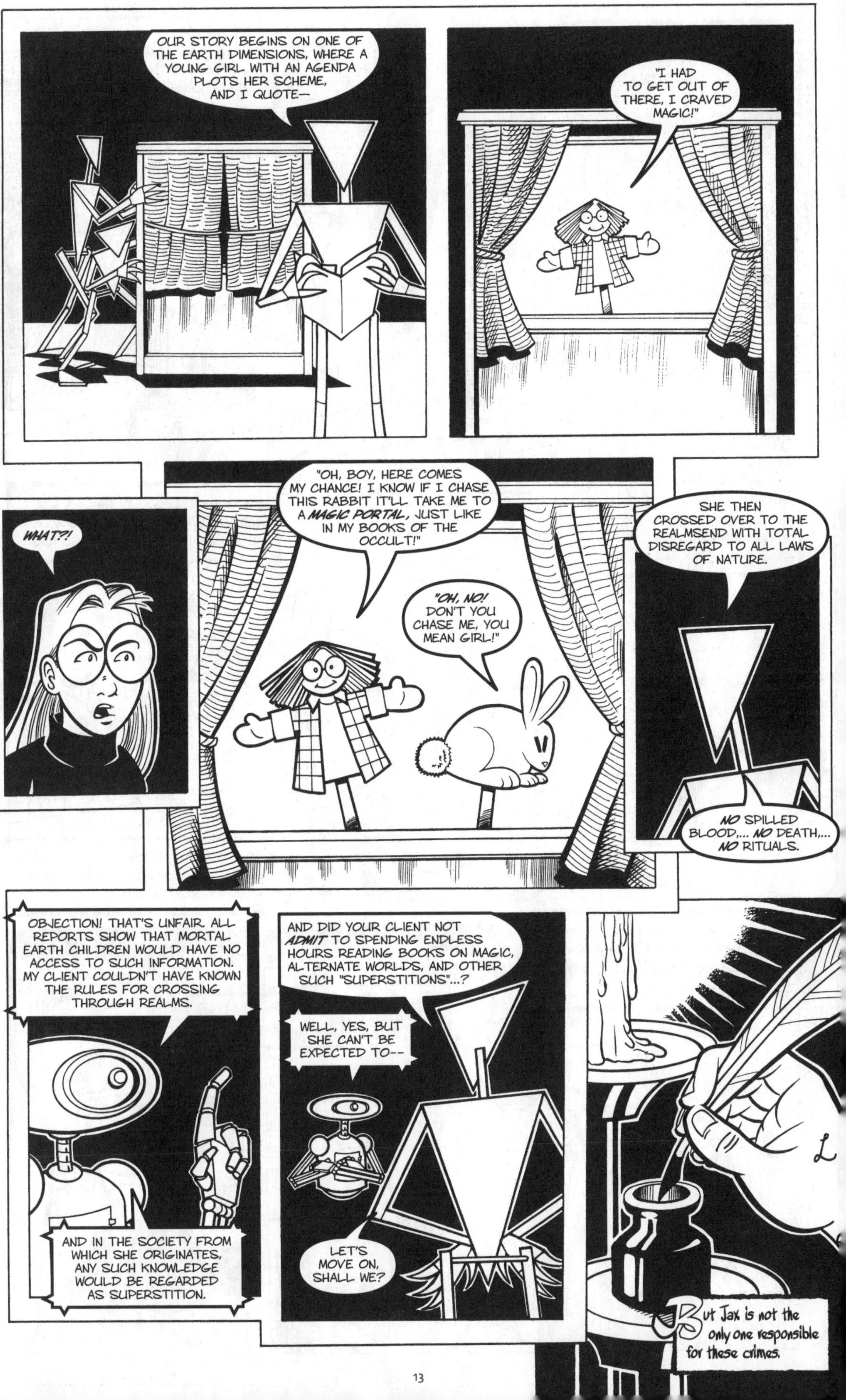

OUR STORY BEGINS ON ONE OF THE EARTH DIMENSIONS, WHERE A YOUNG GIRL WITH AN AGENDA PLOTS HER SCHEME, AND I QUOTE—
"I HAD TO GET OUT OF THERE, I CRAVED MAGIC!"
WHAT?!
"OH, BOY, HERE COMES MY CHANCE! I KNOW IF I CHASE THIS RABBIT IT'LL TAKE ME TO A MAGIC PORTAL, JUST LIKE IN MY BOOKS OF THE OCCULT!"
"OH, NO! DON'T YOU CHASE ME, YOU MEAN GIRL!"
SHE THEN CROSSED OVER TO THE REALMSEND WITH TOTAL DISREGARD TO ALL LAWS OF NATURE.
NO SPILLED BLOOD,... NO DEATH,... NO RITUALS.
OBJECTION! THAT'S UNFAIR. ALL REPORTS SHOW THAT MORTAL EARTH CHILDREN WOULD HAVE NO ACCESS TO SUCH INFORMATION. MY CLIENT COULDN'T HAVE KNOWN THE RULES FOR CROSSING THROUGH REALMS.
AND IN THE SOCIETY FROM WHICH SHE ORIGINATES, ANY SUCH KNOWLEDGE WOULD BE REGARDED AS SUPERSTITION.
AND DID YOUR CLIENT NOT ADMIT TO SPENDING ENDLESS HOURS READING BOOKS ON MAGIC, ALTERNATE WORLDS, AND OTHER SUCH "SUPERSTITIONS"...?
WELL, YES, BUT SHE CAN'T BE EXPECTED TO--
LET'S MOVE ON, SHALL WE?
But Jax is not the only one responsible for these crimes.

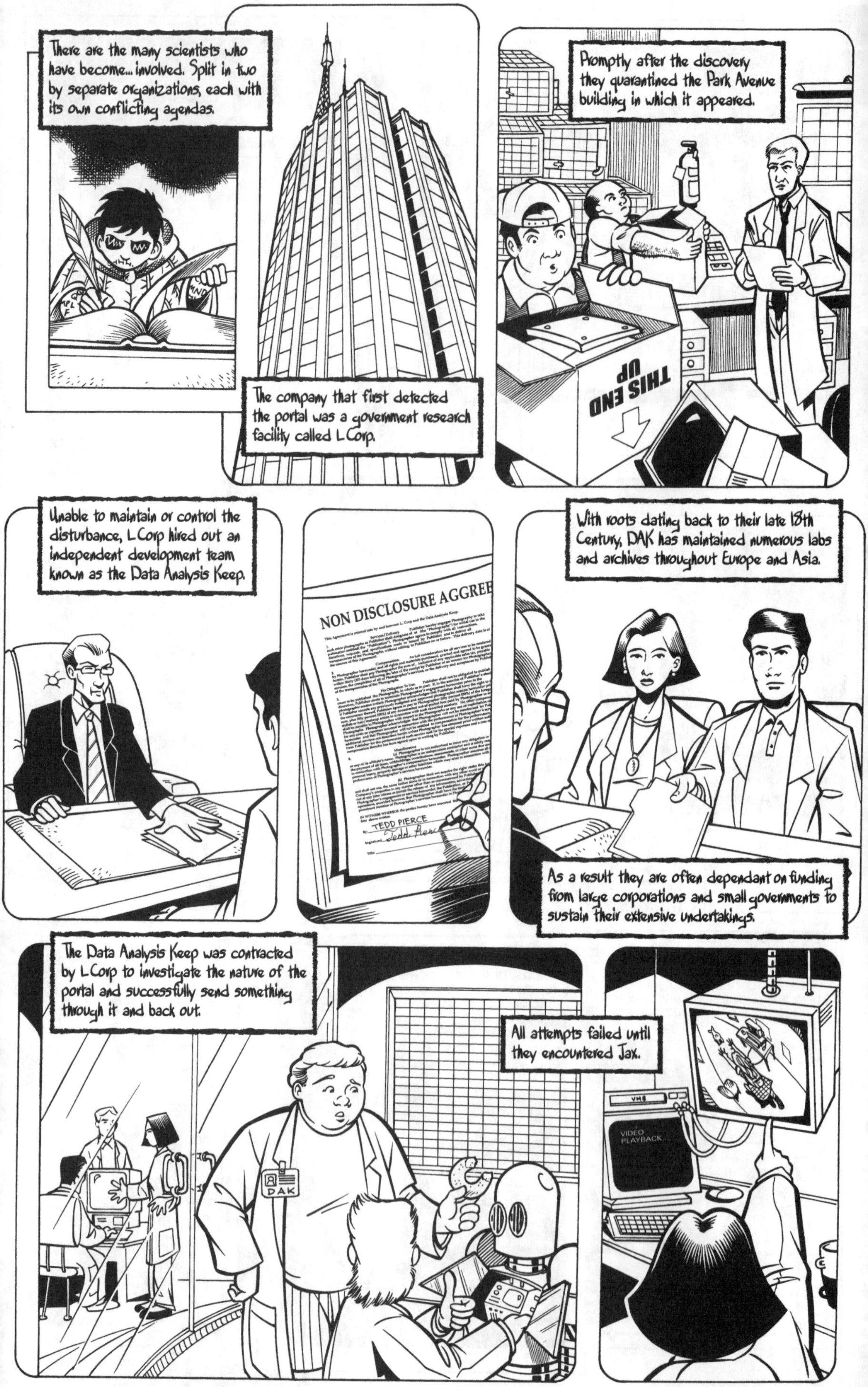
There are the many scientists who have become... involved. Split in two by separate organizations, each with its own conflicting agendas.
The company that first detected the portal was a government research facility called L Corp.
Promptly after the discovery they quarantined the Park Avenue building in which it appeared.
THIS END UP
Unable to maintain or control the disturbance, L Corp hired out an independent development team known as the Data Analysis Keep.
NON DISCLOSURE AGREE
TEDD PIERCE
With roots dating back to their late 18th Century, DAK has maintained numerous labs and archives throughout Europe and Asia.
As a result they are often dependant on funding from large corporations and small governments to sustain their extensive undertakings.
The Data Analysis Keep was contracted by L Corp to investigate the nature of the portal and successfully send something through it and back out.
DAK
All attempts failed until they encountered Jax.
VHS
VIDEO PLAYBACK...

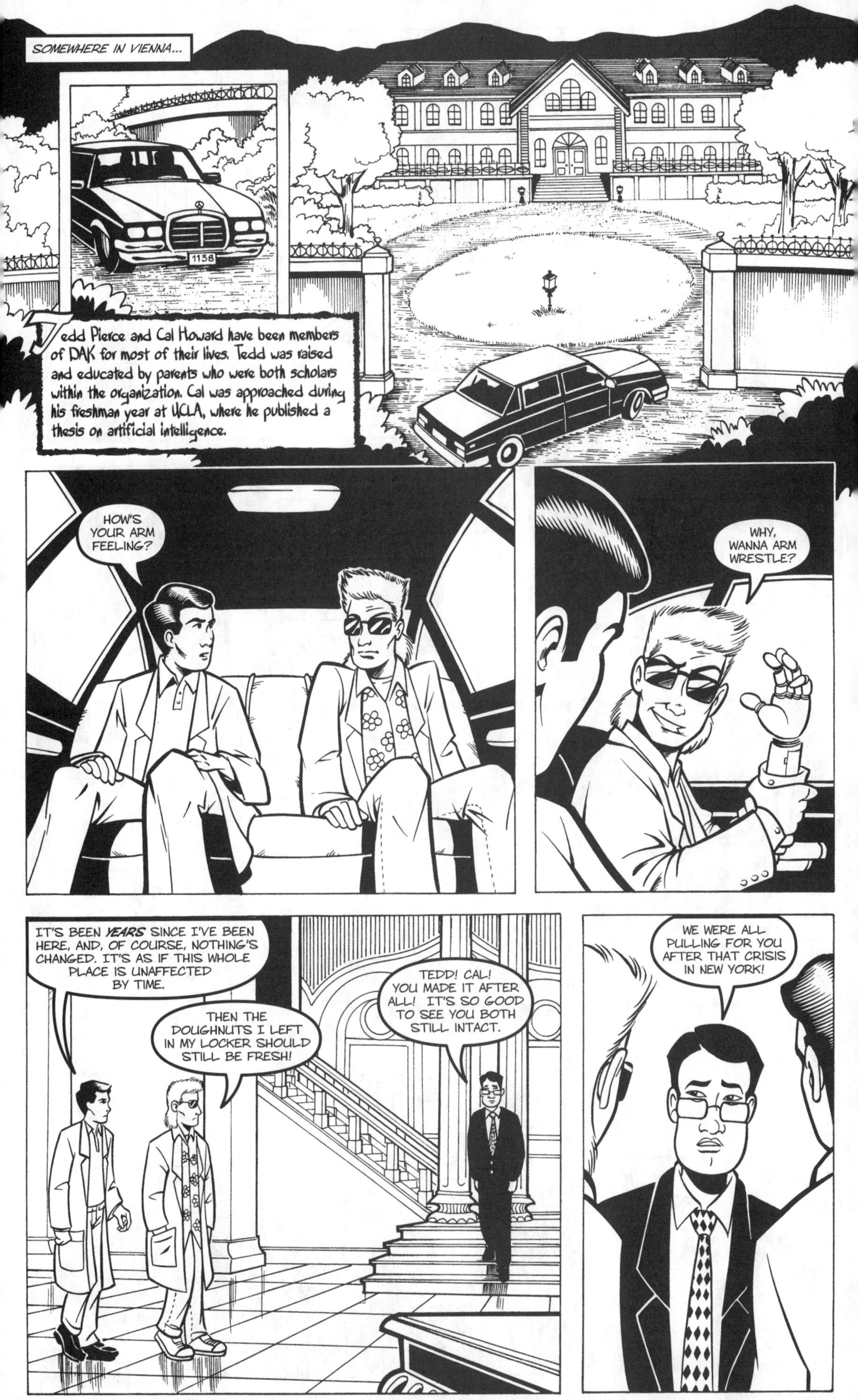

SOMEWHERE IN VIENNA...
1138
Tedd Pierce and Cal Howard have been members of DAK for most of their lives. Tedd was raised and educated by parents who were both scholars within the organization. Cal was approached during his freshman year at UCLA, where he published a thesis on artificial intelligence.
HOW'S YOUR ARM FEELING?
WHY, WANNA ARM WRESTLE?
IT'S BEEN *YEARS* SINCE I'VE BEEN HERE, AND, OF COURSE, NOTHING'S CHANGED. IT'S AS IF THIS WHOLE PLACE IS UNAFFECTED BY TIME.
THEN THE DOUGHNUTS I LEFT IN MY LOCKER SHOULD STILL BE FRESH!
TEDD! CAL! YOU MADE IT AFTER ALL! IT'S SO GOOD TO SEE YOU BOTH STILL INTACT.
WE WERE ALL PULLING FOR YOU AFTER THAT CRISIS IN NEW YORK!

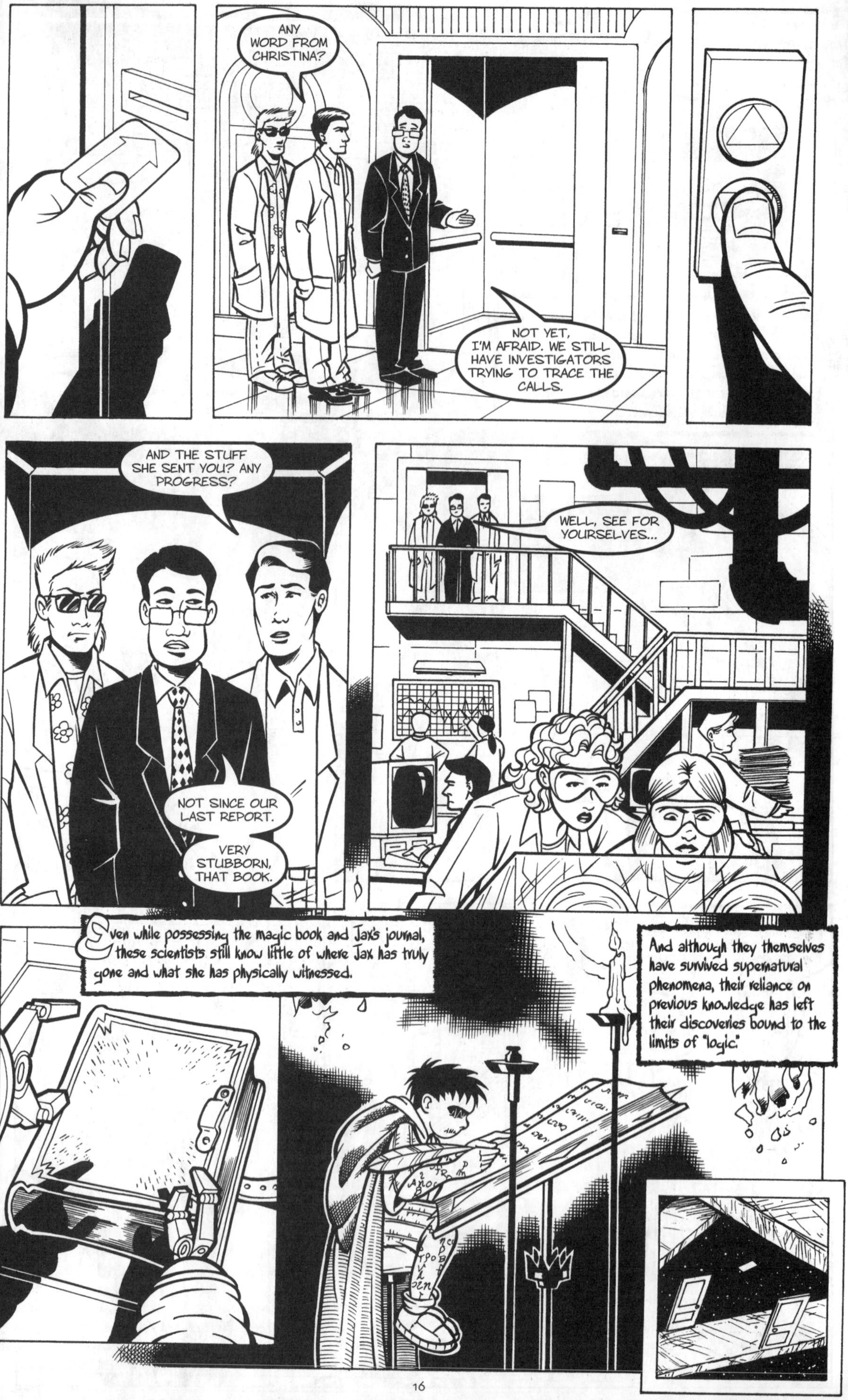
ANY WORD FROM CHRISTINA?
NOT YET, I'M AFRAID. WE STILL HAVE INVESTIGATORS TRYING TO TRACE THE CALLS.
AND THE STUFF SHE SENT YOU? ANY PROGRESS?
NOT SINCE OUR LAST REPORT.
VERY STUBBORN, THAT BOOK.
WELL, SEE FOR YOURSELVES...
Even while possessing the magic book and Jax's journal, these scientists still know little of where Jax has truly gone and what she has physically witnessed.
And although they themselves have survived supernatural phenomena, their reliance on previous knowledge has left their discoveries bound to the limits of "logic."

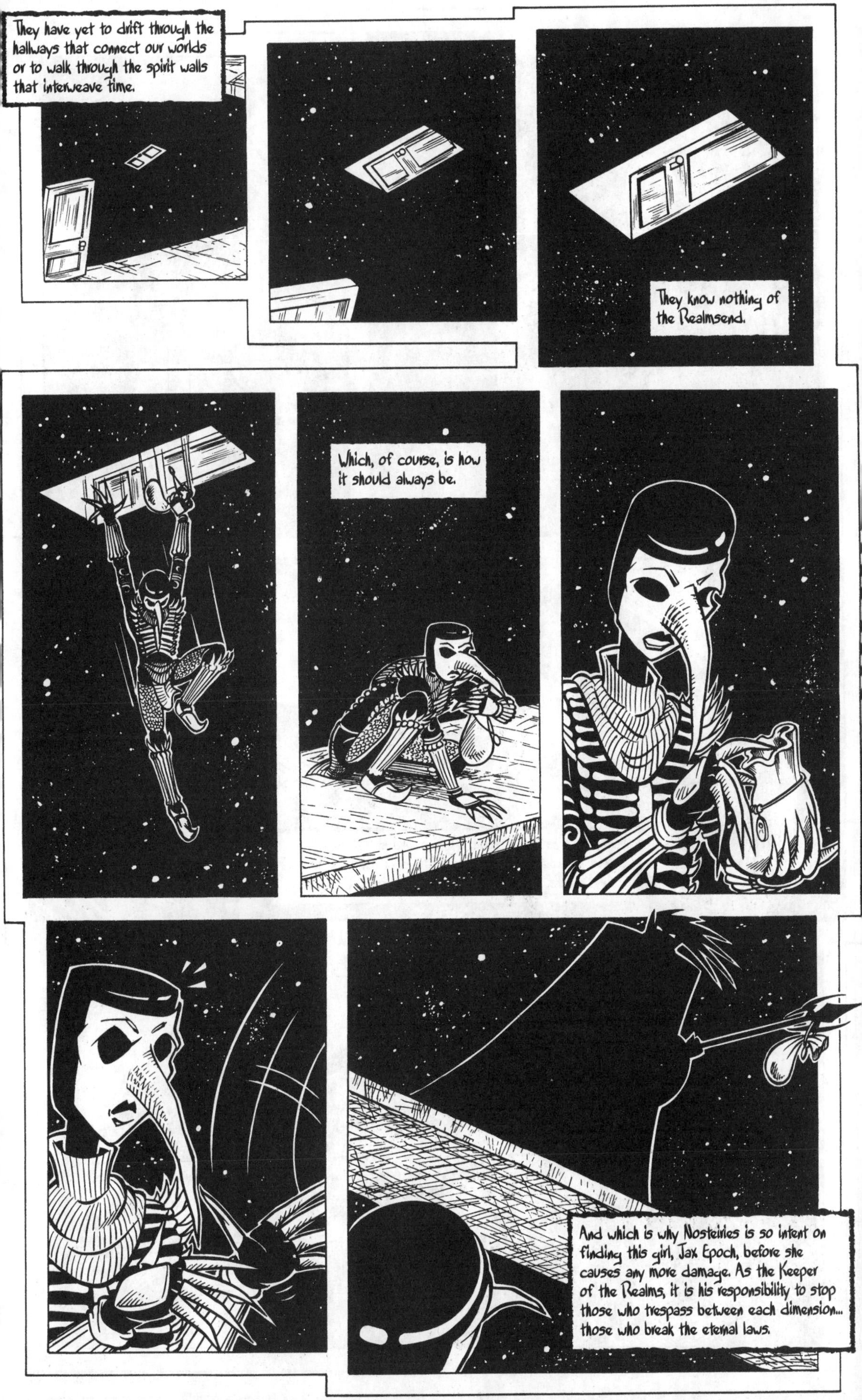
They have yet to drift through the hallways that connect our worlds or to walk through the spirit walls that interweave time.
They know nothing of the Realmsend.
Which, of course, is how it should always be.
And which is why Nosteiries is so intent on finding this girl, Jax Epoch, before she causes any more damage. As the Keeper of the Realms, it is his responsibility to stop those who trespass between each dimension... those who break the eternal laws.

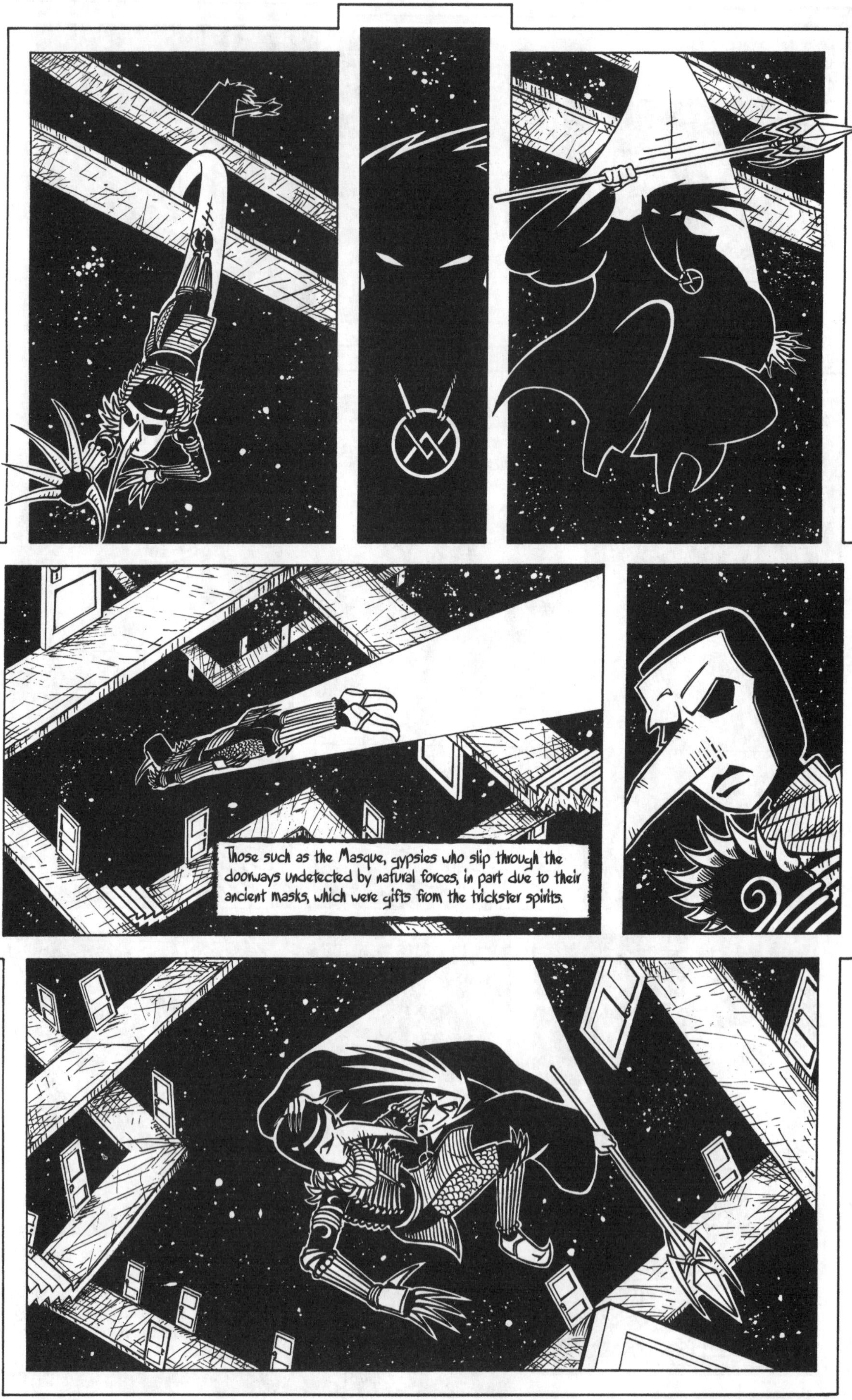
Those such as the Masque, gypsies who slip through the doorways undetected by natural forces, in part due to their ancient masks, which were gifts from the trickster spirits.

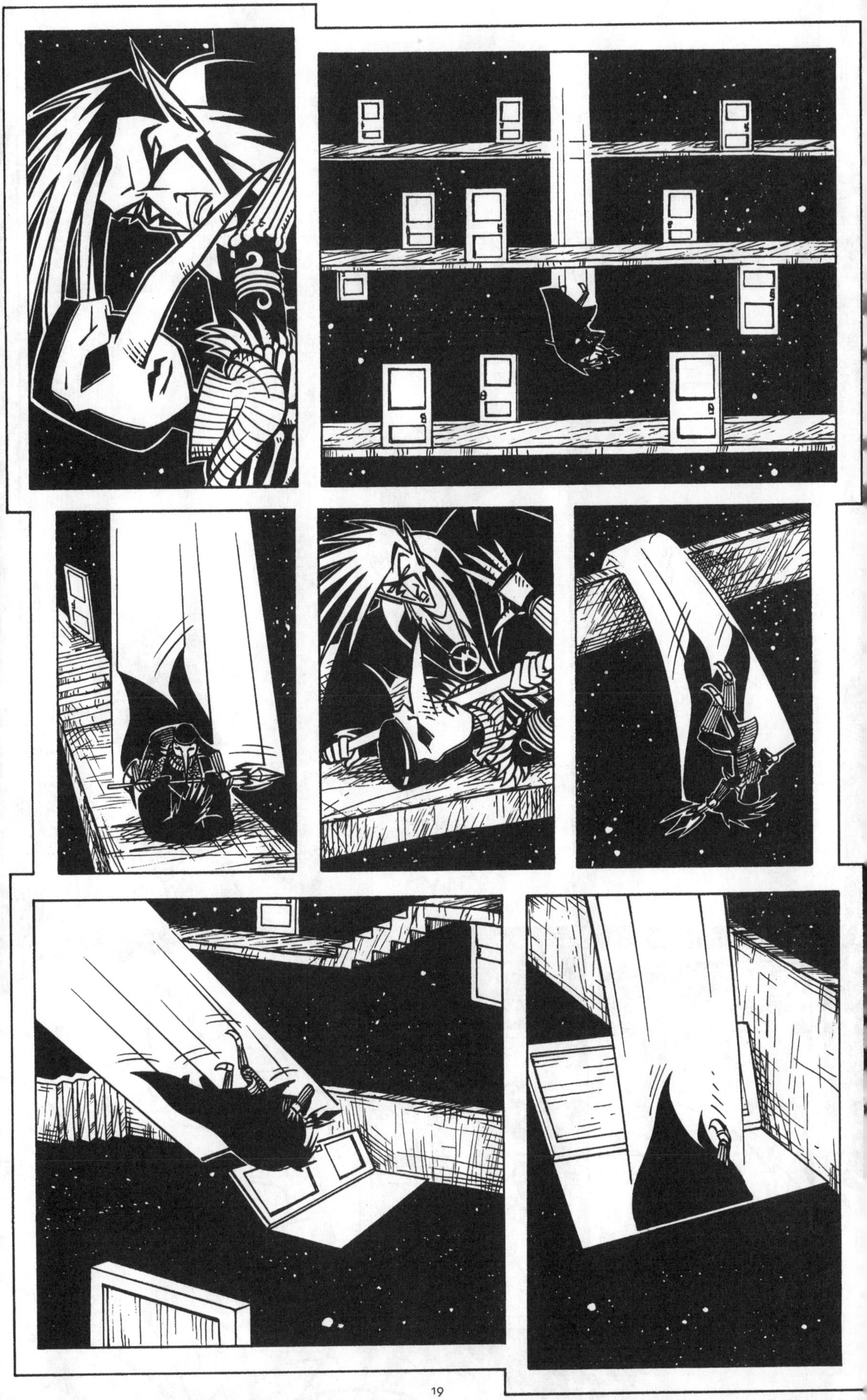

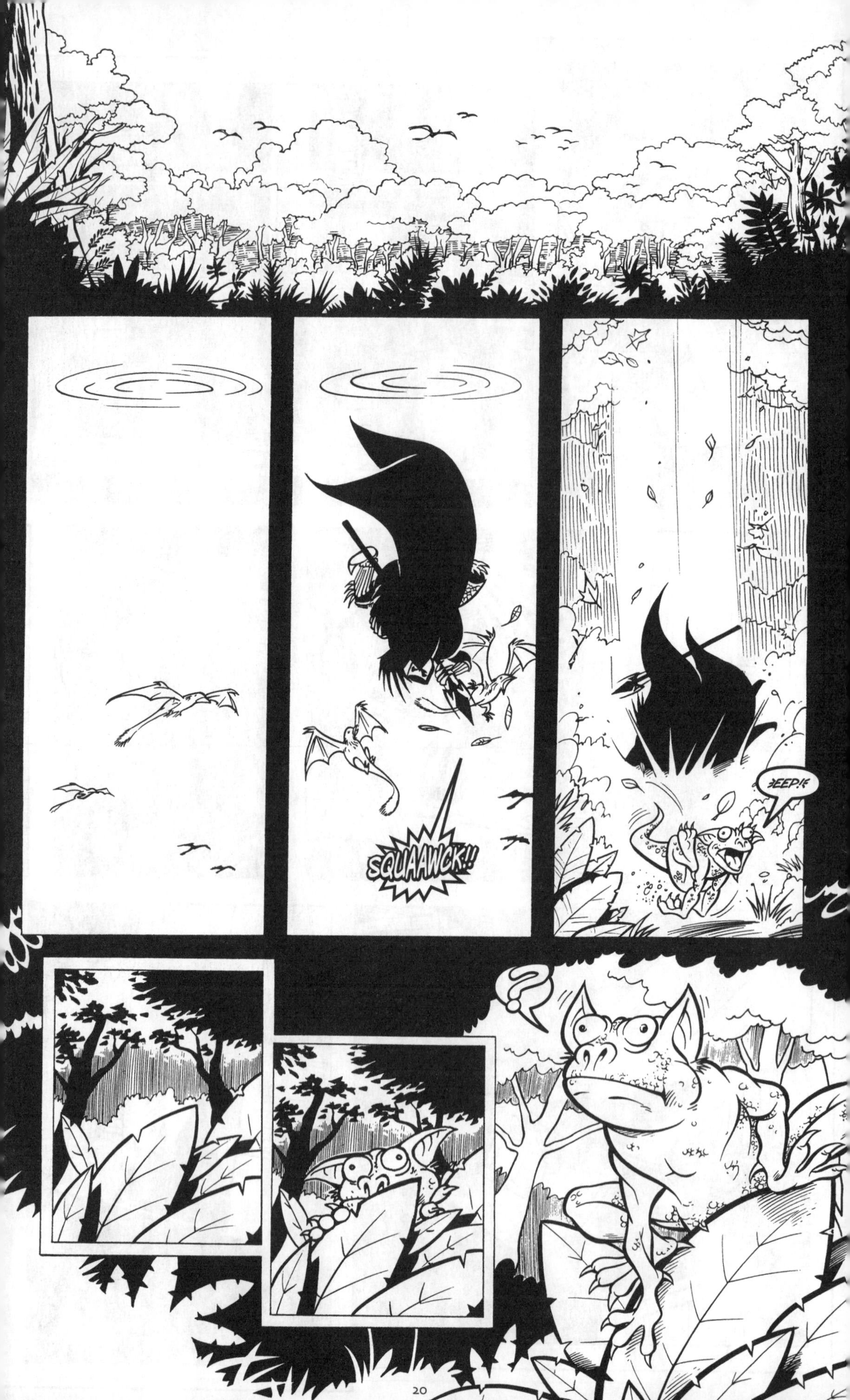
SQUAAWCK!!
EEP!

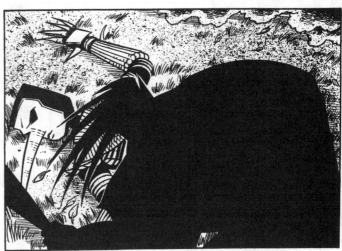

YOU WILL ESCORT ME TO YOUR EMPEROR...

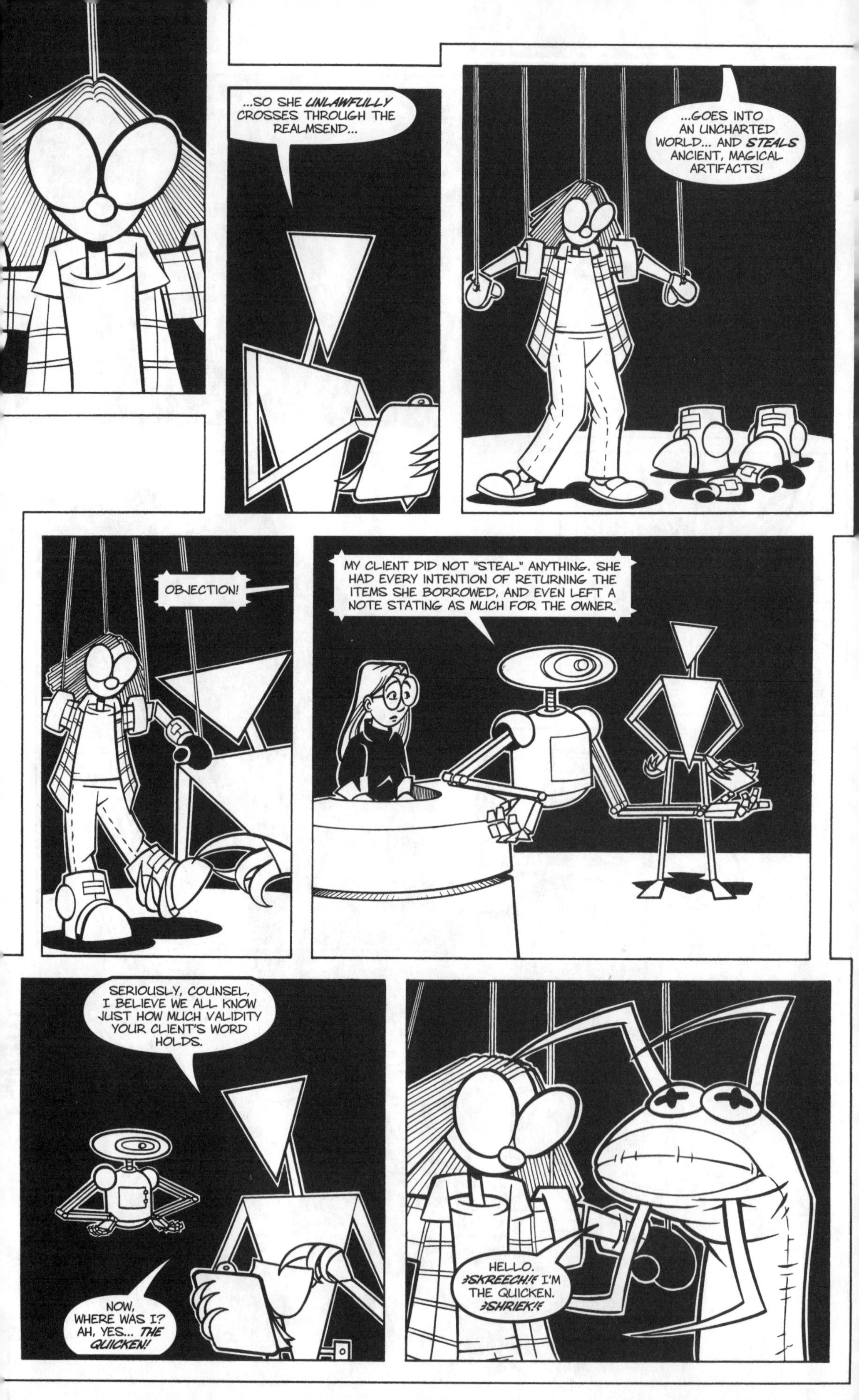

...SO SHE UNLAWFULLY CROSSES THROUGH THE REALMSEND...
...GOES INTO AN UNCHARTED WORLD... AND STEALS ANCIENT, MAGICAL ARTIFACTS!
OBJECTION!
MY CLIENT DID NOT "STEAL" ANYTHING. SHE HAD EVERY INTENTION OF RETURNING THE ITEMS SHE BORROWED, AND EVEN LEFT A NOTE STATING AS MUCH FOR THE OWNER.
SERIOUSLY, COUNSEL, I BELIEVE WE ALL KNOW JUST HOW MUCH VALIDITY YOUR CLIENT'S WORD HOLDS.
NOW, WHERE WAS I? AH, YES... THE QUICKEN!
HELLO. SKREECH! I'M THE QUICKEN. SHRIEK!

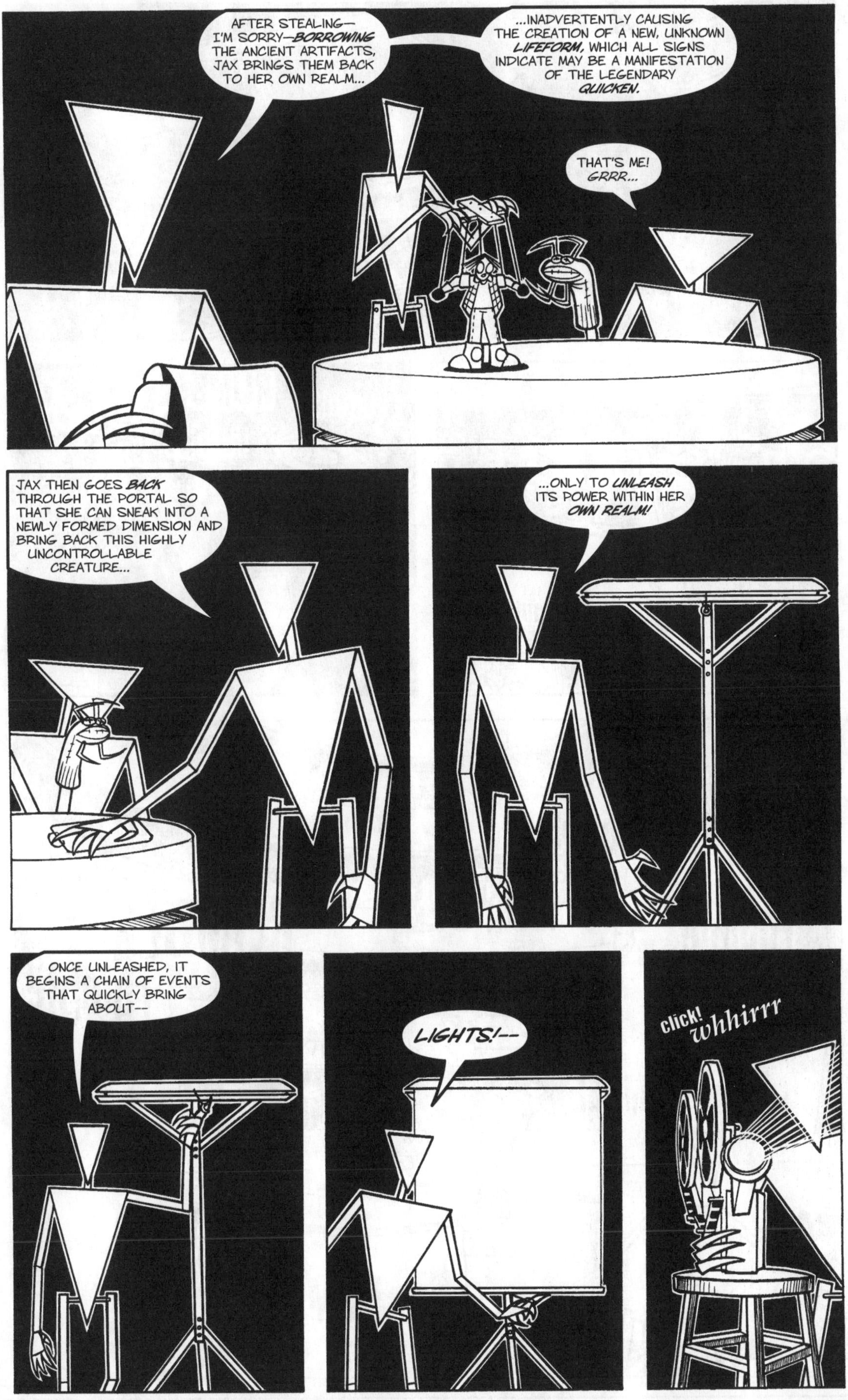
AFTER STEALING— I'M SORRY—BORROWING THE ANCIENT ARTIFACTS, JAX BRINGS THEM BACK TO HER OWN REALM...
...INADVERTENTLY CAUSING THE CREATION OF A NEW, UNKNOWN LIFEFORM, WHICH ALL SIGNS INDICATE MAY BE A MANIFESTATION OF THE LEGENDARY QUICKEN.
THAT'S ME! GRRR...
JAX THEN GOES BACK THROUGH THE PORTAL SO THAT SHE CAN SNEAK INTO A NEWLY FORMED DIMENSION AND BRING BACK THIS HIGHLY UNCONTROLLABLE CREATURE...
...ONLY TO UNLEASH ITS POWER WITHIN HER OWN REALM!
ONCE UNLEASHED, IT BEGINS A CHAIN OF EVENTS THAT QUICKLY BRING ABOUT--
LIGHTS!--
click! whhirrr

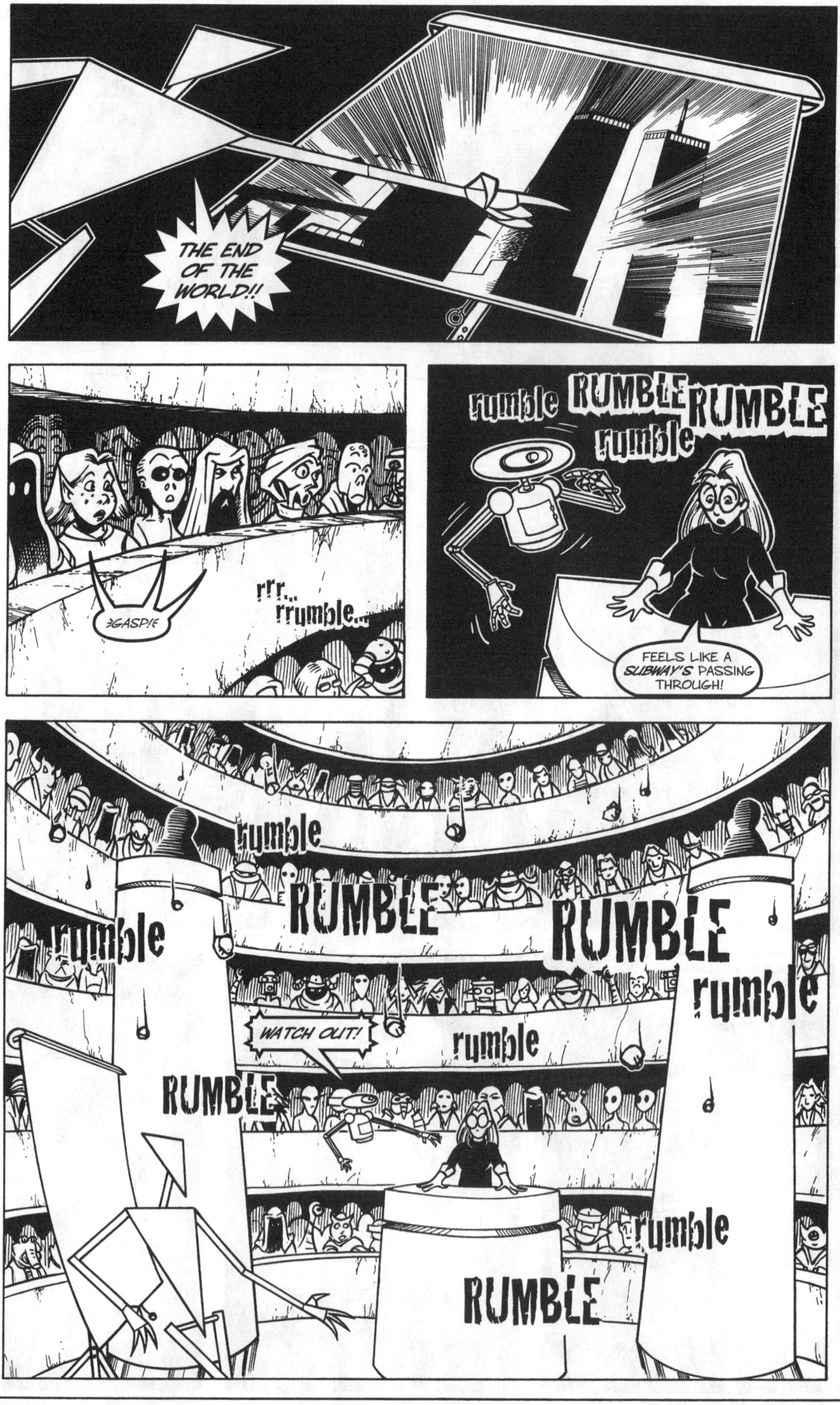
THE END OF THE WORLD!!
GASP!
rrr.. rrumble..
rumble RUMBLE RUMBLE rumble
FEELS LIKE A SUBWAY'S PASSING THROUGH!
rumble
RUMBLE
rumble
RUMBLE
rumble
WATCH OUT!
rumble
RUMBLE
rumble
RUMBLE

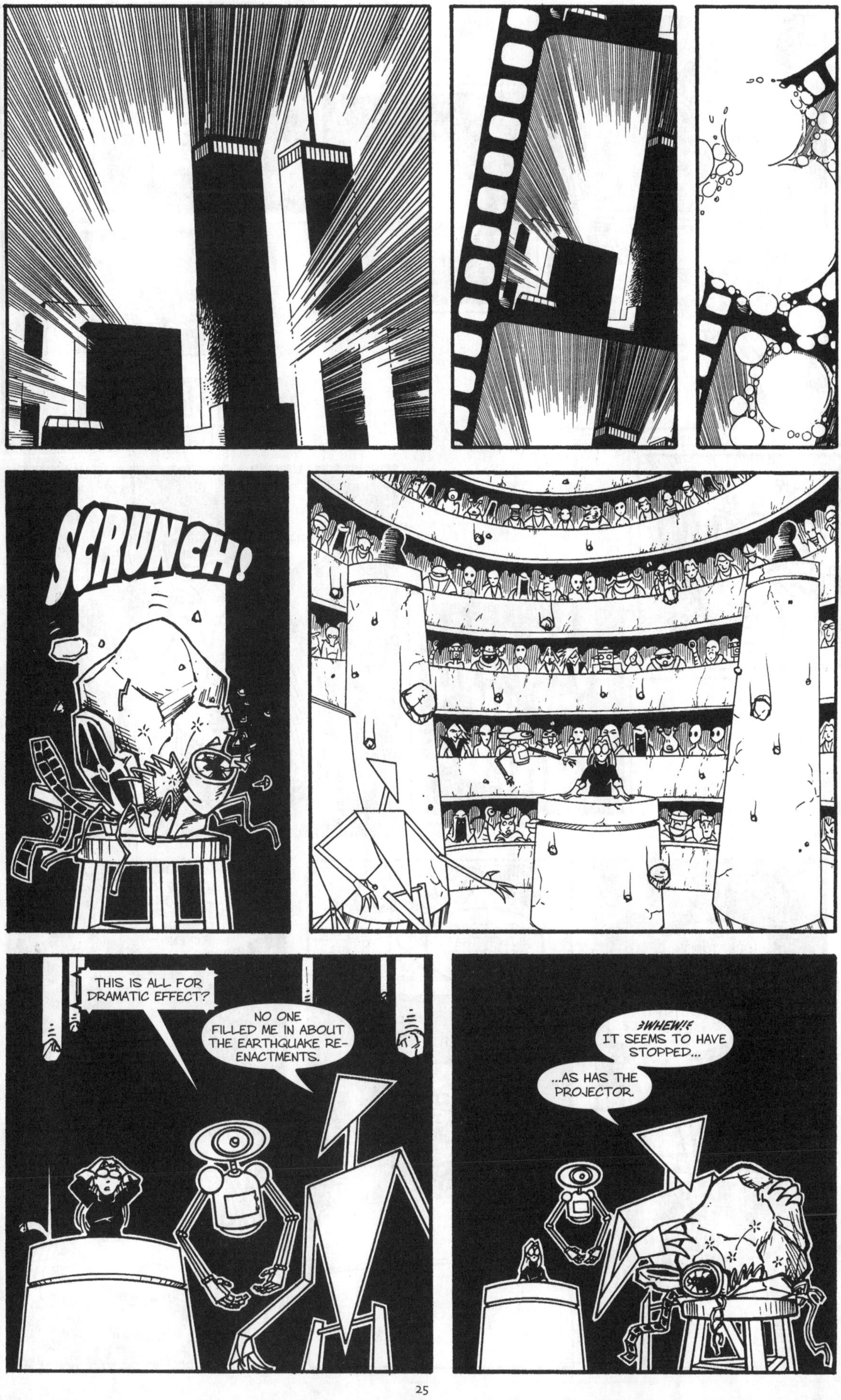
SCRUNCH!
THIS IS ALL FOR DRAMATIC EFFECT?
NO ONE FILLED ME IN ABOUT THE EARTHQUAKE RE-ENACTMENTS.
WHEW!
IT SEEMS TO HAVE STOPPED...
...AS HAS THE PROJECTOR.

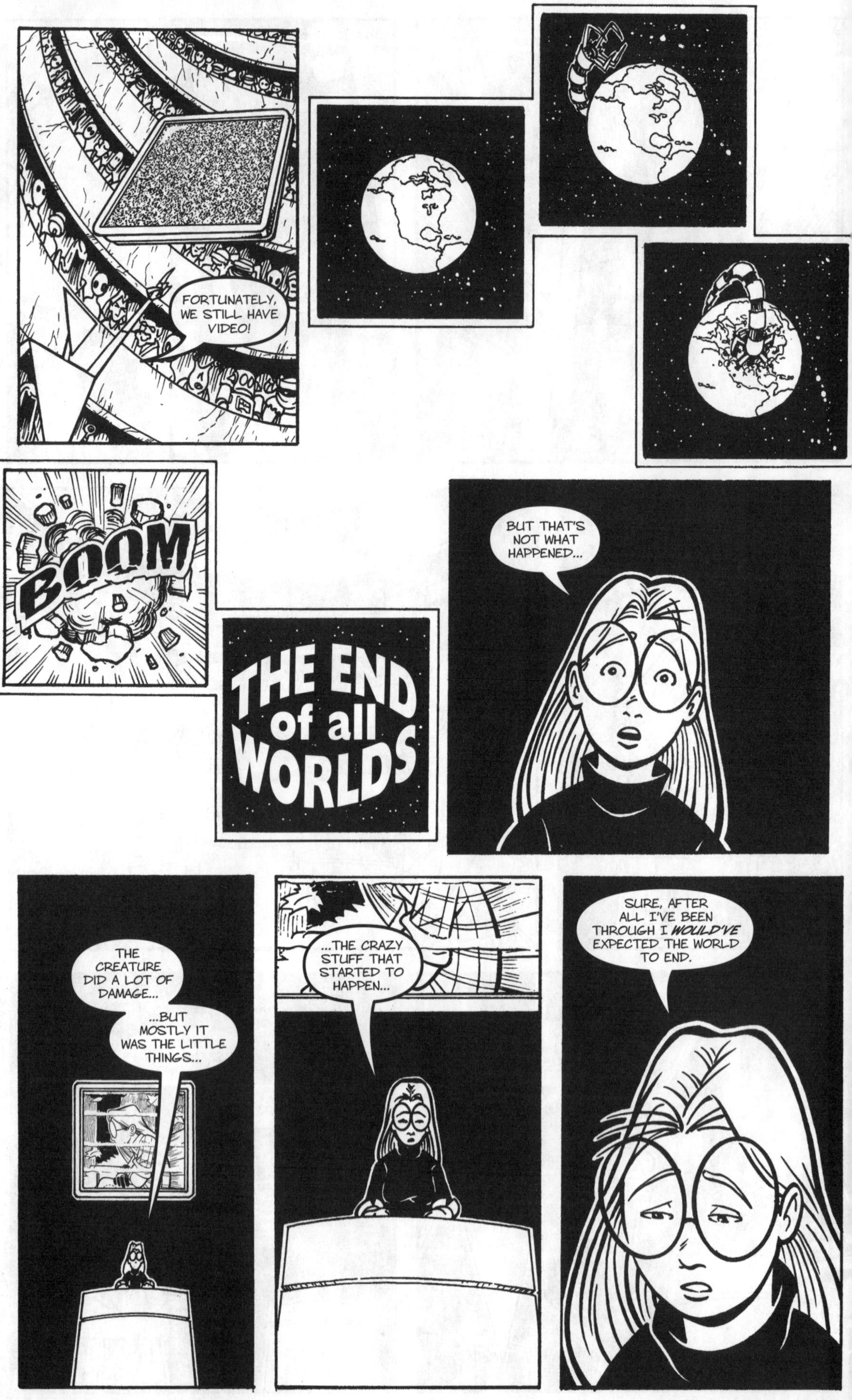
FORTUNATELY, WE STILL HAVE VIDEO!
BOOM
THE END of all WORLDS
BUT THAT'S NOT WHAT HAPPENED...
THE CREATURE DID A LOT OF DAMAGE...
...BUT MOSTLY IT WAS THE LITTLE THINGS...
...THE CRAZY STUFF THAT STARTED TO HAPPEN...
SURE, AFTER ALL I'VE BEEN THROUGH I *WOULD'VE* EXPECTED THE WORLD TO END.

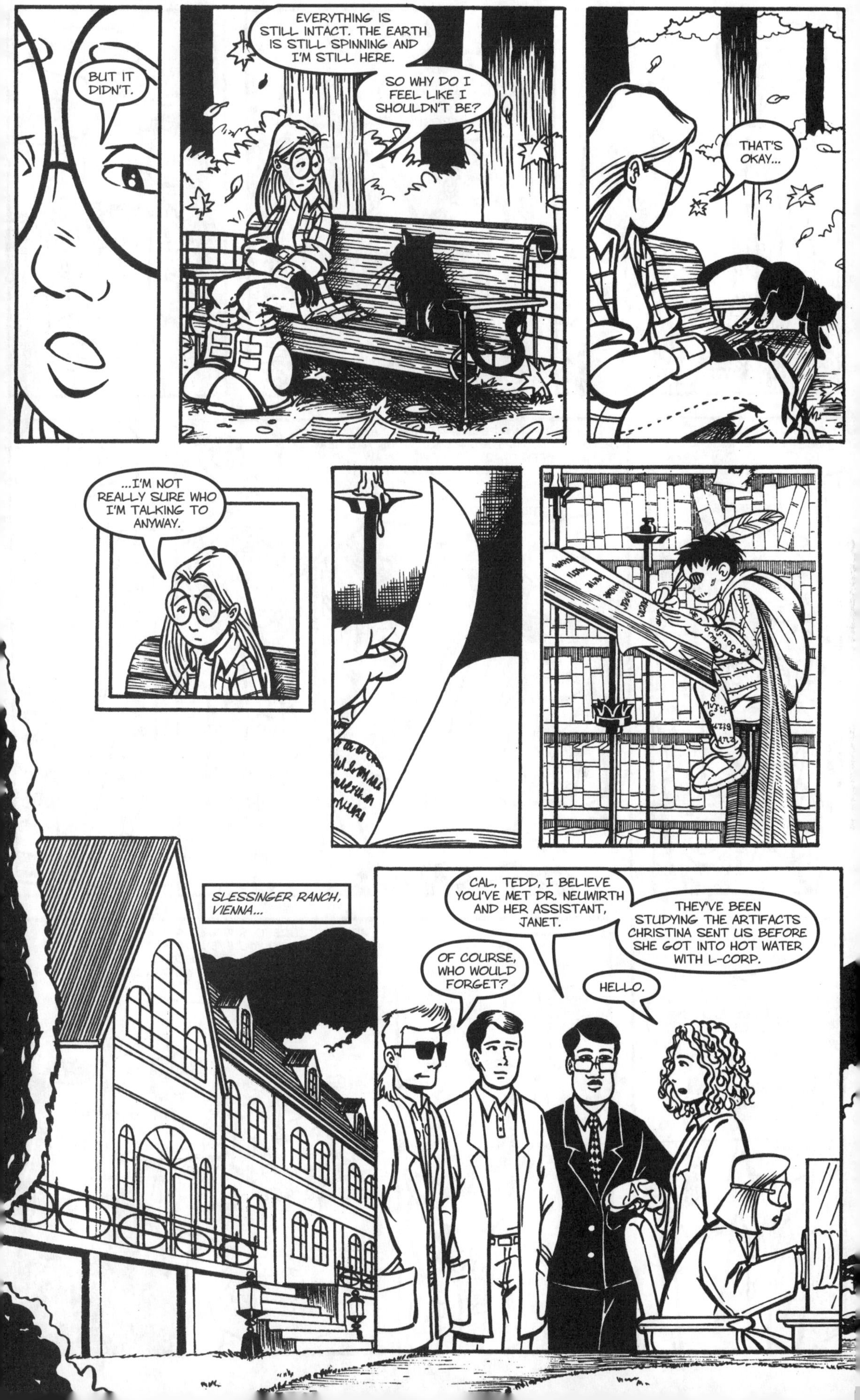
BUT IT DIDN'T.
EVERYTHING IS STILL INTACT. THE EARTH IS STILL SPINNING AND I'M STILL HERE.
SO WHY DO I FEEL LIKE I SHOULDN'T BE?
THAT'S OKAY...
...I'M NOT REALLY SURE WHO I'M TALKING TO ANYWAY.
SLESSINGER RANCH, VIENNA...
CAL, TEDD, I BELIEVE YOU'VE MET DR. NEUWIRTH AND HER ASSISTANT, JANET.
THEY'VE BEEN STUDYING THE ARTIFACTS CHRISTINA SENT US BEFORE SHE GOT INTO HOT WATER WITH L-CORP.
OF COURSE, WHO WOULD FORGET?
HELLO.

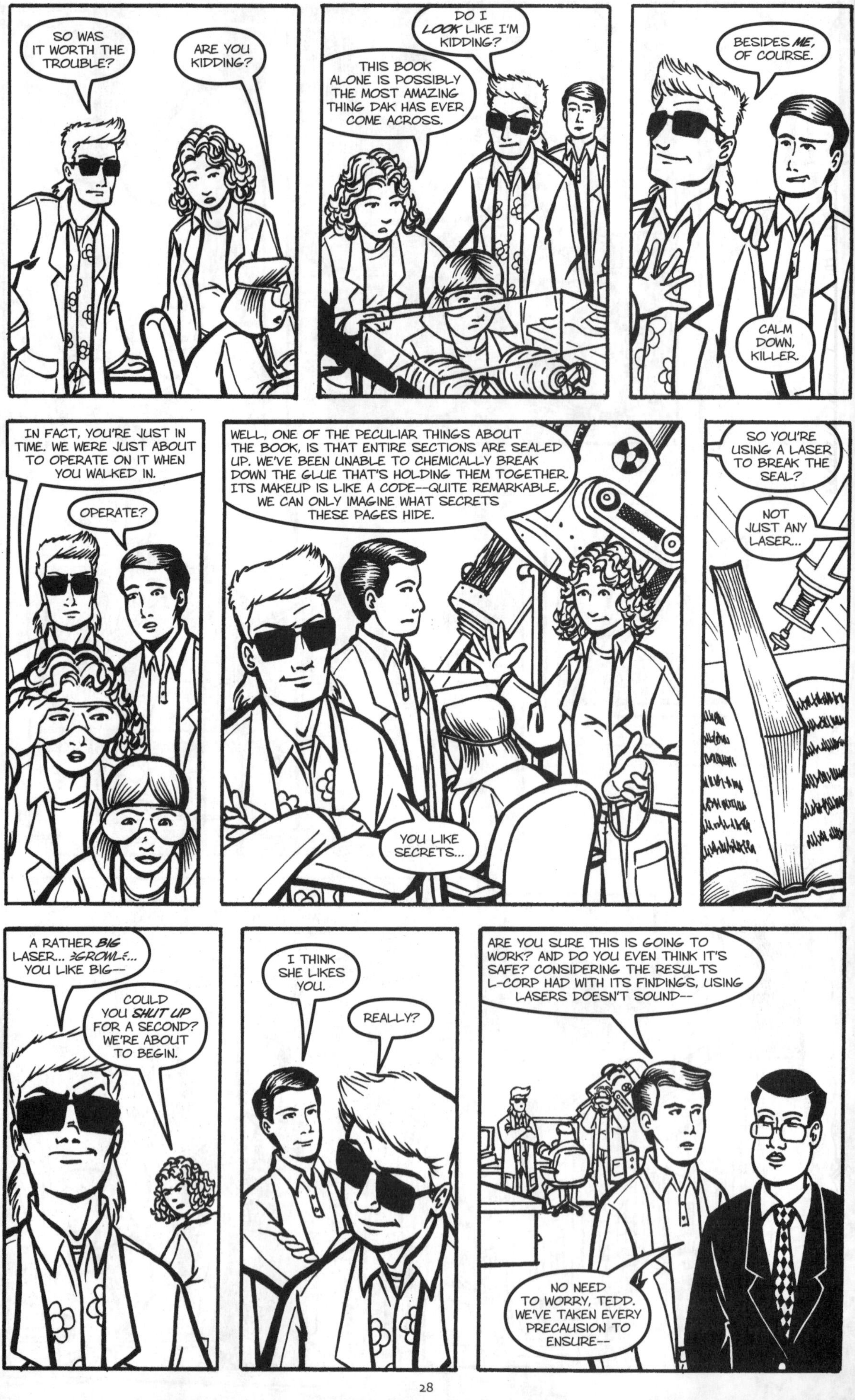

SO WAS IT WORTH THE TROUBLE?
ARE YOU KIDDING?
DO I LOOK LIKE I'M KIDDING?
THIS BOOK ALONE IS POSSIBLY THE MOST AMAZING THING DAK HAS EVER COME ACROSS.
BESIDES ME, OF COURSE.
CALM DOWN, KILLER.
IN FACT, YOU'RE JUST IN TIME. WE WERE JUST ABOUT TO OPERATE ON IT WHEN YOU WALKED IN.
OPERATE?
WELL, ONE OF THE PECULIAR THINGS ABOUT THE BOOK, IS THAT ENTIRE SECTIONS ARE SEALED UP. WE'VE BEEN UNABLE TO CHEMICALLY BREAK DOWN THE GLUE THAT'S HOLDING THEM TOGETHER. ITS MAKEUP IS LIKE A CODE--QUITE REMARKABLE. WE CAN ONLY IMAGINE WHAT SECRETS THESE PAGES HIDE.
YOU LIKE SECRETS...
SO YOU'RE USING A LASER TO BREAK THE SEAL?
NOT JUST ANY LASER...
A RATHER BIG LASER... GROWL... YOU LIKE BIG--
COULD YOU SHUT UP FOR A SECOND? WE'RE ABOUT TO BEGIN.
I THINK SHE LIKES YOU.
REALLY?
ARE YOU SURE THIS IS GOING TO WORK? AND DO YOU EVEN THINK IT'S SAFE? CONSIDERING THE RESULTS L-CORP HAD WITH ITS FINDINGS, USING LASERS DOESN'T SOUND--
NO NEED TO WORRY, TEDD. WE'VE TAKEN EVERY PRECAUSION TO ENSURE--

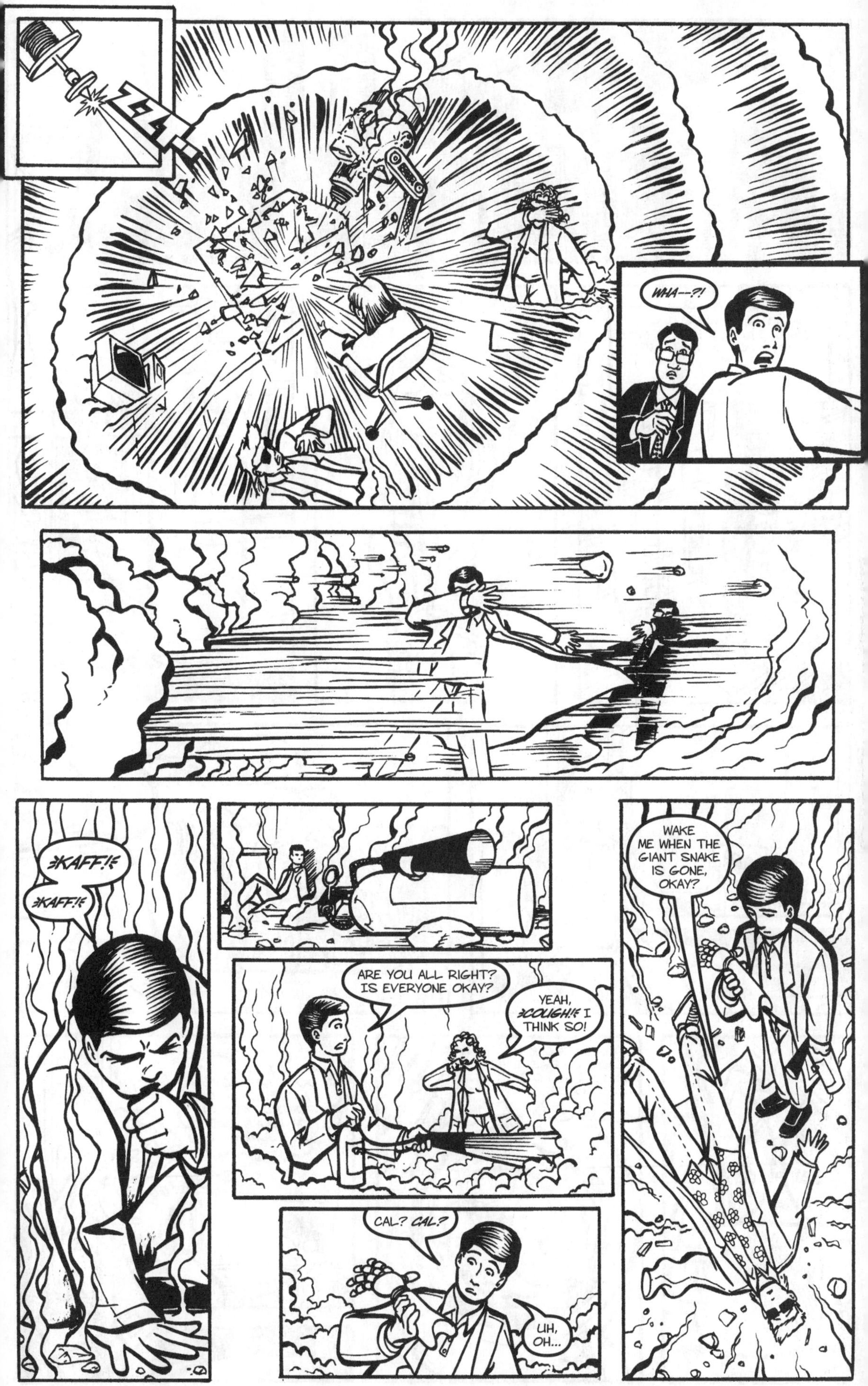
ZZZ...
WHA--?!
≯KAFF!≮
≯KAFF!≮
ARE YOU ALL RIGHT? IS EVERYONE OKAY?
YEAH, ≯COUGH!≮ I THINK SO!
CAL? CAL?
UH, OH...
WAKE ME WHEN THE GIANT SNAKE IS GONE, OKAY?

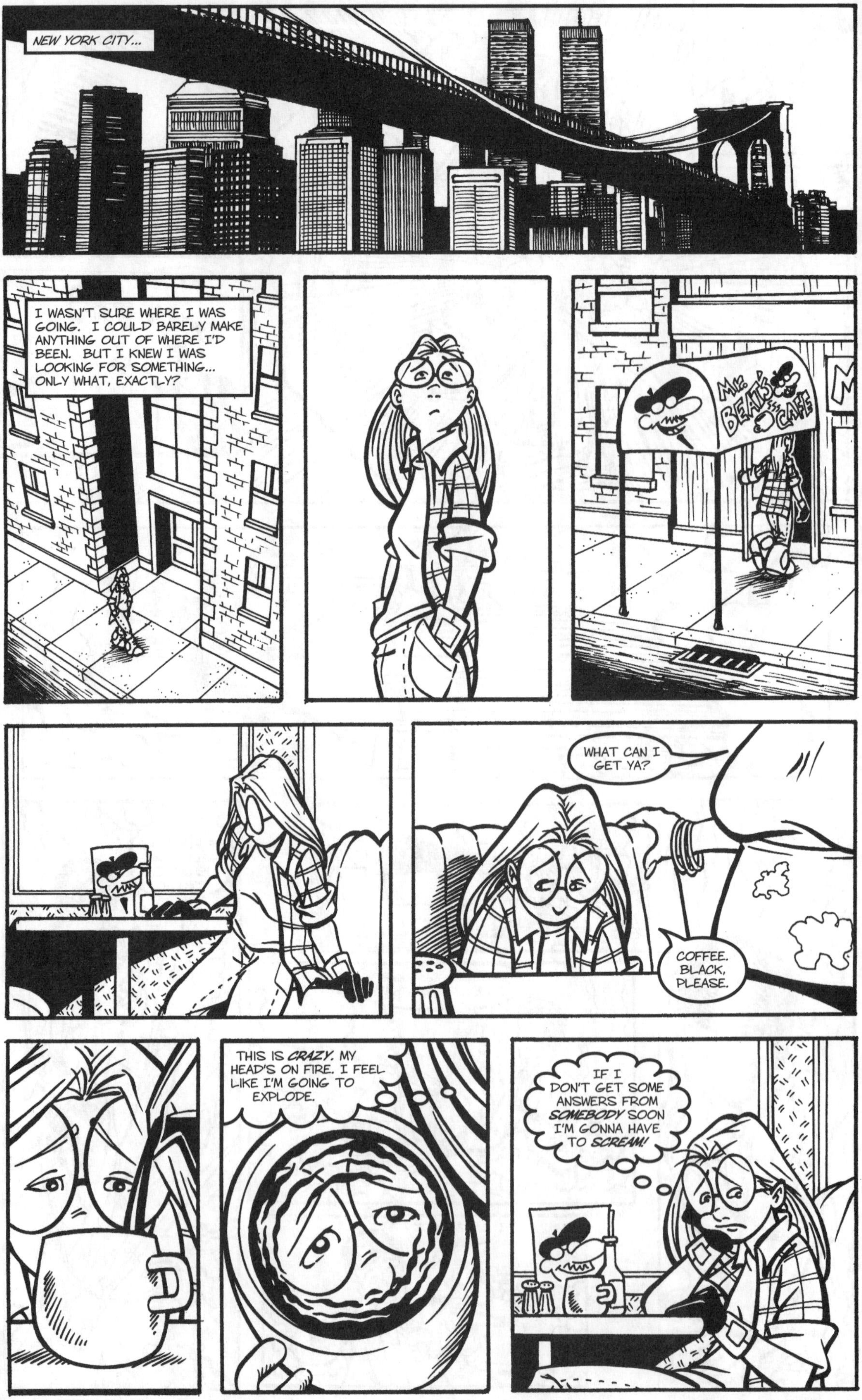
NEW YORK CITY...
I WASN'T SURE WHERE I WAS GOING. I COULD BARELY MAKE ANYTHING OUT OF WHERE I'D BEEN. BUT I KNEW I WAS LOOKING FOR SOMETHING... ONLY WHAT, EXACTLY?
MR. BEAT'S CAFE
WHAT CAN I GET YA?
COFFEE. BLACK, PLEASE.
THIS IS CRAZY. MY HEAD'S ON FIRE. I FEEL LIKE I'M GOING TO EXPLODE.
IF I DON'T GET SOME ANSWERS FROM SOMEBODY SOON I'M GONNA HAVE TO SCREAM!

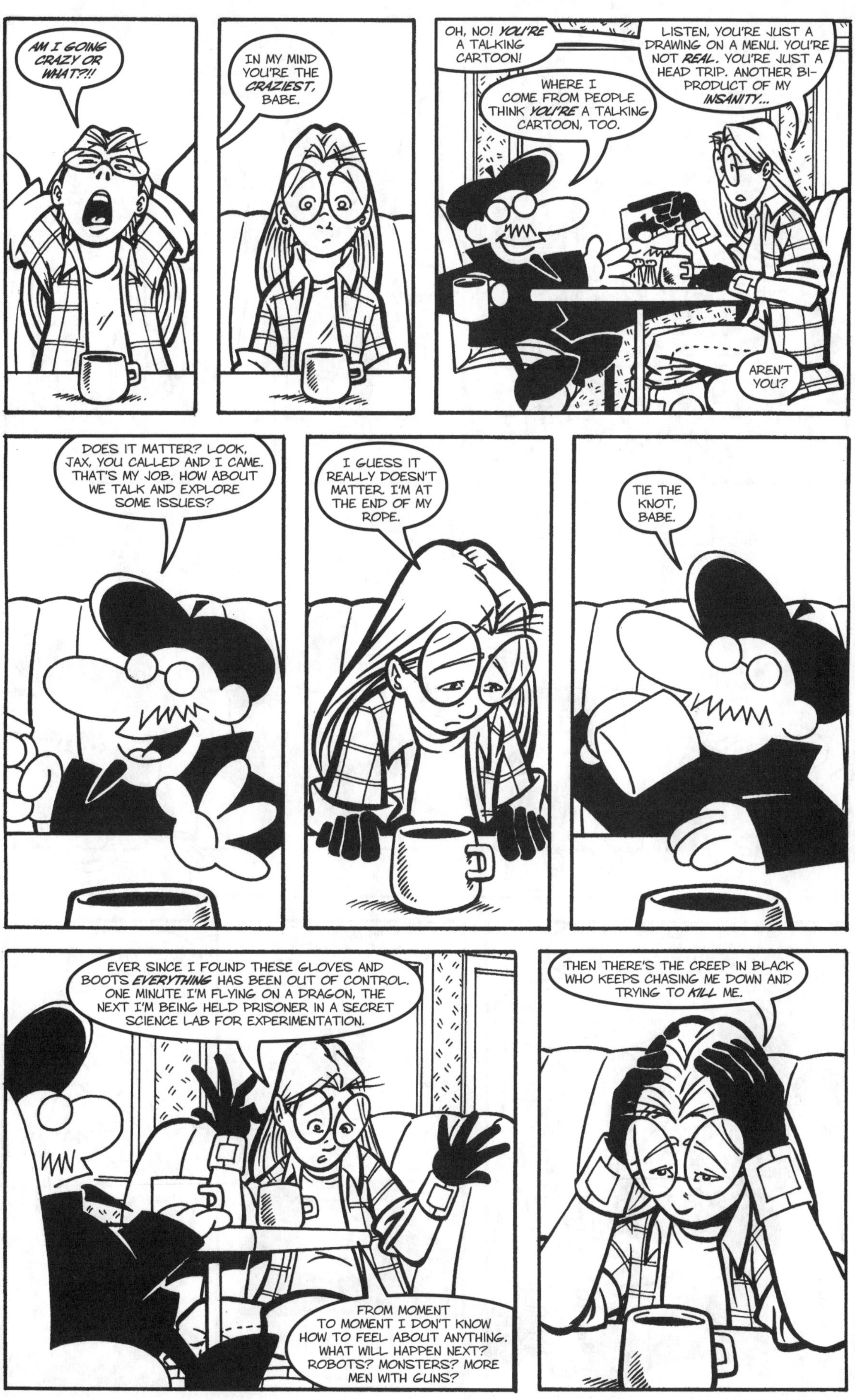
AM I GOING CRAZY OR WHAT?!!
IN MY MIND YOU'RE THE CRAZIEST, BABE.
OH, NO! YOU'RE A TALKING CARTOON!
WHERE I COME FROM PEOPLE THINK YOU'RE A TALKING CARTOON, TOO.
LISTEN, YOU'RE JUST A DRAWING ON A MENU. YOU'RE NOT REAL. YOU'RE JUST A HEAD TRIP. ANOTHER BI-PRODUCT OF MY INSANITY...
AREN'T YOU?
DOES IT MATTER? LOOK, JAX, YOU CALLED AND I CAME. THAT'S MY JOB. HOW ABOUT WE TALK AND EXPLORE SOME ISSUES?
I GUESS IT REALLY DOESN'T MATTER. I'M AT THE END OF MY ROPE.
TIE THE KNOT, BABE.
EVER SINCE I FOUND THESE GLOVES AND BOOTS EVERYTHING HAS BEEN OUT OF CONTROL. ONE MINUTE I'M FLYING ON A DRAGON, THE NEXT I'M BEING HELD PRISONER IN A SECRET SCIENCE LAB FOR EXPERIMENTATION.
FROM MOMENT TO MOMENT I DON'T KNOW HOW TO FEEL ABOUT ANYTHING. WHAT WILL HAPPEN NEXT? ROBOTS? MONSTERS? MORE MEN WITH GUNS?
THEN THERE'S THE CREEP IN BLACK WHO KEEPS CHASING ME DOWN AND TRYING TO KILL ME.

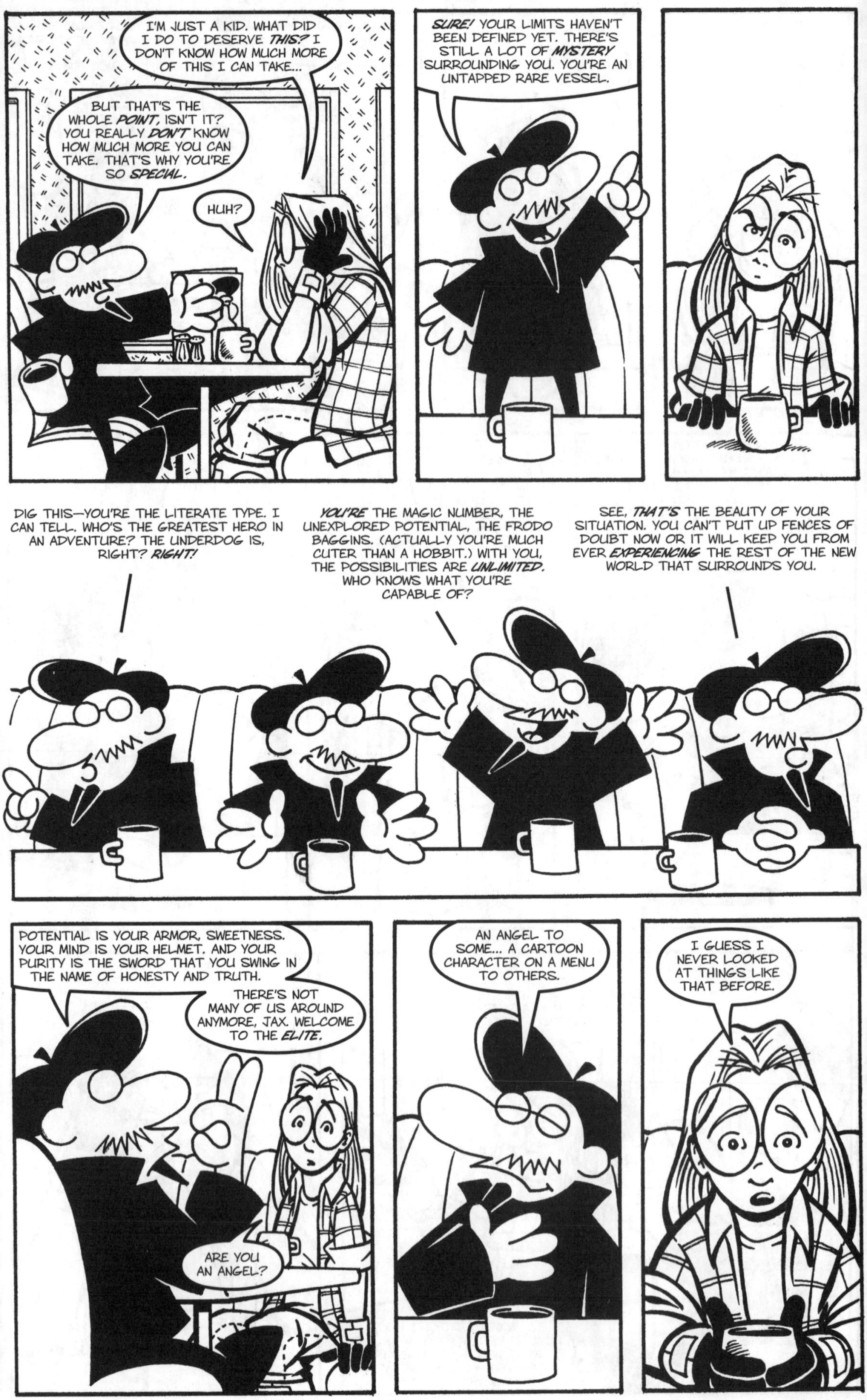
I'M JUST A KID. WHAT DID I DO TO DESERVE THIS? I DON'T KNOW HOW MUCH MORE OF THIS I CAN TAKE...
BUT THAT'S THE WHOLE POINT, ISN'T IT? YOU REALLY DON'T KNOW HOW MUCH MORE YOU CAN TAKE. THAT'S WHY YOU'RE SO SPECIAL.
HUH?
SURE! YOUR LIMITS HAVEN'T BEEN DEFINED YET. THERE'S STILL A LOT OF MYSTERY SURROUNDING YOU. YOU'RE AN UNTAPPED RARE VESSEL.
DIG THIS—YOU'RE THE LITERATE TYPE. I CAN TELL. WHO'S THE GREATEST HERO IN AN ADVENTURE? THE UNDERDOG IS, RIGHT? RIGHT!
YOU'RE THE MAGIC NUMBER, THE UNEXPLORED POTENTIAL, THE FRODO BAGGINS. (ACTUALLY YOU'RE MUCH CUTER THAN A HOBBIT.) WITH YOU, THE POSSIBILITIES ARE UNLIMITED. WHO KNOWS WHAT YOU'RE CAPABLE OF?
SEE, THAT'S THE BEAUTY OF YOUR SITUATION. YOU CAN'T PUT UP FENCES OF DOUBT NOW OR IT WILL KEEP YOU FROM EVER EXPERIENCING THE REST OF THE NEW WORLD THAT SURROUNDS YOU.
POTENTIAL IS YOUR ARMOR, SWEETNESS. YOUR MIND IS YOUR HELMET. AND YOUR PURITY IS THE SWORD THAT YOU SWING IN THE NAME OF HONESTY AND TRUTH.
THERE'S NOT MANY OF US AROUND ANYMORE, JAX. WELCOME TO THE ELITE.
ARE YOU AN ANGEL?
AN ANGEL TO SOME... A CARTOON CHARACTER ON A MENU TO OTHERS.
I GUESS I NEVER LOOKED AT THINGS LIKE THAT BEFORE.

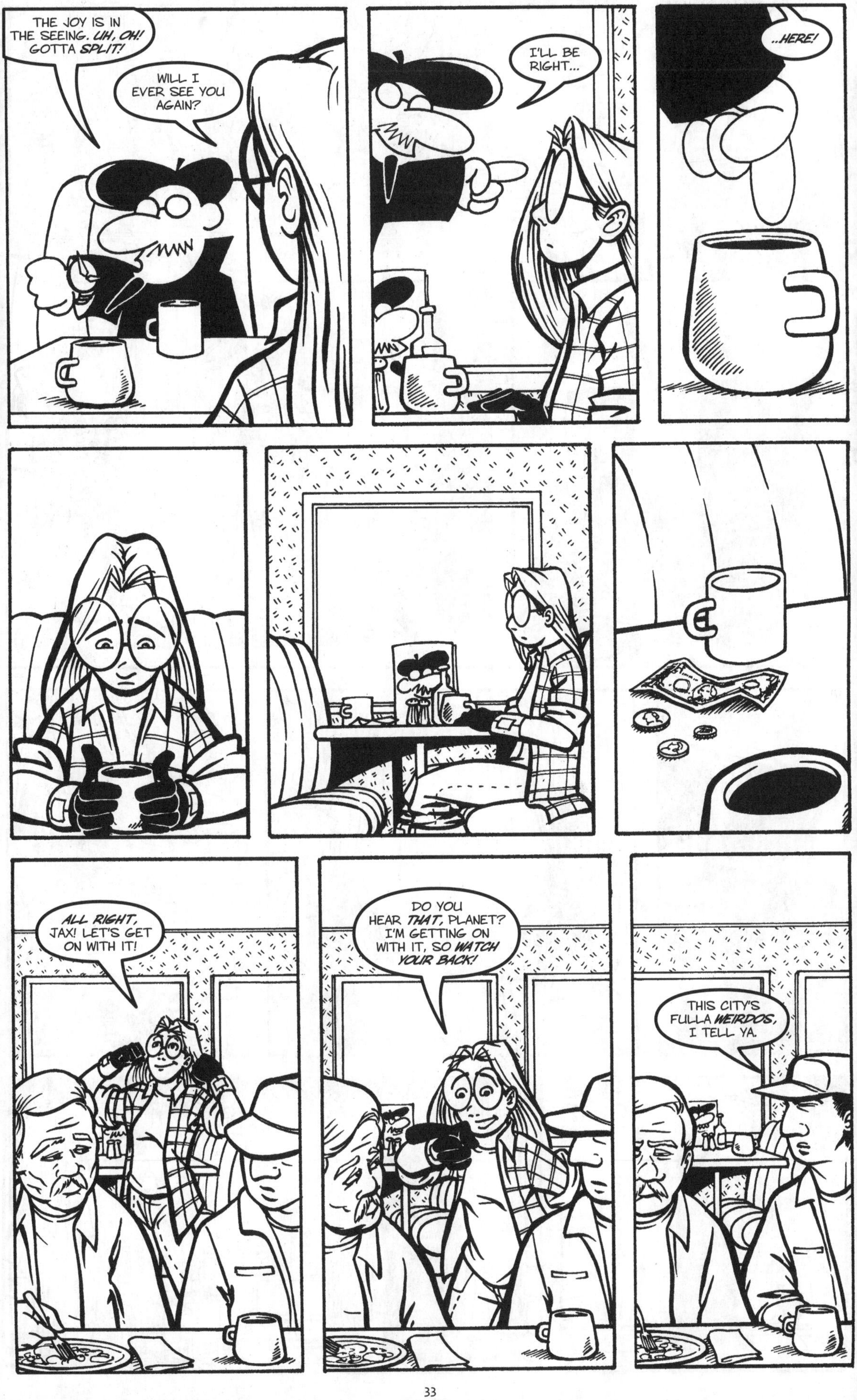
THE JOY IS IN THE SEEING. UH, OH! GOTTA SPLIT!
WILL I EVER SEE YOU AGAIN?
I'LL BE RIGHT...
..HERE!
ALL RIGHT, JAX! LET'S GET ON WITH IT!
DO YOU HEAR THAT, PLANET? I'M GETTING ON WITH IT, SO WATCH YOUR BACK!
THIS CITY'S FULLA WEIRDOS, I TELL YA.

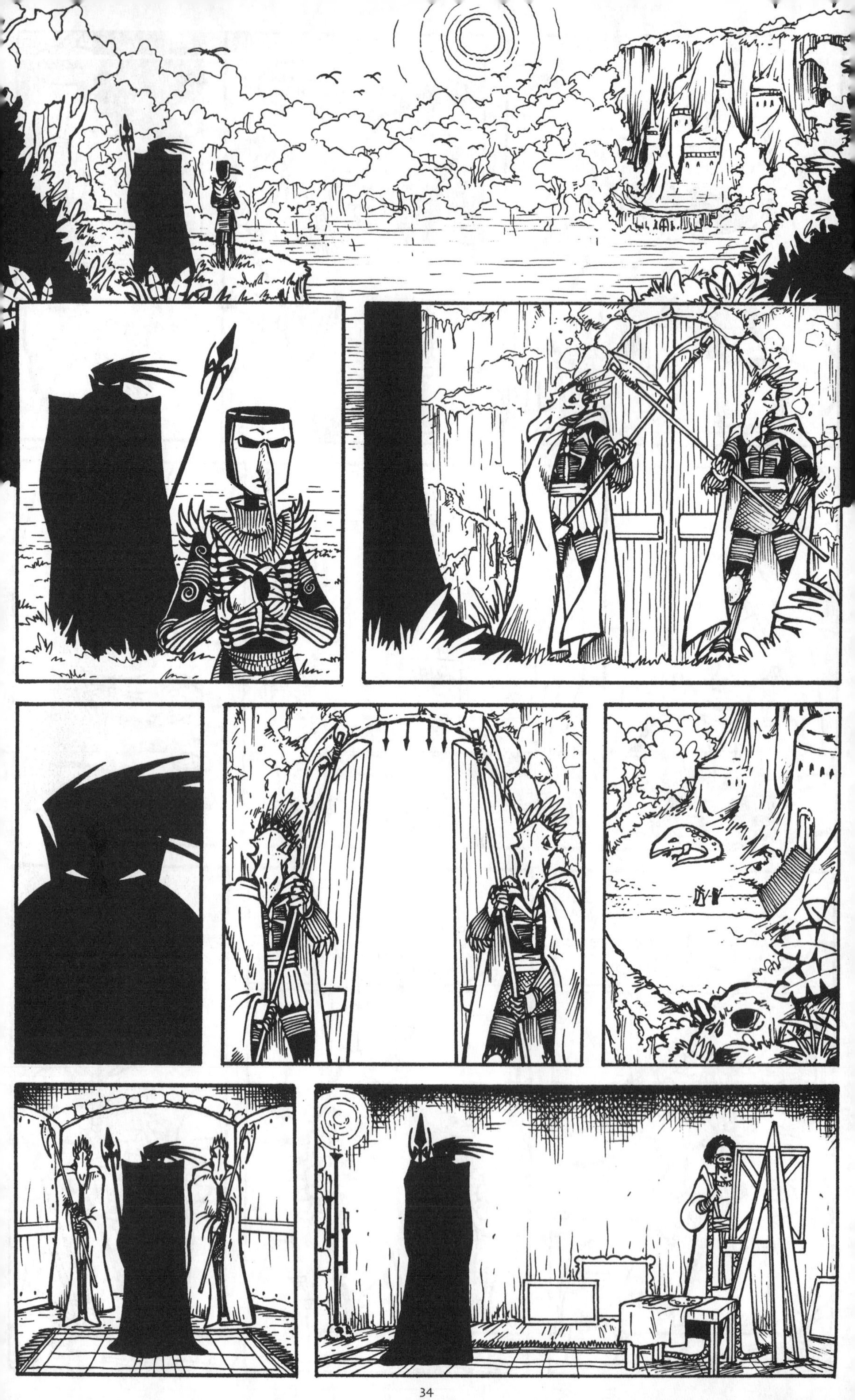

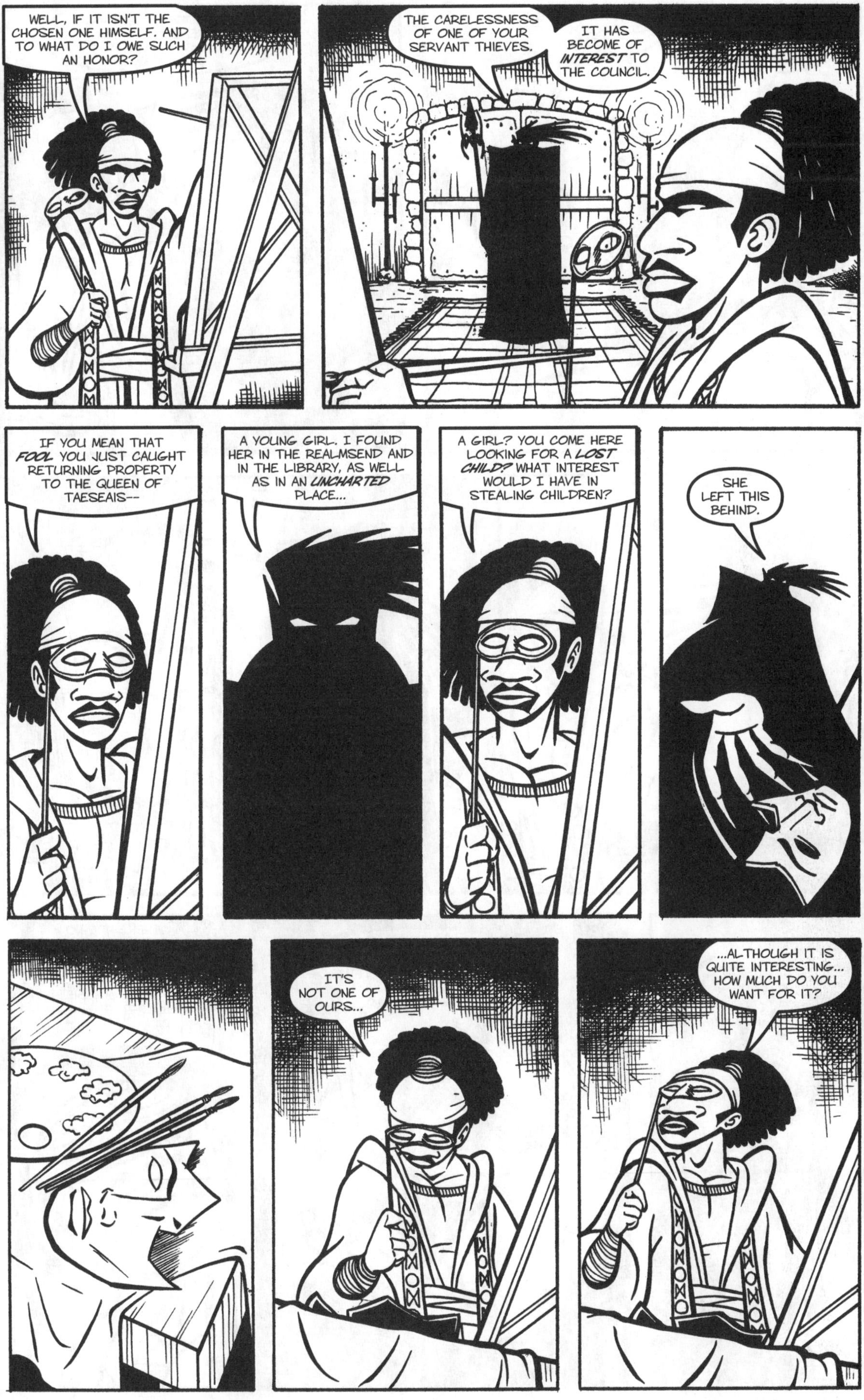
WELL, IF IT ISN'T THE CHOSEN ONE HIMSELF. AND TO WHAT DO I OWE SUCH AN HONOR?
THE CARELESSNESS OF ONE OF YOUR SERVANT THIEVES.
IT HAS BECOME OF INTEREST TO THE COUNCIL.
IF YOU MEAN THAT FOOL YOU JUST CAUGHT RETURNING PROPERTY TO THE QUEEN OF TAESEAIS--
A YOUNG GIRL. I FOUND HER IN THE REALMSEND AND IN THE LIBRARY, AS WELL AS IN AN UNCHARTED PLACE...
A GIRL? YOU COME HERE LOOKING FOR A LOST CHILD? WHAT INTEREST WOULD I HAVE IN STEALING CHILDREN?
SHE LEFT THIS BEHIND.
IT'S NOT ONE OF OURS...
...ALTHOUGH IT IS QUITE INTERESTING... HOW MUCH DO YOU WANT FOR IT?

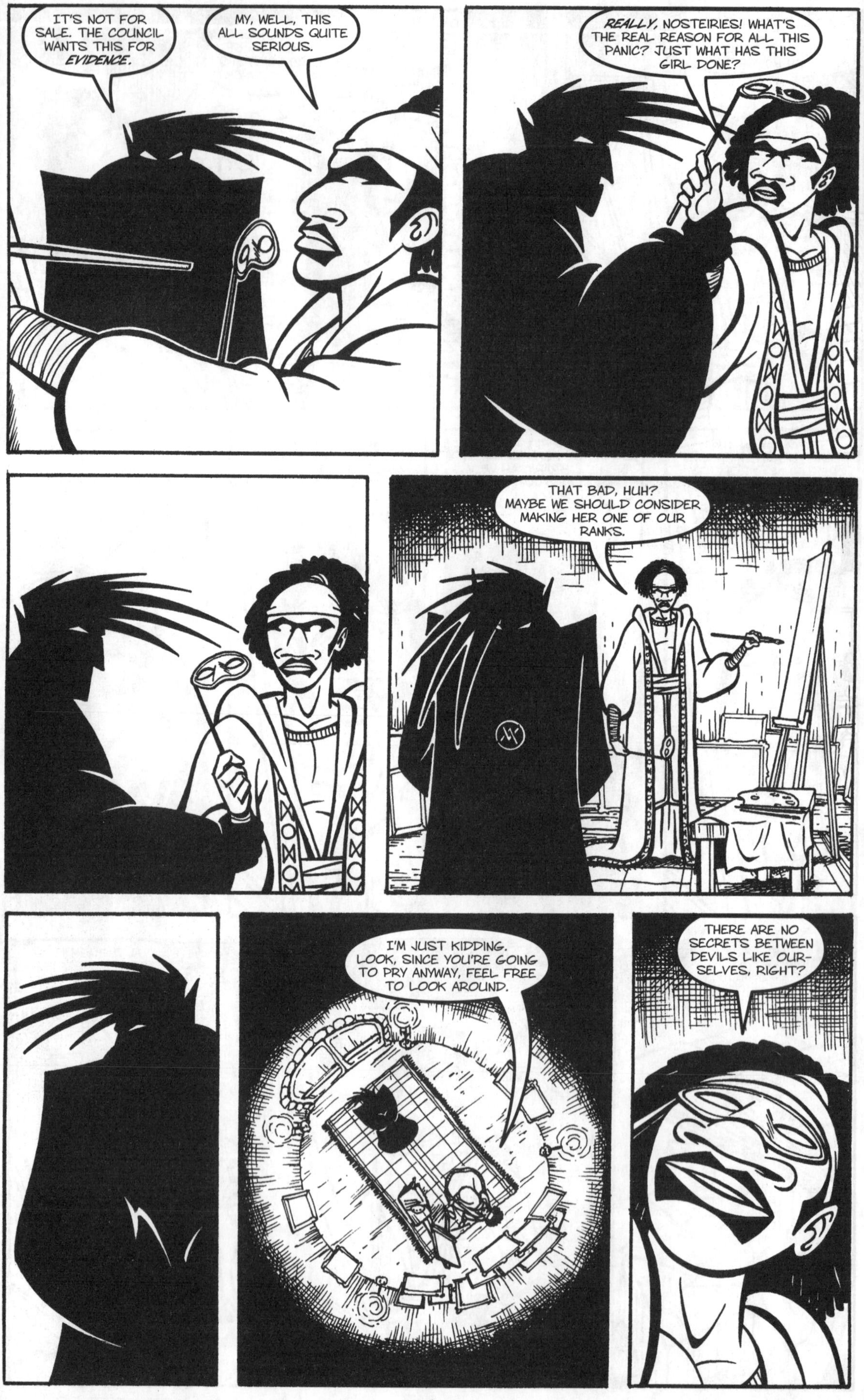

IT'S NOT FOR SALE. THE COUNCIL WANTS THIS FOR *EVIDENCE.*
MY, WELL, THIS ALL SOUNDS QUITE SERIOUS.
REALLY, NOSTEIRIES! WHAT'S THE REAL REASON FOR ALL THIS PANIC? JUST WHAT HAS THIS GIRL DONE?
THAT BAD, HUH? MAYBE WE SHOULD CONSIDER MAKING HER ONE OF OUR RANKS.
I'M JUST KIDDING. LOOK, SINCE YOU'RE GOING TO PRY ANYWAY, FEEL FREE TO LOOK AROUND.
THERE ARE NO SECRETS BETWEEN DEVILS LIKE OUR-SELVES, RIGHT?

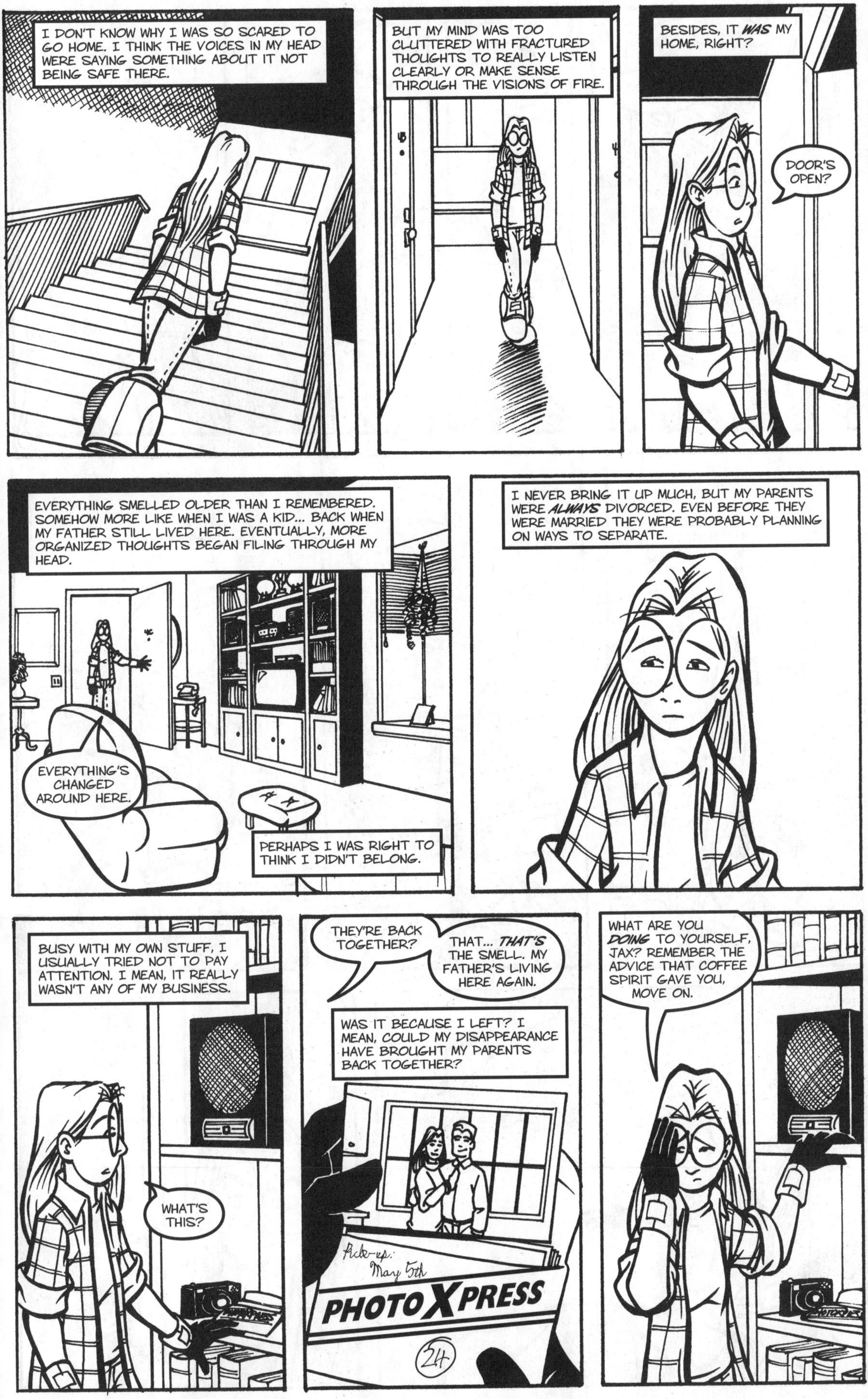

I DON'T KNOW WHY I WAS SO SCARED TO GO HOME. I THINK THE VOICES IN MY HEAD WERE SAYING SOMETHING ABOUT IT NOT BEING SAFE THERE.
BUT MY MIND WAS TOO CLUTTERED WITH FRACTURED THOUGHTS TO REALLY LISTEN CLEARLY OR MAKE SENSE THROUGH THE VISIONS OF FIRE.
BESIDES, IT *WAS* MY HOME, RIGHT?
DOOR'S OPEN?
EVERYTHING SMELLED OLDER THAN I REMEMBERED. SOMEHOW MORE LIKE WHEN I WAS A KID... BACK WHEN MY FATHER STILL LIVED HERE. EVENTUALLY, MORE ORGANIZED THOUGHTS BEGAN FILING THROUGH MY HEAD.
EVERYTHING'S CHANGED AROUND HERE.
PERHAPS I WAS RIGHT TO THINK I DIDN'T BELONG.
I NEVER BRING IT UP MUCH, BUT MY PARENTS WERE *ALWAYS* DIVORCED. EVEN BEFORE THEY WERE MARRIED THEY WERE PROBABLY PLANNING ON WAYS TO SEPARATE.
BUSY WITH MY OWN STUFF, I USUALLY TRIED NOT TO PAY ATTENTION. I MEAN, IT REALLY WASN'T ANY OF MY BUSINESS.
WHAT'S THIS?
THEY'RE BACK TOGETHER?
THAT... *THAT'S* THE SMELL. MY FATHER'S LIVING HERE AGAIN.
WAS IT BECAUSE I LEFT? I MEAN, COULD MY DISAPPEARANCE HAVE BROUGHT MY PARENTS BACK TOGETHER?
Pick-up: May 5th
PHOTO X PRESS
24
WHAT ARE YOU *DOING* TO YOURSELF, JAX? REMEMBER THE ADVICE THAT COFFEE SPIRIT GAVE YOU, MOVE ON.

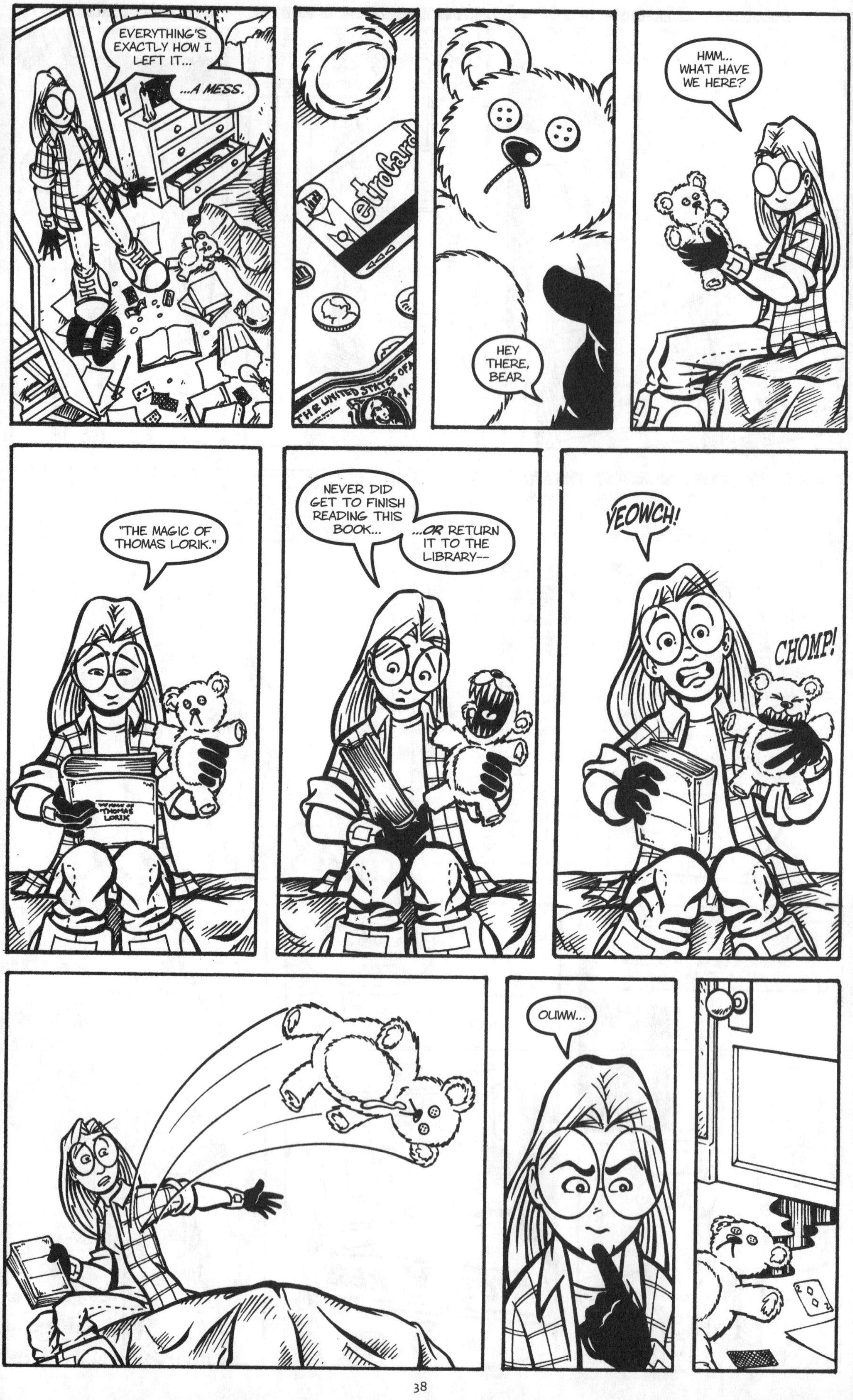
EVERYTHING'S EXACTLY HOW I LEFT IT...
...A MESS.
MetroCard
THE UNITED STATES OF A
HEY THERE, BEAR.
HMM... WHAT HAVE WE HERE?
"THE MAGIC OF THOMAS LORIK."
THOMAS LORIK
NEVER DID GET TO FINISH READING THIS BOOK...
...OR RETURN IT TO THE LIBRARY--
YEOWCH!
CHOMP!
OUWW...

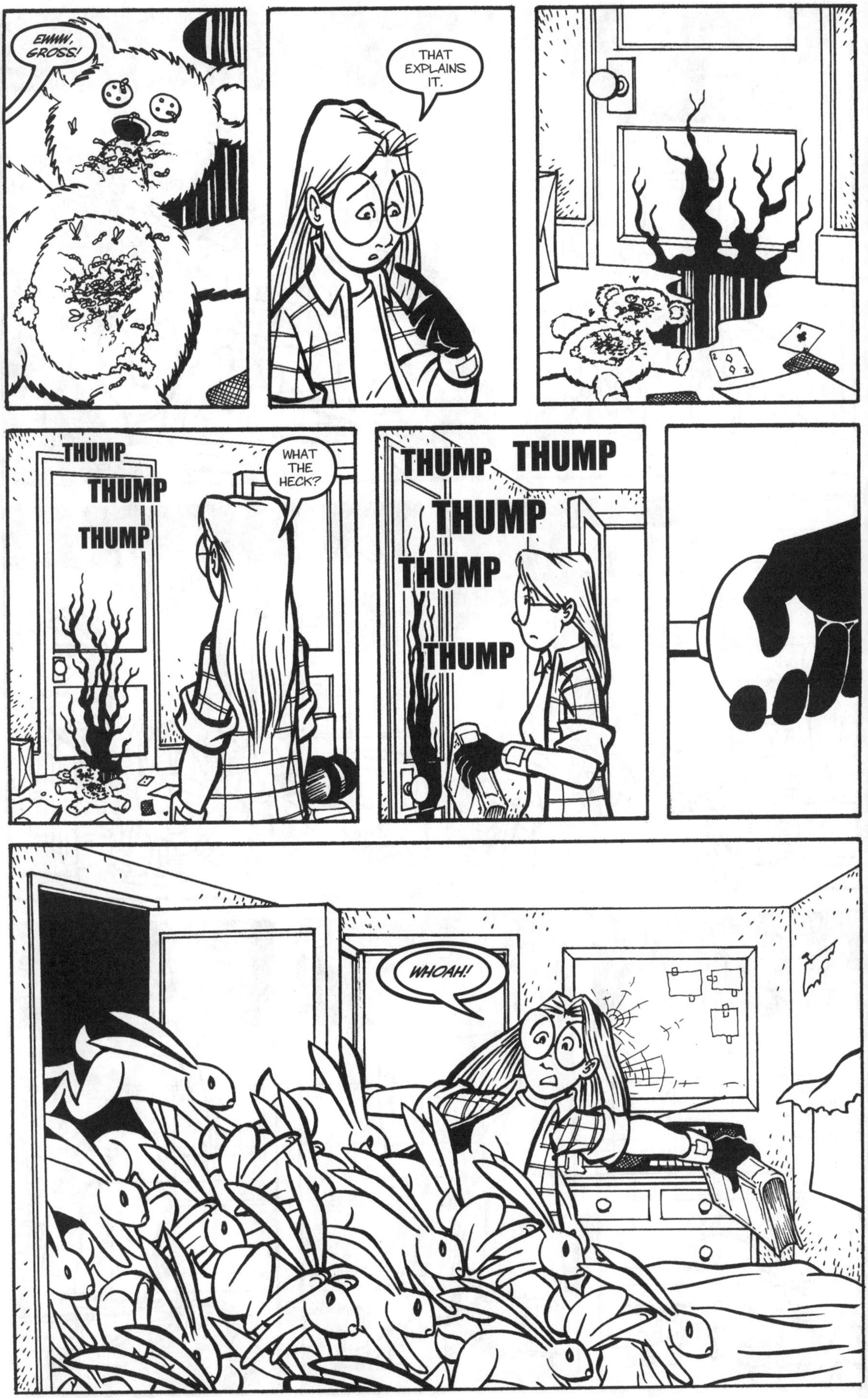
EWWW, GROSS!
THAT EXPLAINS IT.
THUMP
THUMP
THUMP
WHAT THE HECK?
THUMP THUMP
THUMP
THUMP
THUMP
WHOAH!

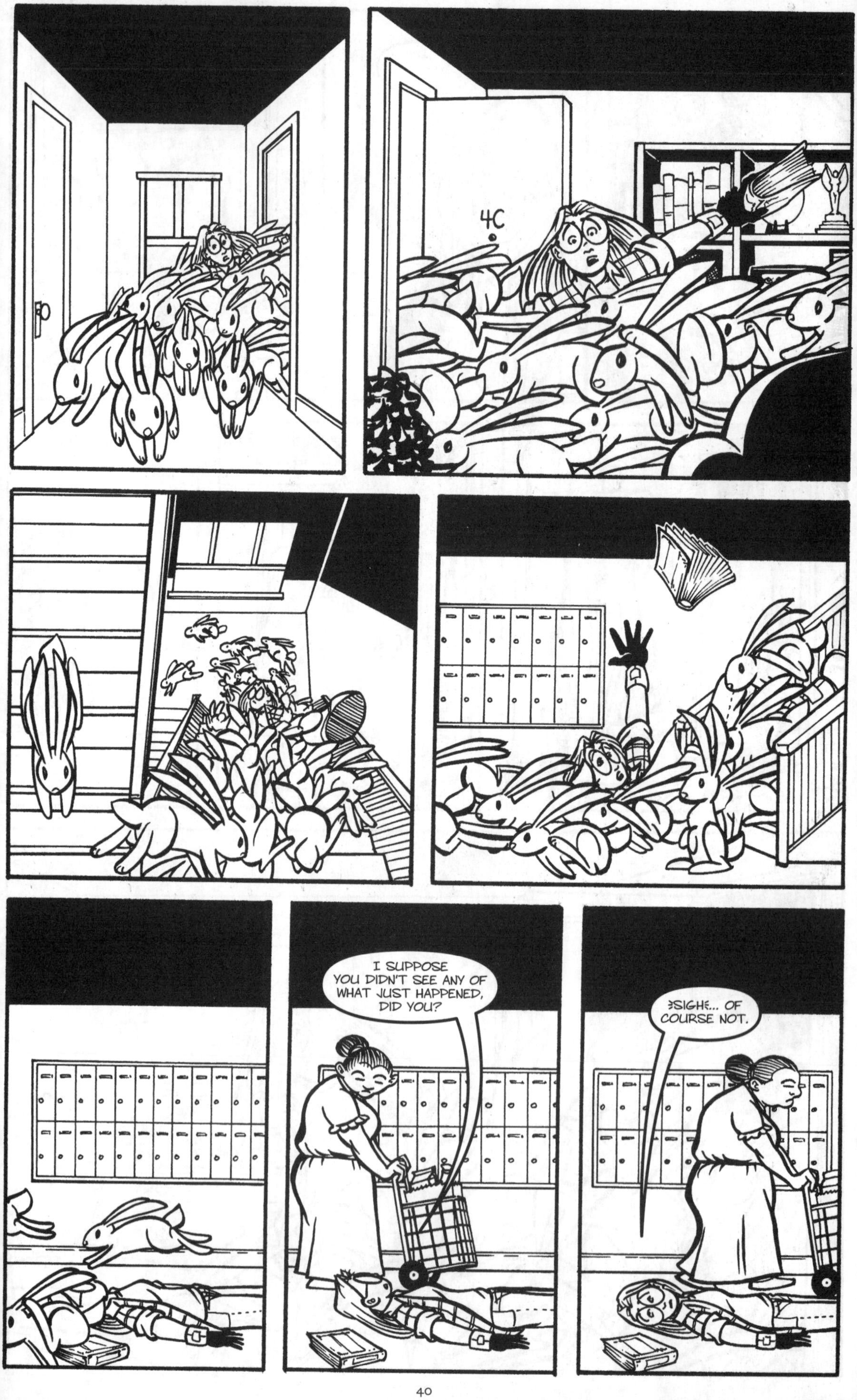
4C
I SUPPOSE YOU DIDN'T SEE ANY OF WHAT JUST HAPPENED, DID YOU?
ƎSIGHƐ... OF COURSE NOT.

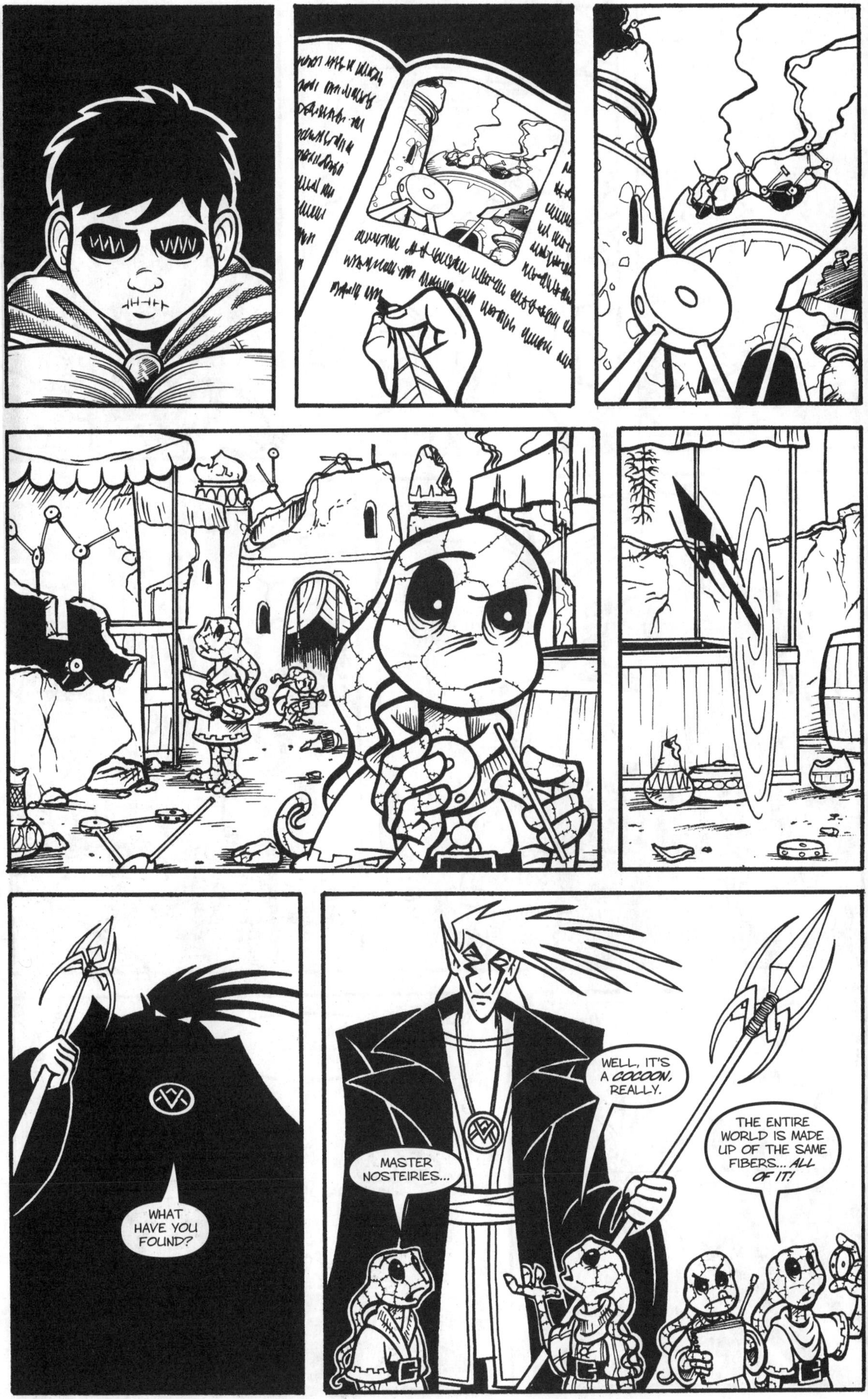
WHAT HAVE YOU FOUND?
MASTER NOSTEIRIES...
WELL, IT'S A *COCOON*, REALLY.
THE ENTIRE WORLD IS MADE UP OF THE SAME FIBERS... *ALL OF IT!*

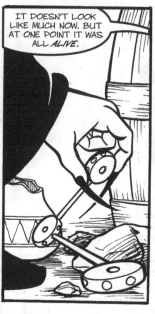

IT DOESN'T LOOK LIKE MUCH NOW, BUT AT ONE POINT IT WAS ALL *ALIVE.*

THIS REALM GAVE THE CREATURE THE NUTRIENTS TO BUILD ITSELF UP.

BUT WHEN IT GOT UP AND LEFT, THIS *WHOLE PLACE* CRUMBLED INTO, WELL--

TOYS?

I THINK.

WHATEVER THAT BEING WAS, IT'S GONE... COMPLETELY.

COULD IT HAVE GONE WITH THE GIRL?

THAT'S A POSSIBILITY. THE THING MIGHT HAVE SOMEHOW ATTACHED ITSELF TO HER WITHOUT HER EVEN KNOWING IT.

OR SHE MAY HAVE *WILLINGLY* TAKEN IT WITH HER. WE STILL HAVE NO CLEAR SENSE OF WHAT HER *MOTIVES* ARE.

rumble

rumble

rumble

rumble

UH, OH... M-M-MORE SHAKING...

THIS WHOLE PLACE IS *COLLAPSING...* WE'D BETTER--

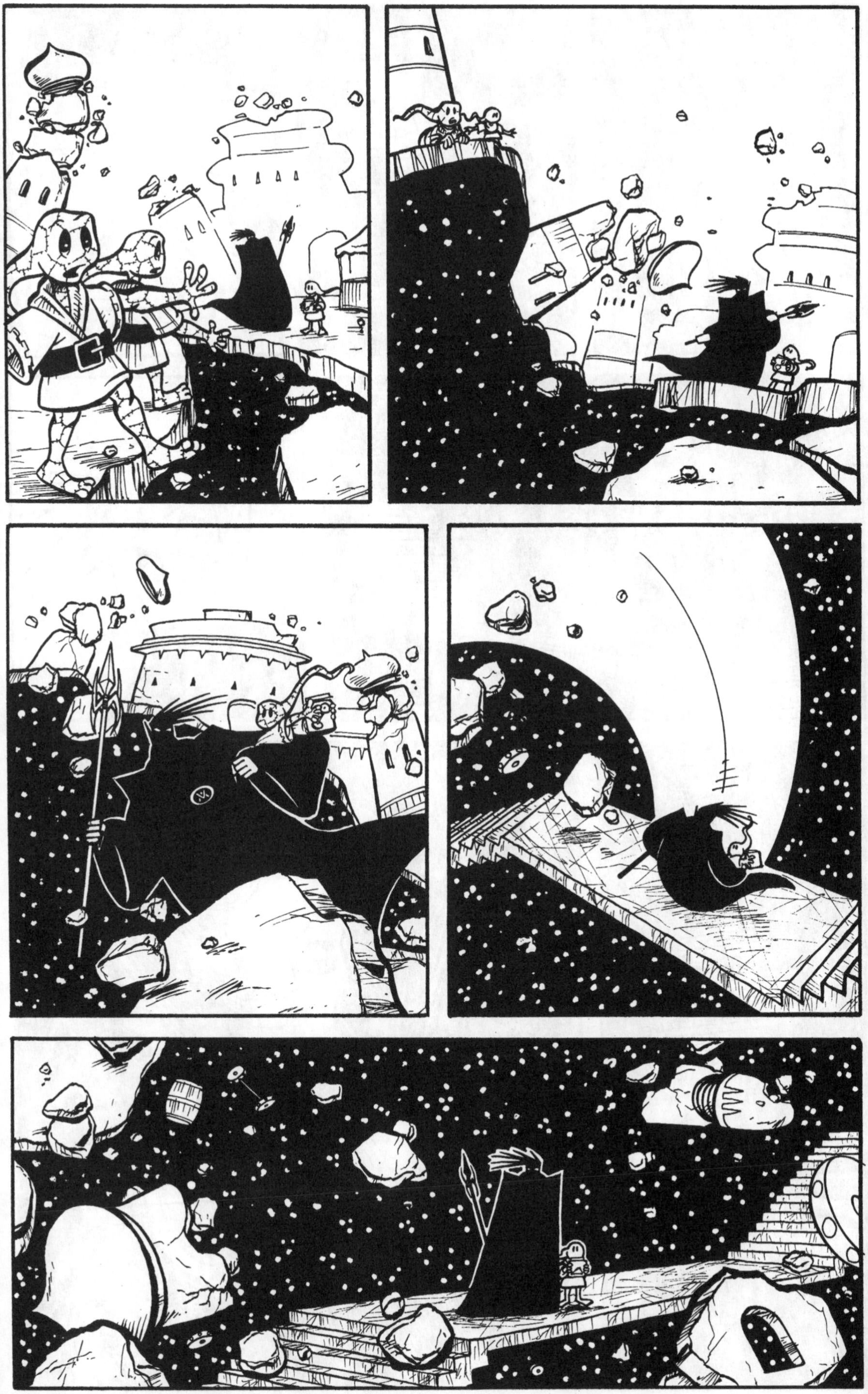

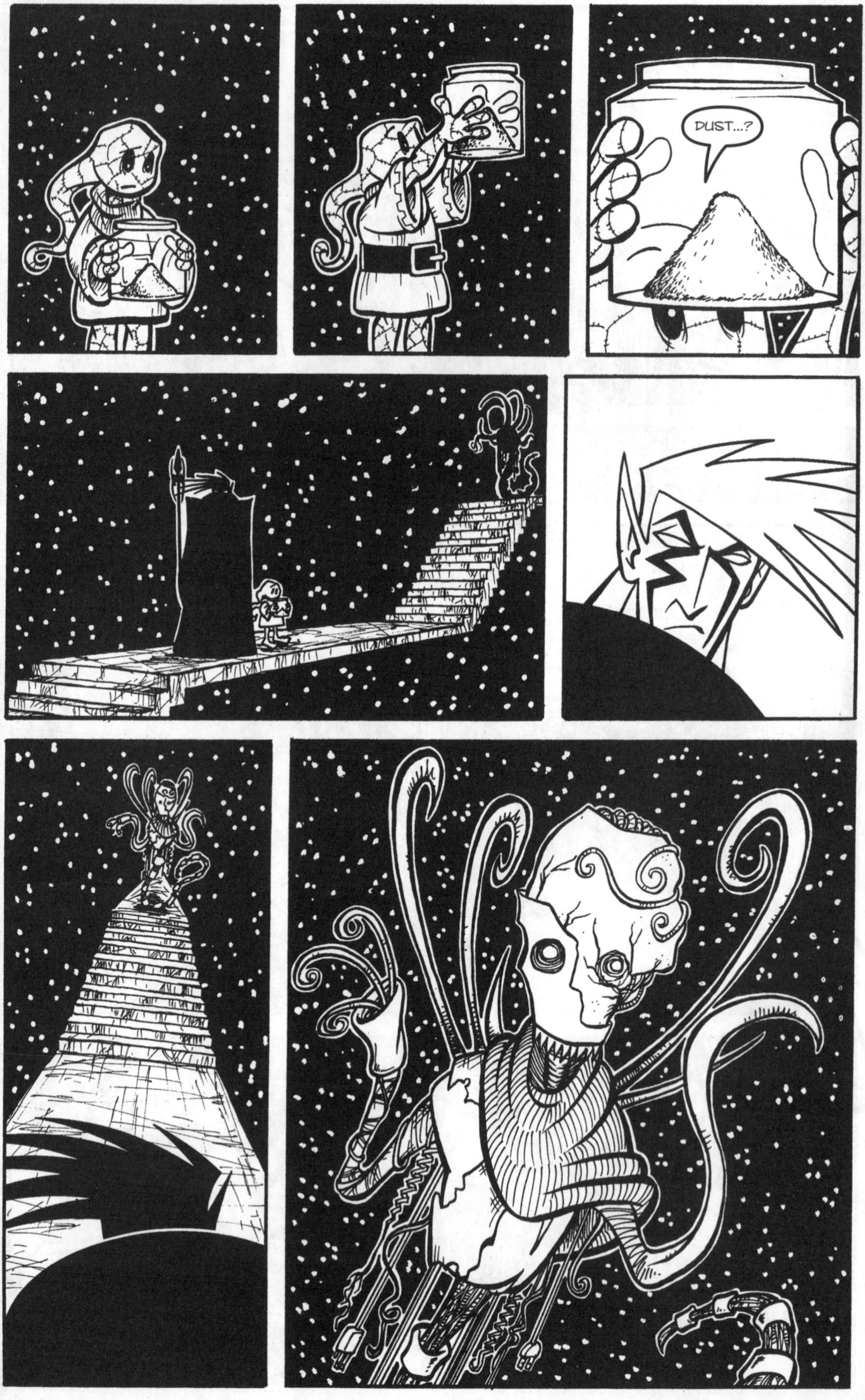
DUST...?

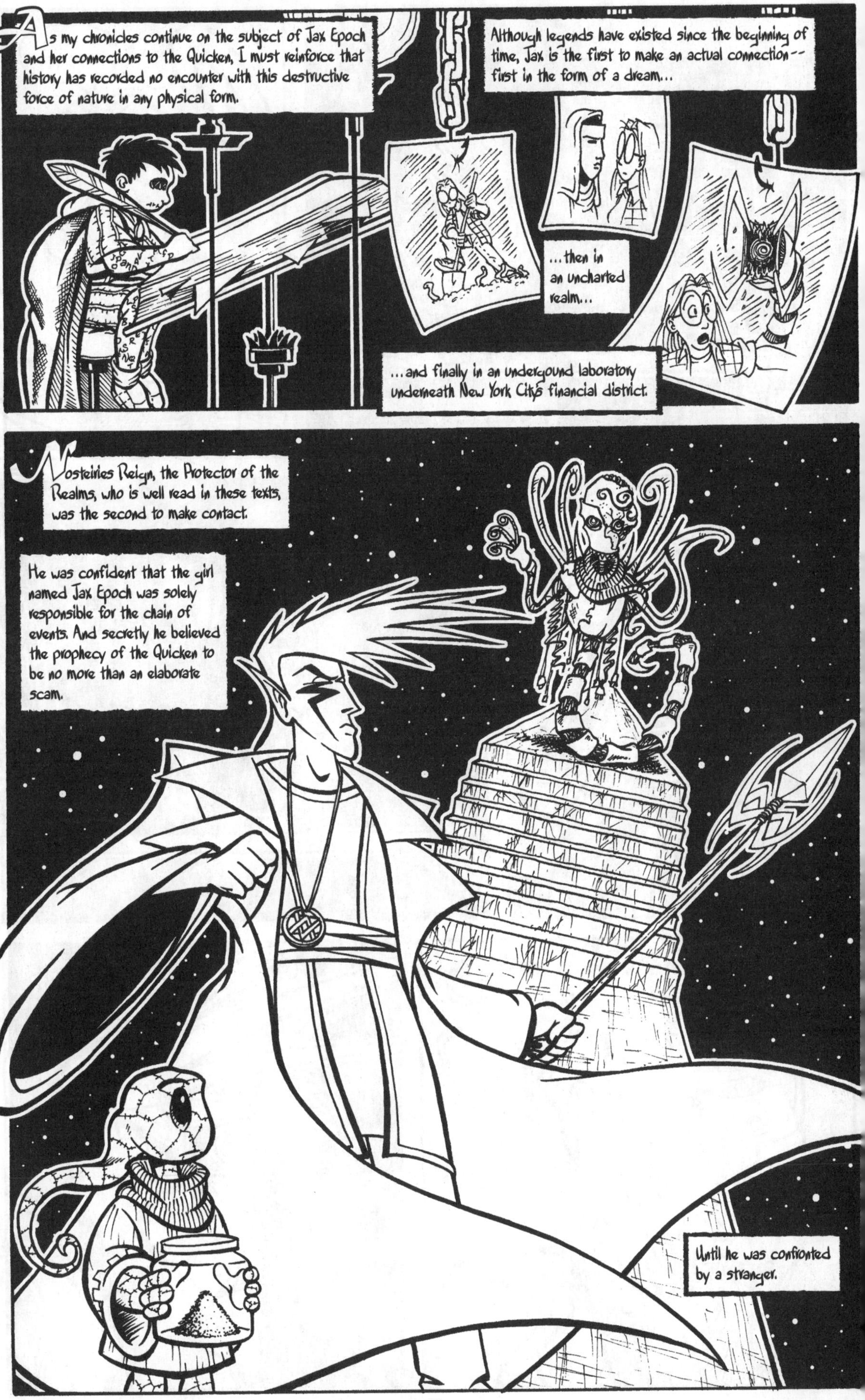
As my chronicles continue on the subject of Jax Epoch and her connections to the Quicken, I must reinforce that history has recorded no encounter with this destructive force of nature in any physical form.
Although legends have existed since the beginning of time, Jax is the first to make an actual connection--first in the form of a dream...
...then in an uncharted realm...
...and finally in an undergound laboratory underneath New York City's financial district.
Nosteiries Reign, the Protector of the Realms, who is well read in these texts, was the second to make contact.
He was confident that the girl named Jax Epoch was solely responsible for the chain of events. And secretly he believed the prophecy of the Quicken to be no more than an elaborate scam.
Until he was confronted by a stranger.

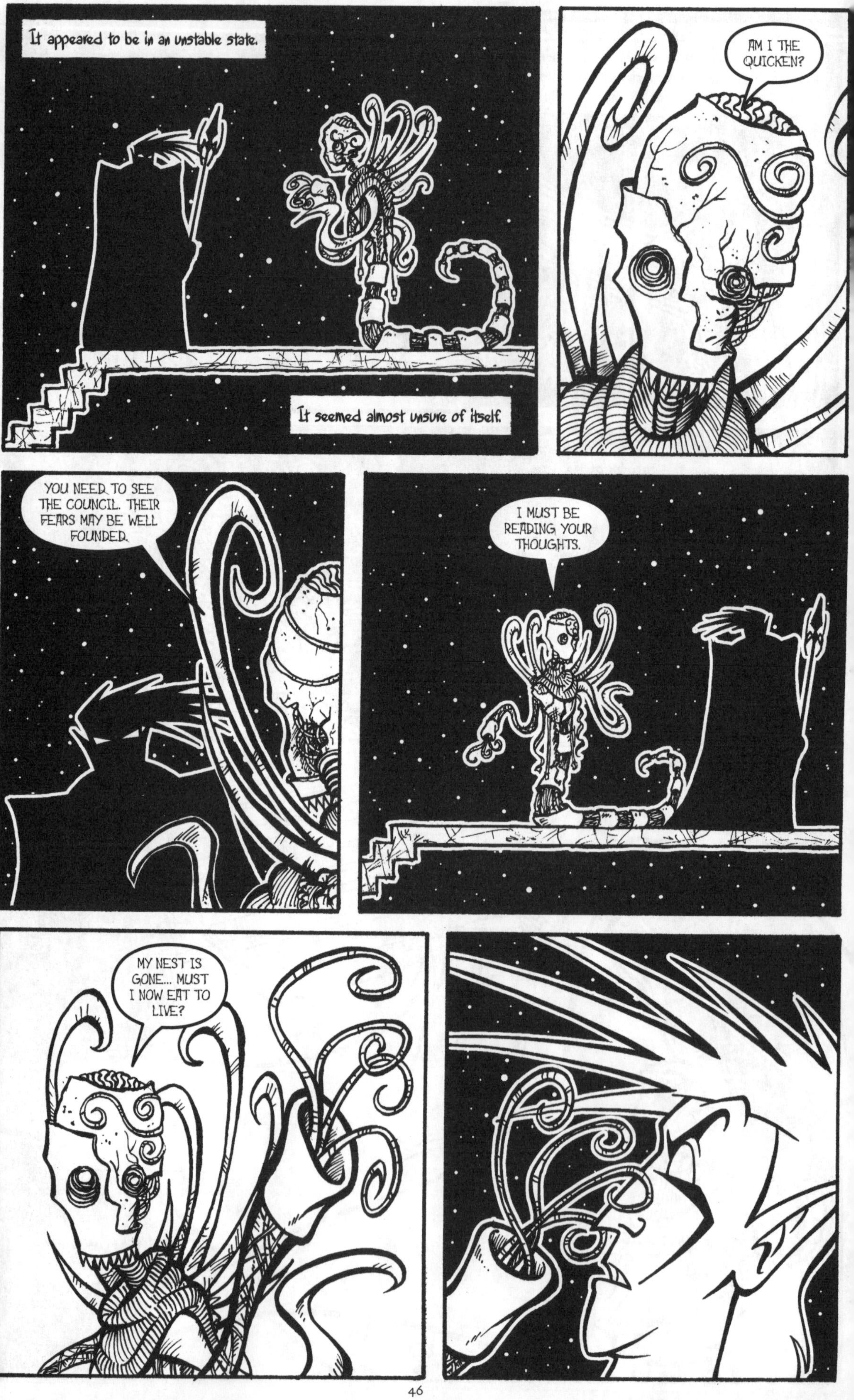
It appeared to be in an unstable state.
It seemed almost unsure of itself.
AM I THE QUICKEN?
YOU NEED TO SEE THE COUNCIL. THEIR FEARS MAY BE WELL FOUNDED.
I MUST BE READING YOUR THOUGHTS.
MY NEST IS GONE... MUST I NOW EAT TO LIVE?

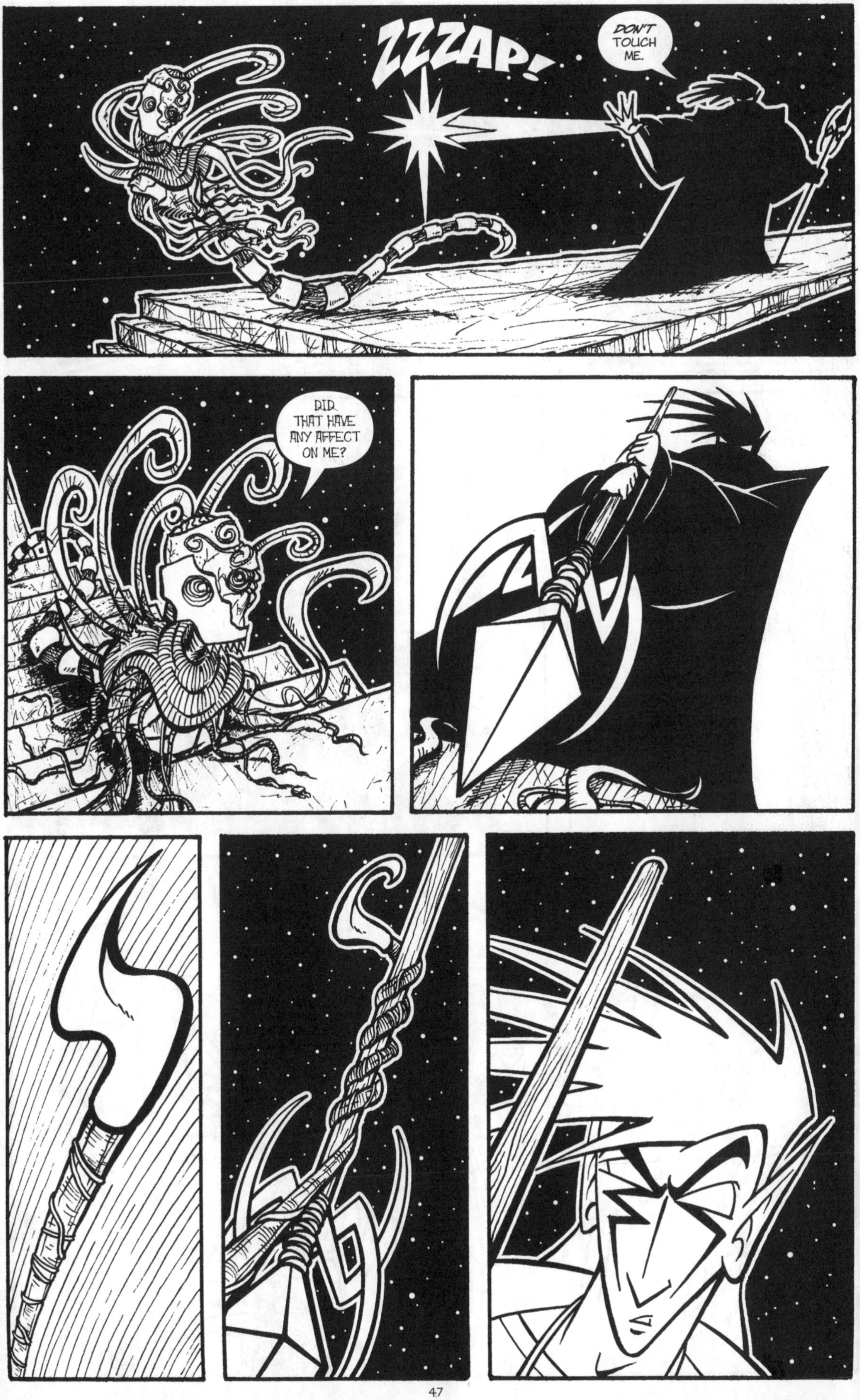
ZZZAP!
DON'T TOUCH ME.
DID THAT HAVE ANY AFFECT ON ME?

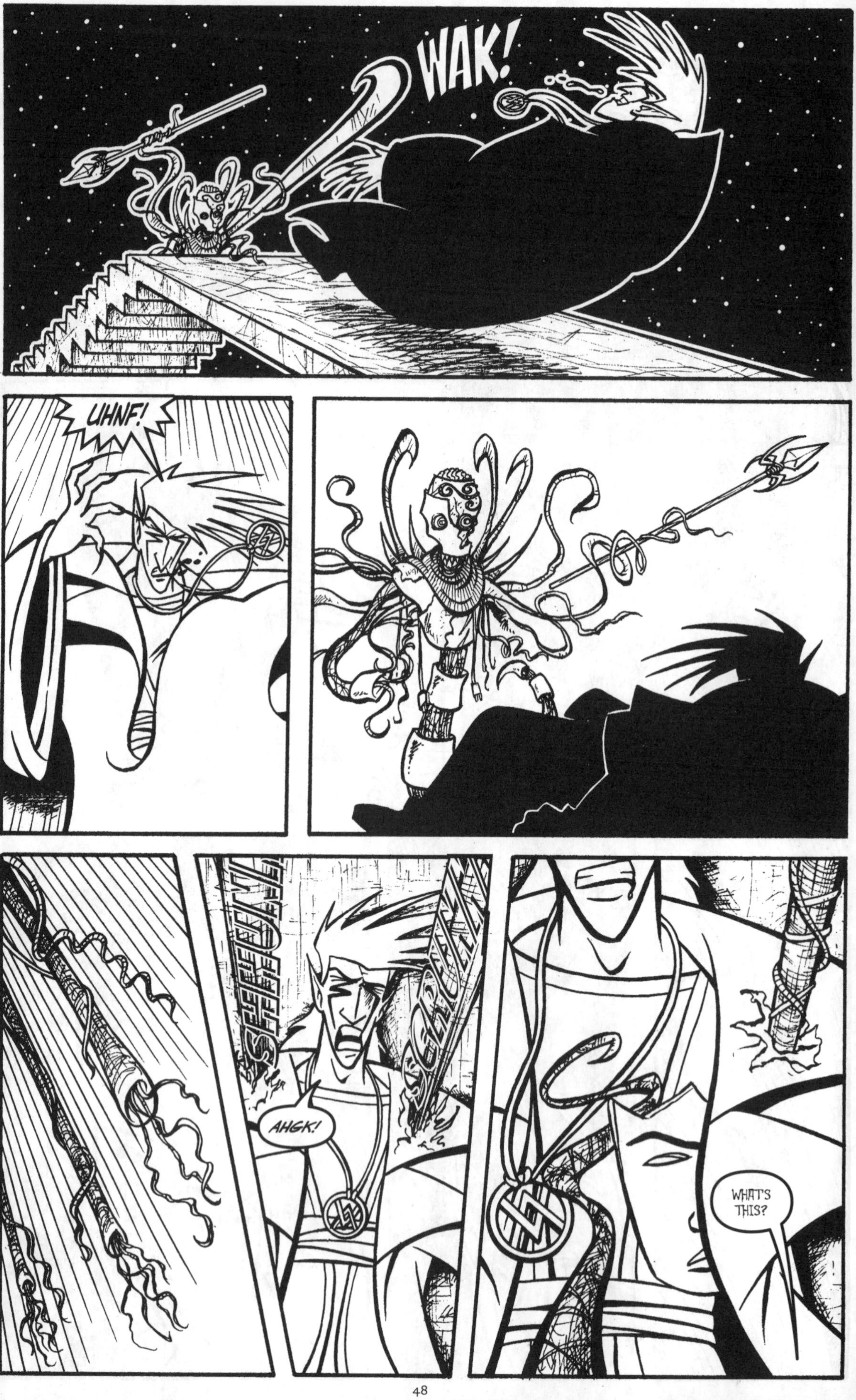
WAK!
UHNF!
AHGK!
WHAT'S THIS?

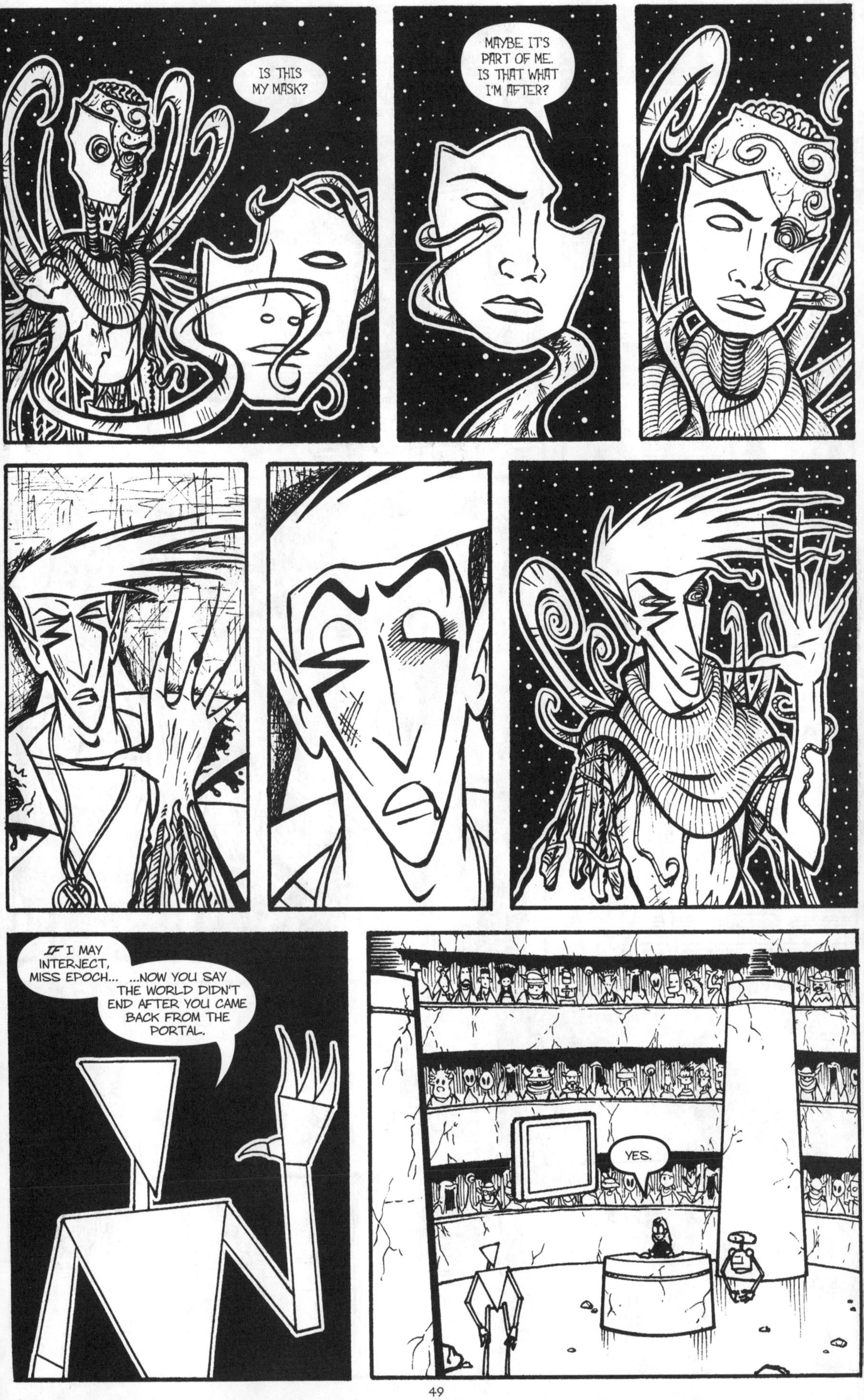

IS THIS MY MASK?
MAYBE IT'S PART OF ME. IS THAT WHAT I'M AFTER?
IF I MAY INTERJECT, MISS EPOCH...
...NOW YOU SAY THE WORLD DIDN'T END AFTER YOU CAME BACK FROM THE PORTAL.
YES.

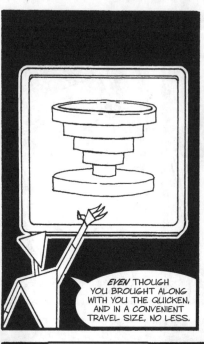

YOU SAY IT WAS JUST THE *LITTLE THINGS* THAT STARTED HAPPENENING IN YOUR WORLD THAT LED YOU TO BELIEVE REALITY WAS FALLING APART--

WELL I *DID* ALMOST DROWN FROM A CLOSET FULL OF *RABBITS.*

YES, BUT DID YOU EVER STOP TO THINK WHERE ALL THIS *MADNESS* CAME FROM? THE FLYING DRAGONS, THE TALKING MARSHMALLOWS?

EVEN THOUGH YOU BROUGHT ALONG WITH YOU THE QUICKEN, AND IN A CONVENIENT TRAVEL SIZE, NO LESS.

DID YOU EVER STOP TO THINK THAT WHILE *FANTASY* WAS LEAKING INTO YOUR WORLD, WHICH IS BUILT ON THE FOUNDATION OF REALITY...

REALITY | FANTAS

...*REALITY* MIGHT BE POURING IN AND DESTROYING THE WORLDS OF *FANTASY?*

SHE LOOKS CONFUSED. PERHAPS WE NEED MORE VISUAL AIDS?

I BELIEVE A FIELD TRIP IS IN ORDER.

vreeeee

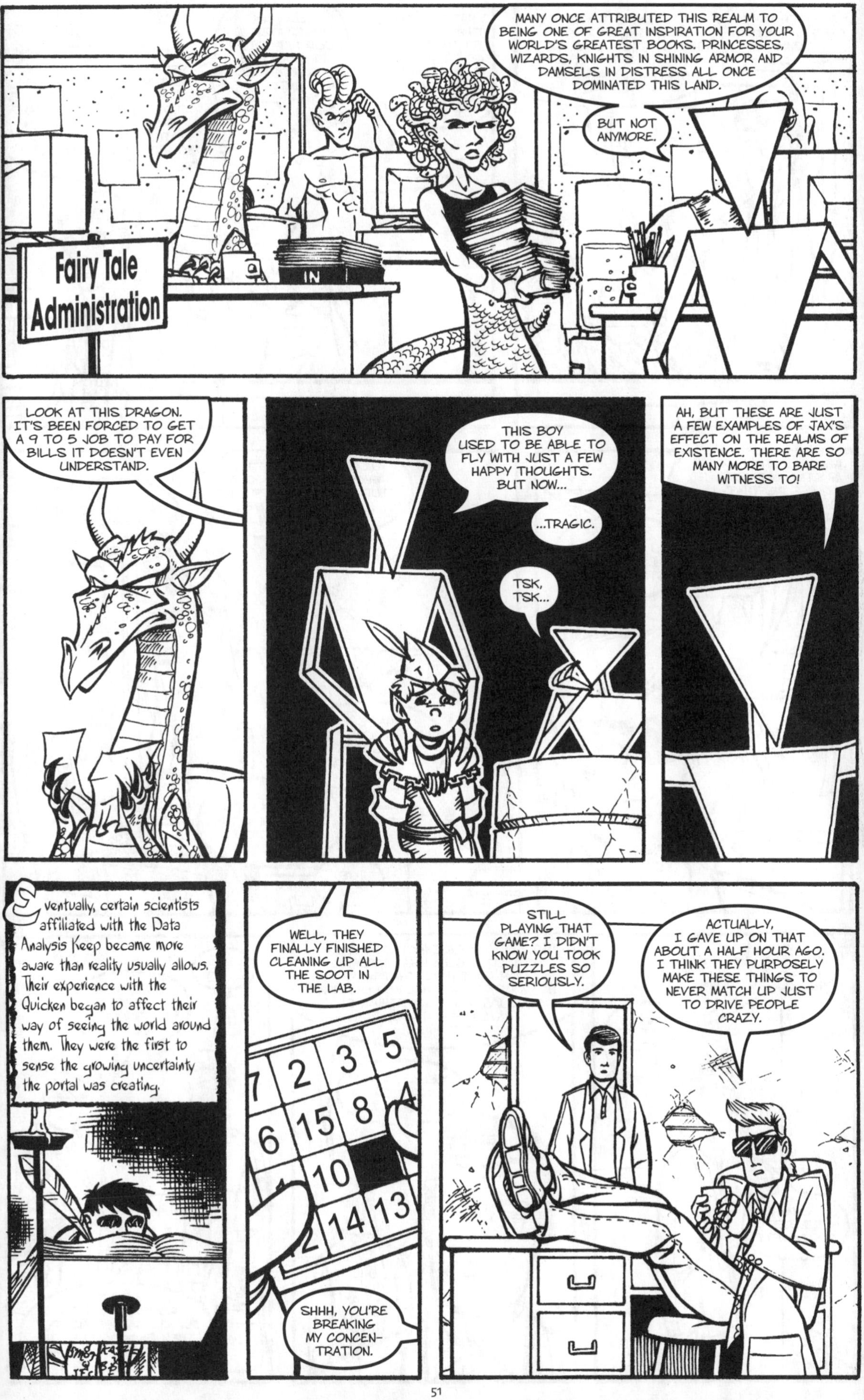

Fairy Tale Administration
MANY ONCE ATTRIBUTED THIS REALM TO BEING ONE OF GREAT INSPIRATION FOR YOUR WORLD'S GREATEST BOOKS. PRINCESSES, WIZARDS, KNIGHTS IN SHINING ARMOR AND DAMSELS IN DISTRESS ALL ONCE DOMINATED THIS LAND.
BUT NOT ANYMORE.
IN
LOOK AT THIS DRAGON. IT'S BEEN FORCED TO GET A 9 TO 5 JOB TO PAY FOR BILLS IT DOESN'T EVEN UNDERSTAND.
THIS BOY USED TO BE ABLE TO FLY WITH JUST A FEW HAPPY THOUGHTS. BUT NOW...
...TRAGIC.
TSK, TSK...
AH, BUT THESE ARE JUST A FEW EXAMPLES OF JAX'S EFFECT ON THE REALMS OF EXISTENCE. THERE ARE SO MANY MORE TO BARE WITNESS TO!
Eventually, certain scientists affiliated with the Data Analysis Keep became more aware than reality usually allows. Their experience with the Quicken began to affect their way of seeing the world around them. They were the first to sense the growing uncertainty the portal was creating.
WELL, THEY FINALLY FINISHED CLEANING UP ALL THE SOOT IN THE LAB.
SHHH, YOU'RE BREAKING MY CONCEN-TRATION.
STILL PLAYING THAT GAME? I DIDN'T KNOW YOU TOOK PUZZLES SO SERIOUSLY.
ACTUALLY, I GAVE UP ON THAT ABOUT A HALF HOUR AGO. I THINK THEY PURPOSELY MAKE THESE THINGS TO NEVER MATCH UP JUST TO DRIVE PEOPLE CRAZY.

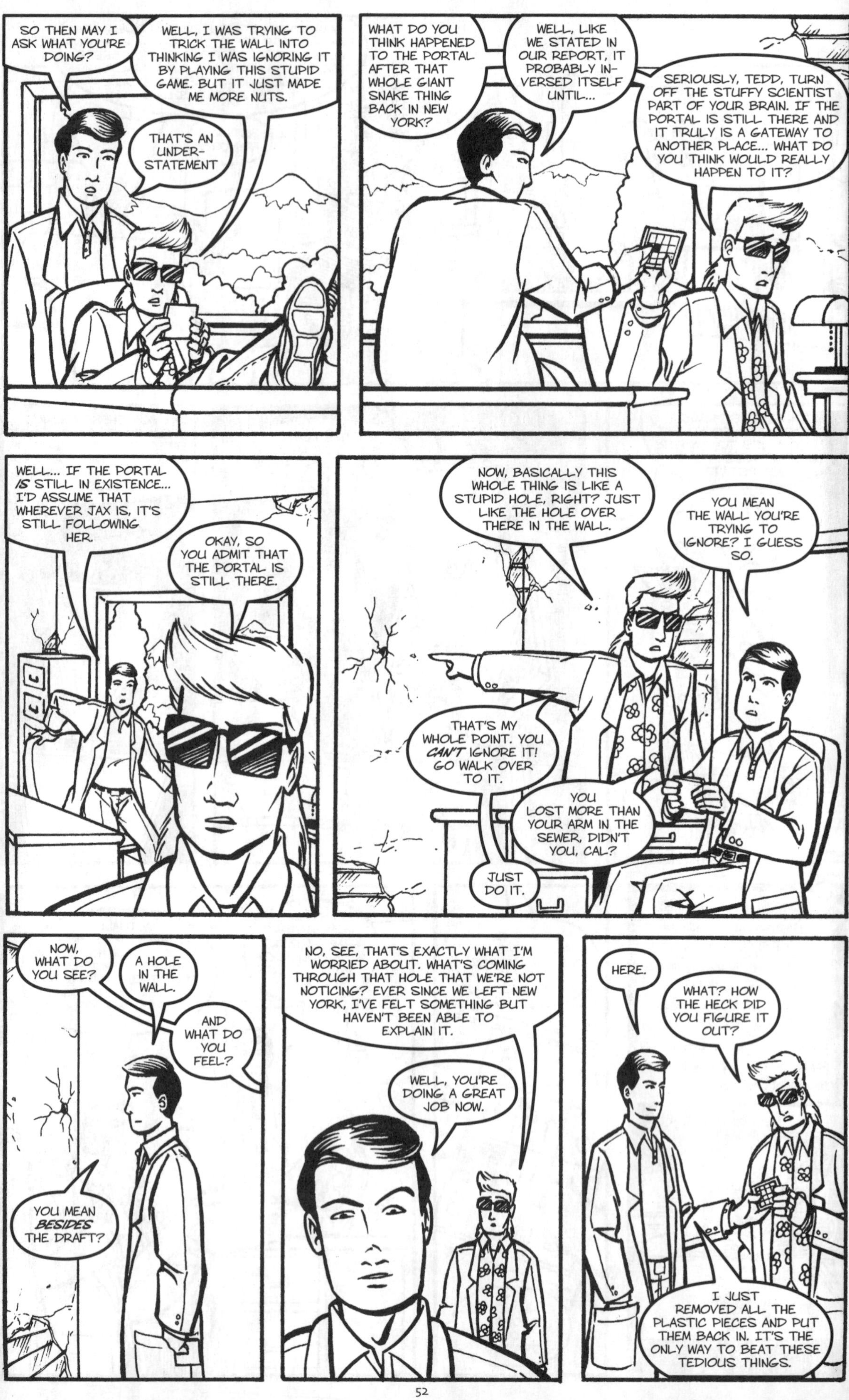
SO THEN MAY I ASK WHAT YOU'RE DOING?
WELL, I WAS TRYING TO TRICK THE WALL INTO THINKING I WAS IGNORING IT BY PLAYING THIS STUPID GAME. BUT IT JUST MADE ME MORE NUTS.
THAT'S AN UNDER-STATEMENT
WHAT DO YOU THINK HAPPENED TO THE PORTAL AFTER THAT WHOLE GIANT SNAKE THING BACK IN NEW YORK?
WELL, LIKE WE STATED IN OUR REPORT, IT PROBABLY IN-VERSED ITSELF UNTIL...
SERIOUSLY, TEDD, TURN OFF THE STUFFY SCIENTIST PART OF YOUR BRAIN. IF THE PORTAL IS STILL THERE AND IT TRULY IS A GATEWAY TO ANOTHER PLACE... WHAT DO YOU THINK WOULD REALLY HAPPEN TO IT?
WELL... IF THE PORTAL *IS* STILL IN EXISTENCE... I'D ASSUME THAT WHEREVER JAX IS, IT'S STILL FOLLOWING HER.
OKAY, SO YOU ADMIT THAT THE PORTAL IS STILL THERE.
NOW, BASICALLY THIS WHOLE THING IS LIKE A STUPID HOLE, RIGHT? JUST LIKE THE HOLE OVER THERE IN THE WALL.
YOU MEAN THE WALL YOU'RE TRYING TO IGNORE? I GUESS SO.
THAT'S MY WHOLE POINT. YOU *CAN'T* IGNORE IT! GO WALK OVER TO IT.
YOU LOST MORE THAN YOUR ARM IN THE SEWER, DIDN'T YOU, CAL?
JUST DO IT.
NOW, WHAT DO YOU SEE?
A HOLE IN THE WALL.
AND WHAT DO YOU FEEL?
YOU MEAN *BESIDES* THE DRAFT?
NO, SEE, THAT'S EXACTLY WHAT I'M WORRIED ABOUT. WHAT'S COMING THROUGH THAT HOLE THAT WE'RE NOT NOTICING? EVER SINCE WE LEFT NEW YORK, I'VE FELT SOMETHING BUT HAVEN'T BEEN ABLE TO EXPLAIN IT.
WELL, YOU'RE DOING A GREAT JOB NOW.
HERE.
WHAT? HOW THE HECK DID YOU FIGURE IT OUT?
I JUST REMOVED ALL THE PLASTIC PIECES AND PUT THEM BACK IN. IT'S THE ONLY WAY TO BEAT THESE TEDIOUS THINGS.

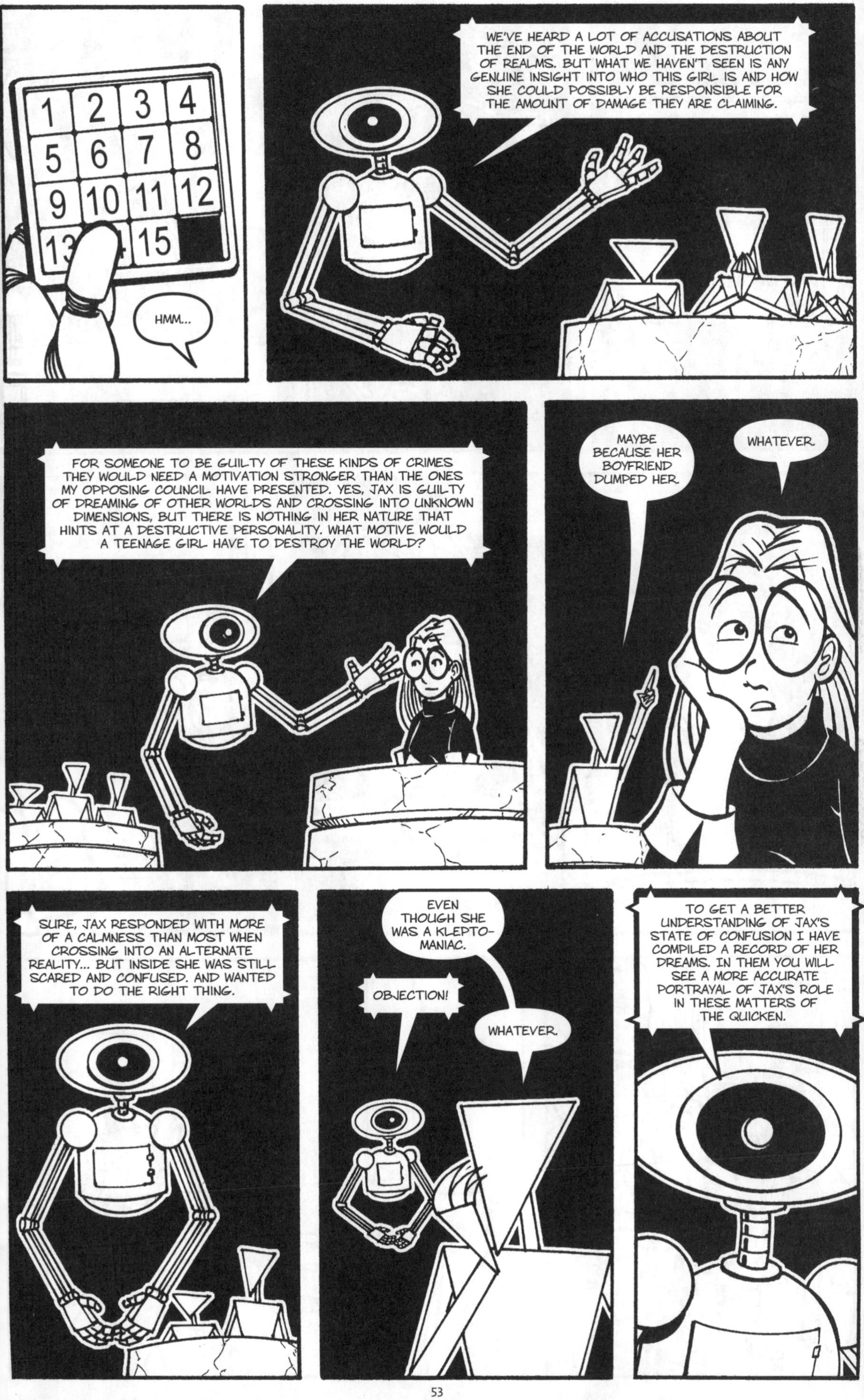
1 2 3 4 5 6 7 8 9 10 11 12 13 14 15
HMM...
WE'VE HEARD A LOT OF ACCUSATIONS ABOUT THE END OF THE WORLD AND THE DESTRUCTION OF REALMS. BUT WHAT WE HAVEN'T SEEN IS ANY GENUINE INSIGHT INTO WHO THIS GIRL IS AND HOW SHE COULD POSSIBLY BE RESPONSIBLE FOR THE AMOUNT OF DAMAGE THEY ARE CLAIMING.
FOR SOMEONE TO BE GUILTY OF THESE KINDS OF CRIMES THEY WOULD NEED A MOTIVATION STRONGER THAN THE ONES MY OPPOSING COUNCIL HAVE PRESENTED. YES, JAX IS GUILTY OF DREAMING OF OTHER WORLDS AND CROSSING INTO UNKNOWN DIMENSIONS, BUT THERE IS NOTHING IN HER NATURE THAT HINTS AT A DESTRUCTIVE PERSONALITY. WHAT MOTIVE WOULD A TEENAGE GIRL HAVE TO DESTROY THE WORLD?
MAYBE BECAUSE HER BOYFRIEND DUMPED HER.
WHATEVER.
SURE, JAX RESPONDED WITH MORE OF A CALMNESS THAN MOST WHEN CROSSING INTO AN ALTERNATE REALITY... BUT INSIDE SHE WAS STILL SCARED AND CONFUSED. AND WANTED TO DO THE RIGHT THING.
EVEN THOUGH SHE WAS A KLEPTO-MANIAC.
OBJECTION!
WHATEVER.
TO GET A BETTER UNDERSTANDING OF JAX'S STATE OF CONFUSION I HAVE COMPILED A RECORD OF HER DREAMS. IN THEM YOU WILL SEE A MORE ACCURATE PORTRAYAL OF JAX'S ROLE IN THESE MATTERS OF THE QUICKEN.

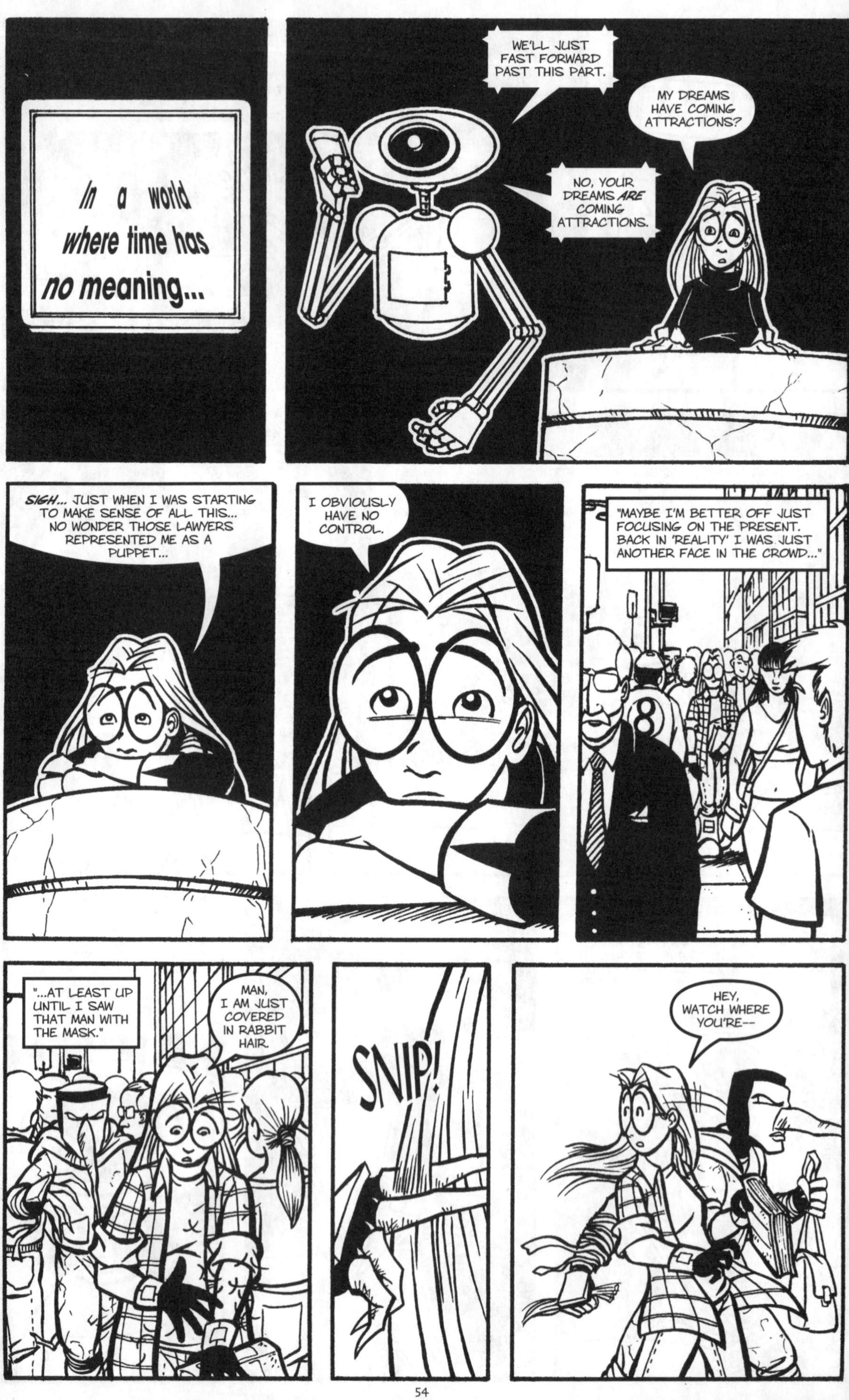
In a world where time has no meaning...
WE'LL JUST FAST FORWARD PAST THIS PART.
MY DREAMS HAVE COMING ATTRACTIONS?
NO, YOUR DREAMS *ARE* COMING ATTRACTIONS.
SIGH... JUST WHEN I WAS STARTING TO MAKE SENSE OF ALL THIS... NO WONDER THOSE LAWYERS REPRESENTED ME AS A PUPPET...
I OBVIOUSLY HAVE NO CONTROL.
"MAYBE I'M BETTER OFF JUST FOCUSING ON THE PRESENT. BACK IN 'REALITY' I WAS JUST ANOTHER FACE IN THE CROWD..."
"...AT LEAST UP UNTIL I SAW THAT MAN WITH THE MASK."
MAN, I AM JUST COVERED IN RABBIT HAIR.
SNIP!
HEY, WATCH WHERE YOU'RE--

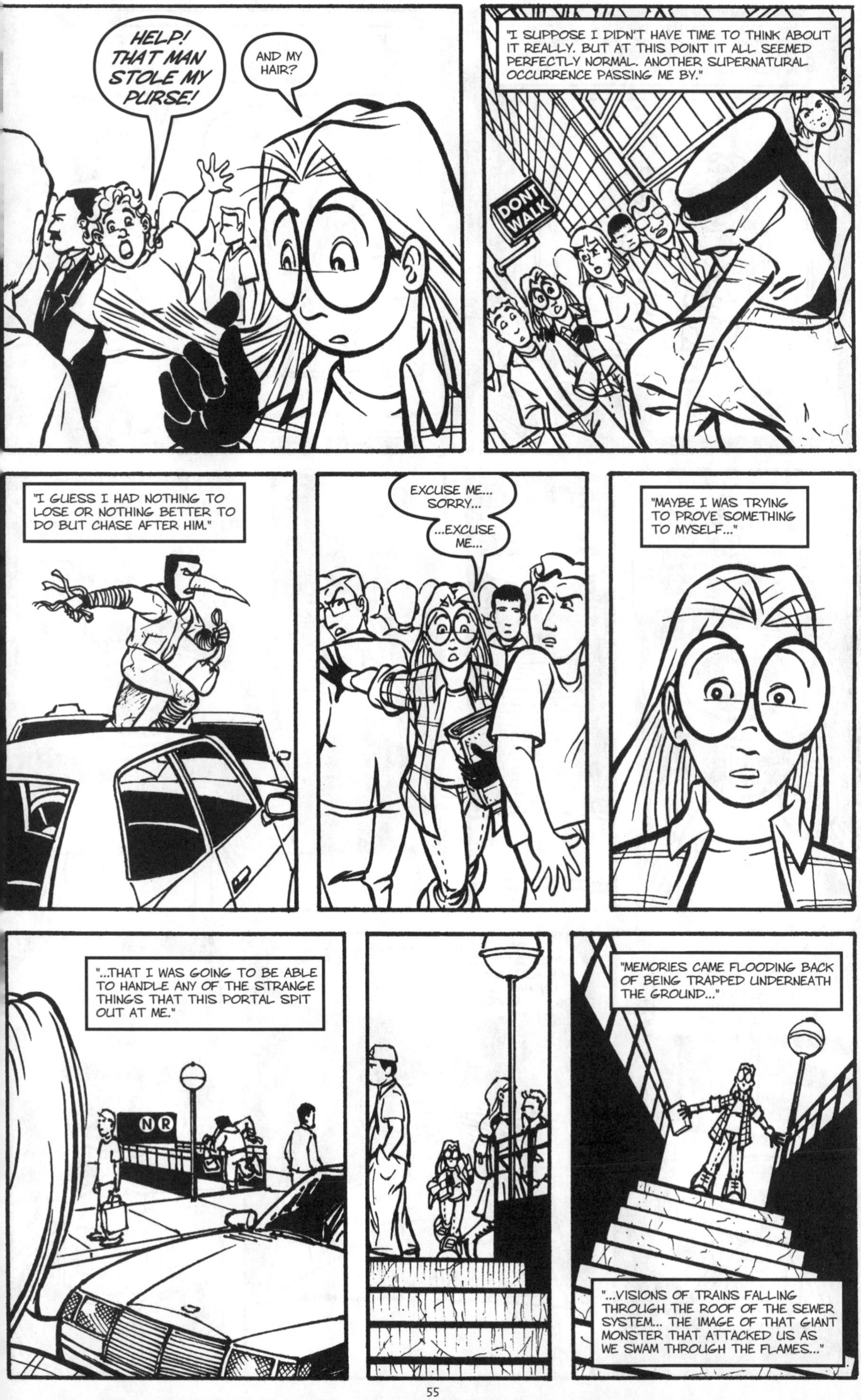
HELP! THAT MAN STOLE MY PURSE!
AND MY HAIR?
"I SUPPOSE I DIDN'T HAVE TIME TO THINK ABOUT IT REALLY. BUT AT THIS POINT IT ALL SEEMED PERFECTLY NORMAL. ANOTHER SUPERNATURAL OCCURRENCE PASSING ME BY."
DONT WALK
"I GUESS I HAD NOTHING TO LOSE OR NOTHING BETTER TO DO BUT CHASE AFTER HIM."
EXCUSE ME... SORRY...
...EXCUSE ME...
"MAYBE I WAS TRYING TO PROVE SOMETHING TO MYSELF..."
"...THAT I WAS GOING TO BE ABLE TO HANDLE ANY OF THE STRANGE THINGS THAT THIS PORTAL SPIT OUT AT ME."
N R
"MEMORIES CAME FLOODING BACK OF BEING TRAPPED UNDERNEATH THE GROUND..."
"...VISIONS OF TRAINS FALLING THROUGH THE ROOF OF THE SEWER SYSTEM... THE IMAGE OF THAT GIANT MONSTER THAT ATTACKED US AS WE SWAM THROUGH THE FLAMES..."

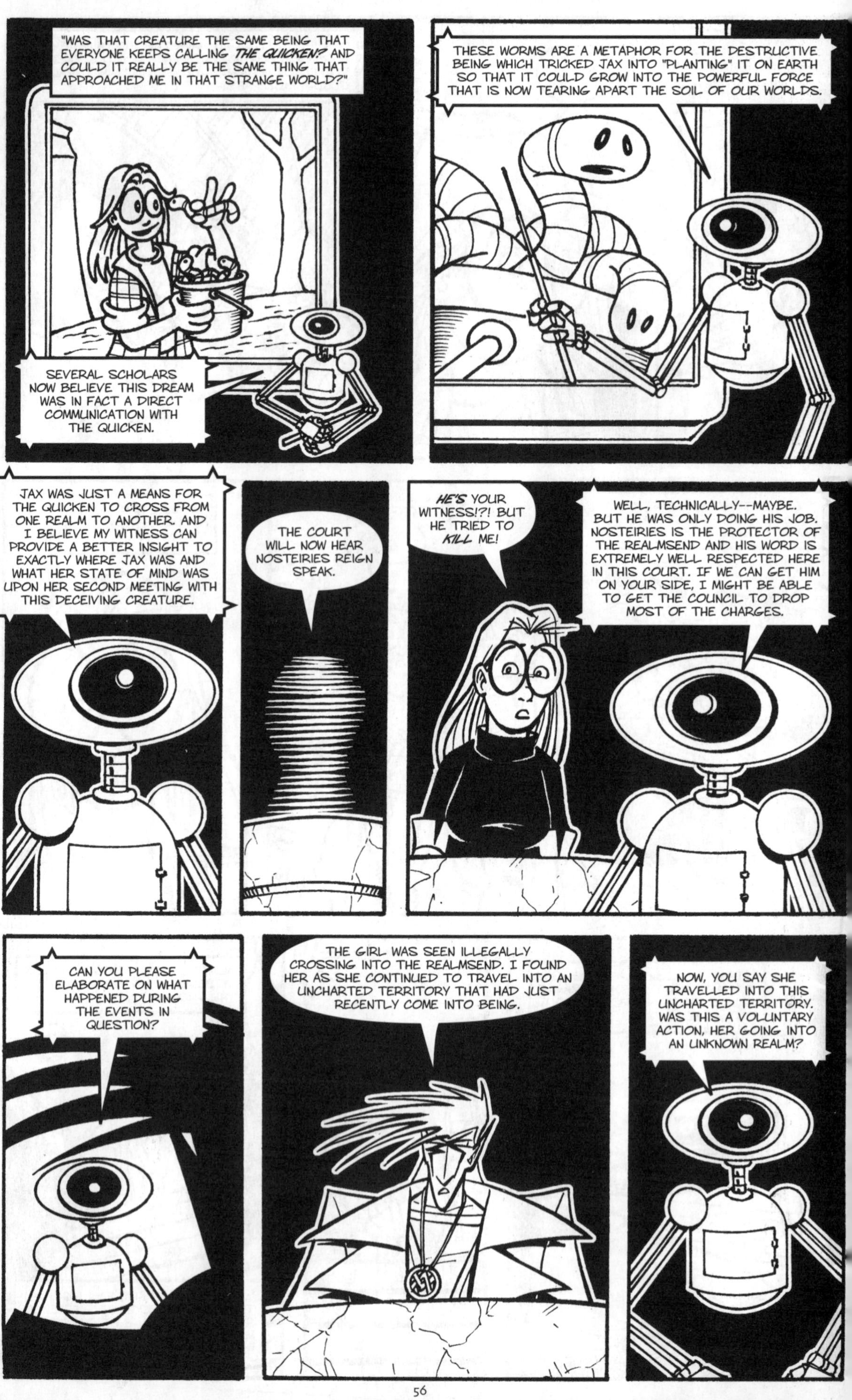
"WAS THAT CREATURE THE SAME BEING THAT EVERYONE KEEPS CALLING *THE QUICKEN?* AND COULD IT REALLY BE THE SAME THING THAT APPROACHED ME IN THAT STRANGE WORLD?"
SEVERAL SCHOLARS NOW BELIEVE THIS DREAM WAS IN FACT A DIRECT COMMUNICATION WITH THE QUICKEN.
THESE WORMS ARE A METAPHOR FOR THE DESTRUCTIVE BEING WHICH TRICKED JAX INTO "PLANTING" IT ON EARTH SO THAT IT COULD GROW INTO THE POWERFUL FORCE THAT IS NOW TEARING APART THE SOIL OF OUR WORLDS.
JAX WAS JUST A MEANS FOR THE QUICKEN TO CROSS FROM ONE REALM TO ANOTHER. AND I BELIEVE MY WITNESS CAN PROVIDE A BETTER INSIGHT TO EXACTLY WHERE JAX WAS AND WHAT HER STATE OF MIND WAS UPON HER SECOND MEETING WITH THIS DECEIVING CREATURE.
THE COURT WILL NOW HEAR NOSTEIRIES REIGN SPEAK.
HE'S YOUR WITNESS!?! BUT HE TRIED TO *KILL* ME!
WELL, TECHNICALLY--MAYBE. BUT HE WAS ONLY DOING HIS JOB. NOSTEIRIES IS THE PROTECTOR OF THE REALMSEND AND HIS WORD IS EXTREMELY WELL RESPECTED HERE IN THIS COURT. IF WE CAN GET HIM ON YOUR SIDE, I MIGHT BE ABLE TO GET THE COUNCIL TO DROP MOST OF THE CHARGES.
CAN YOU PLEASE ELABORATE ON WHAT HAPPENED DURING THE EVENTS IN QUESTION?
THE GIRL WAS SEEN ILLEGALLY CROSSING INTO THE REALMSEND. I FOUND HER AS SHE CONTINUED TO TRAVEL INTO AN UNCHARTED TERRITORY THAT HAD JUST RECENTLY COME INTO BEING.
NOW, YOU SAY SHE TRAVELLED INTO THIS UNCHARTED TERRITORY. WAS THIS A VOLUNTARY ACTION, HER GOING INTO AN UNKNOWN REALM?

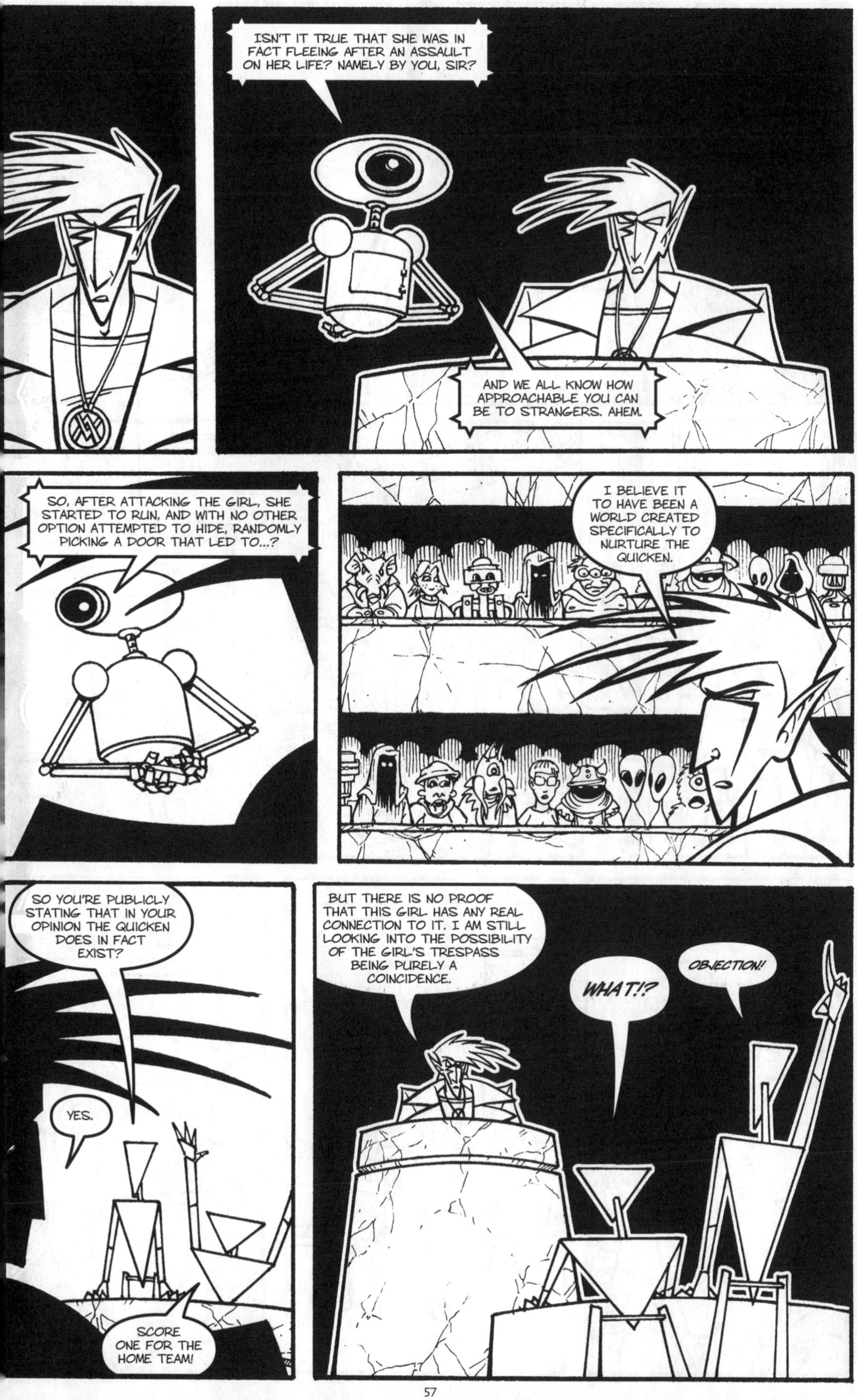
ISN'T IT TRUE THAT SHE WAS IN FACT FLEEING AFTER AN ASSAULT ON HER LIFE? NAMELY BY YOU, SIR?
AND WE ALL KNOW HOW APPROACHABLE YOU CAN BE TO STRANGERS. AHEM.
SO, AFTER ATTACKING THE GIRL, SHE STARTED TO RUN, AND WITH NO OTHER OPTION ATTEMPTED TO HIDE, RANDOMLY PICKING A DOOR THAT LED TO...?
I BELIEVE IT TO HAVE BEEN A WORLD CREATED SPECIFICALLY TO NURTURE THE QUICKEN.
SO YOU'RE PUBLICLY STATING THAT IN YOUR OPINION THE QUICKEN DOES IN FACT EXIST?
YES.
SCORE ONE FOR THE HOME TEAM!
BUT THERE IS NO PROOF THAT THIS GIRL HAS ANY REAL CONNECTION TO IT. I AM STILL LOOKING INTO THE POSSIBILITY OF THE GIRL'S TRESPASS BEING PURELY A COINCIDENCE.
WHAT!?
OBJECTION!

SO YOU HONESTLY BELIEVE THAT THIS GIRL MIGHT BE INNOCENT?

SHE IS DEFINATELY GUILTY OF UNLAWFULLY CROSSING THROUGH THE REALMSEND. BUT FOR CAUSING THE END OF THE WORLD? I VERY MUCH DOUBT IT.

UMM... GREAT. WELL, THEN THE DEFENSE RESTS.

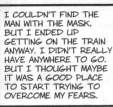

I COULDN'T FIND THE MAN WITH THE MASK, BUT I ENDED UP GETTING ON THE TRAIN ANYWAY. I DIDN'T REALLY HAVE ANYWHERE TO GO. BUT I THOUGHT MAYBE IT WAS A GOOD PLACE TO START TRYING TO OVERCOME MY FEARS.

THUMP!

ATTENTION PASSENGERS. THE TRAIN HAS RUN INTO SOME DEBRIS AHEAD AND HAS BEEN DELAYED TEMPORARILY. WE HAVE ALREADY CONTACTED THE MTA OFFICE AND WILL NOTIFY YOU AS SOON AS WE RECEIVE A SIGNAL TO START MOVING AGAIN.

GREAT. WE PROBABLY HIT SOME STRAY RABBITS.

THE END IS NEAR

MOMMY, WHAT DID THE MAN SAY?

IN THE EVENT WE DO NOT REGAIN POWER, WE'LL GIVE FURTHER INSTRUCTIONS WHEN TO START EXITING THE TRAIN.

SO, DO YOU REALLY THINK THE WORLD WILL END?

EXCUSE ME?

OH, RIGHT. YOU MEAN BECAUSE OF THE SIGN. I THINK ROLAND HERE BELIEVES IT. BUT ME, I'M IN IT JUST FOR THE EXTRA CASH.

THE END IS NEAR

EXTRA CASH?

YEAH, WE GET PAID TEN BUCKS AN HOUR TO STAND IN FRONT OF BANKS WITH THESE THINGS. BOSS SAYS PARANOIA INCREASES SPENDING HABITS AMONG THE MIDDLE AGED.

THAT'S PRETTY SICK.

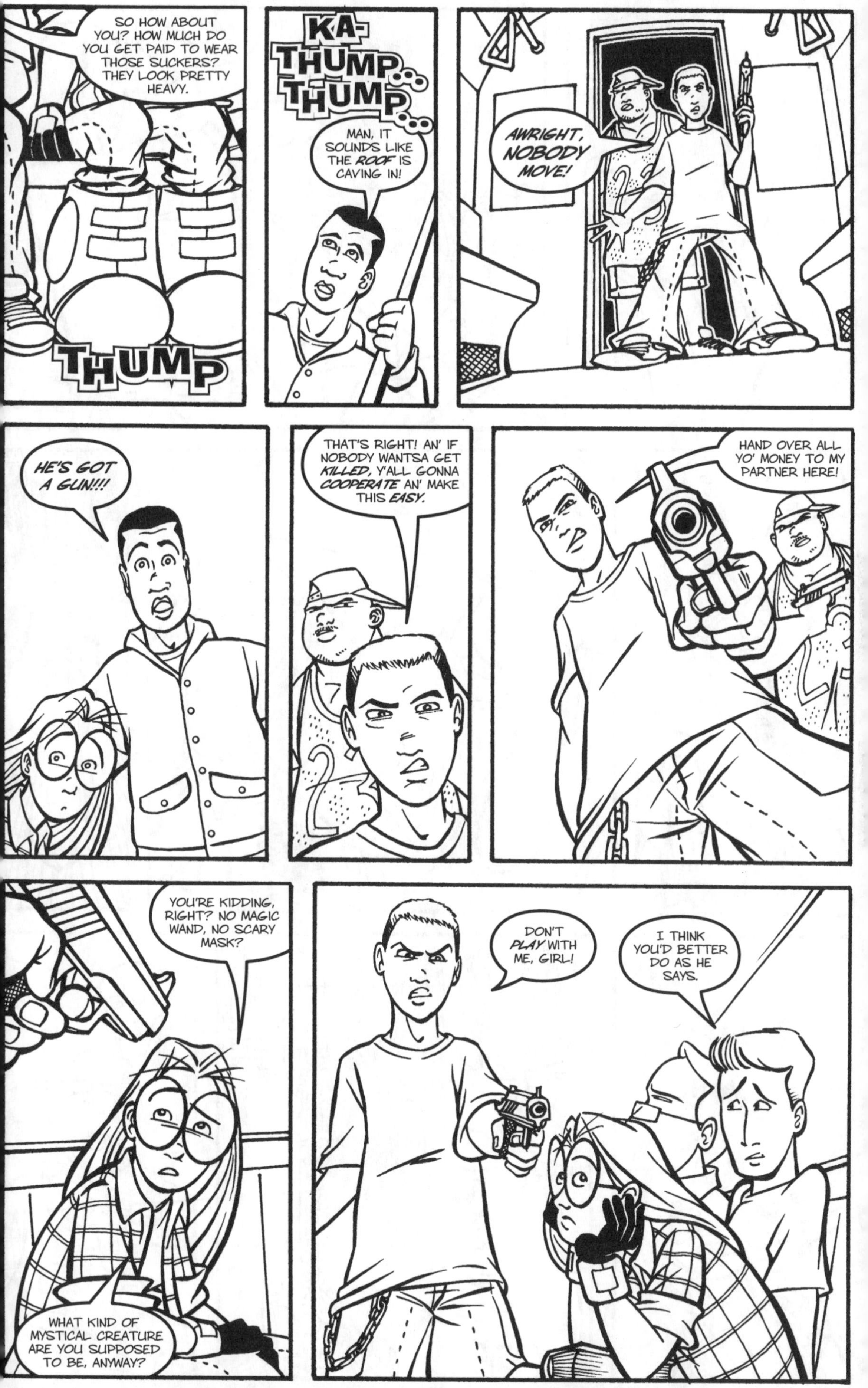
SO HOW ABOUT YOU? HOW MUCH DO YOU GET PAID TO WEAR THOSE SUCKERS? THEY LOOK PRETTY HEAVY.
THUMP
KA-THUMP... THUMP...
MAN, IT SOUNDS LIKE THE ROOF IS CAVING IN!
AWRIGHT, NOBODY MOVE!
HE'S GOT A GUN!!!
THAT'S RIGHT! AN' IF NOBODY WANTSA GET KILLED, Y'ALL GONNA COOPERATE AN' MAKE THIS EASY.
HAND OVER ALL YO' MONEY TO MY PARTNER HERE!
YOU'RE KIDDING, RIGHT? NO MAGIC WAND, NO SCARY MASK?
WHAT KIND OF MYSTICAL CREATURE ARE YOU SUPPOSED TO BE, ANYWAY?
DON'T PLAY WITH ME, GIRL!
I THINK YOU'D BETTER DO AS HE SAYS.

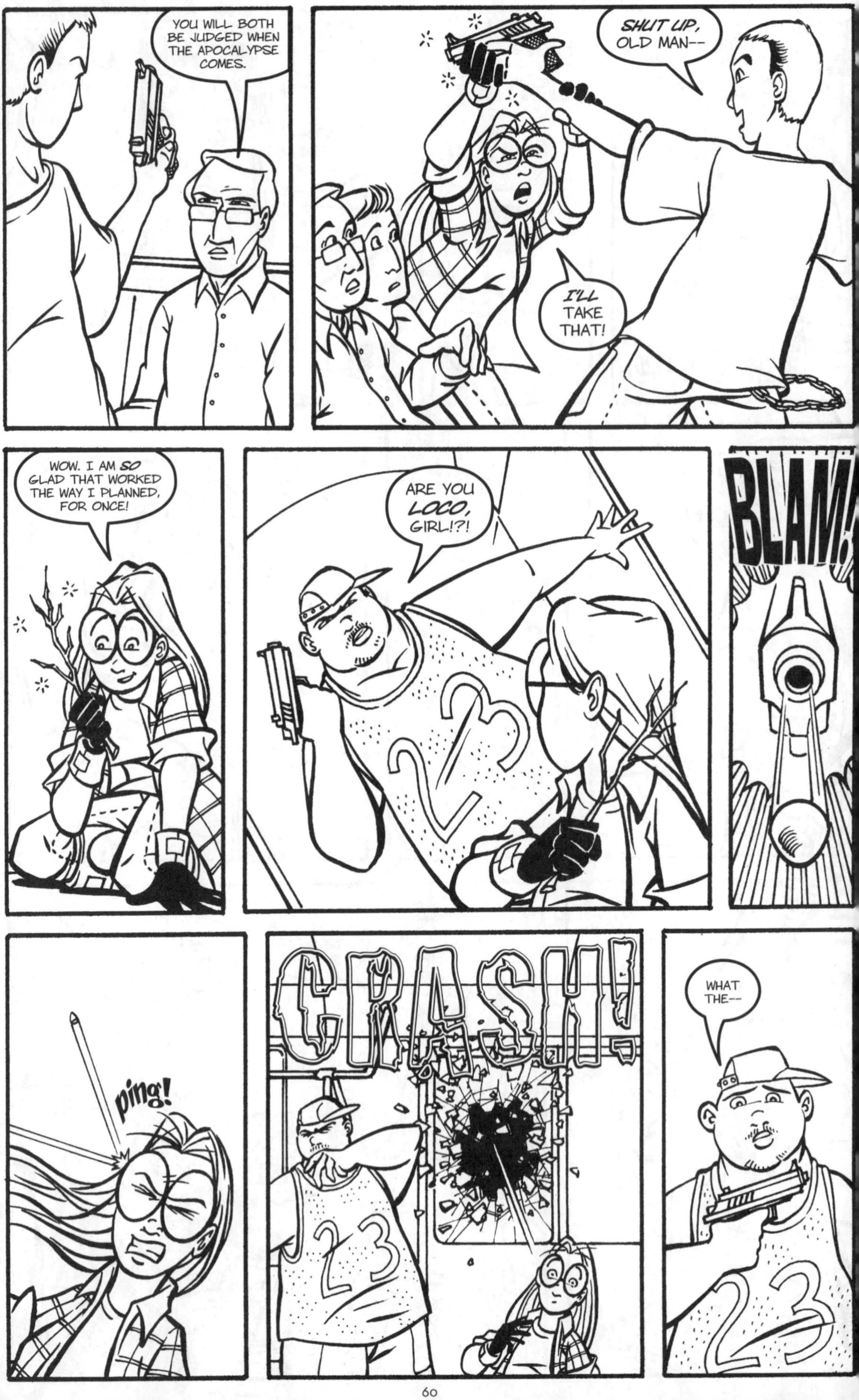
YOU WILL BOTH BE JUDGED WHEN THE APOCALYPSE COMES.
SHUT UP, OLD MAN--
I'LL TAKE THAT!
WOW. I AM SO GLAD THAT WORKED THE WAY I PLANNED, FOR ONCE!
ARE YOU LOCO, GIRL!?!
BLAM!
ping!
CRASH!
WHAT THE--

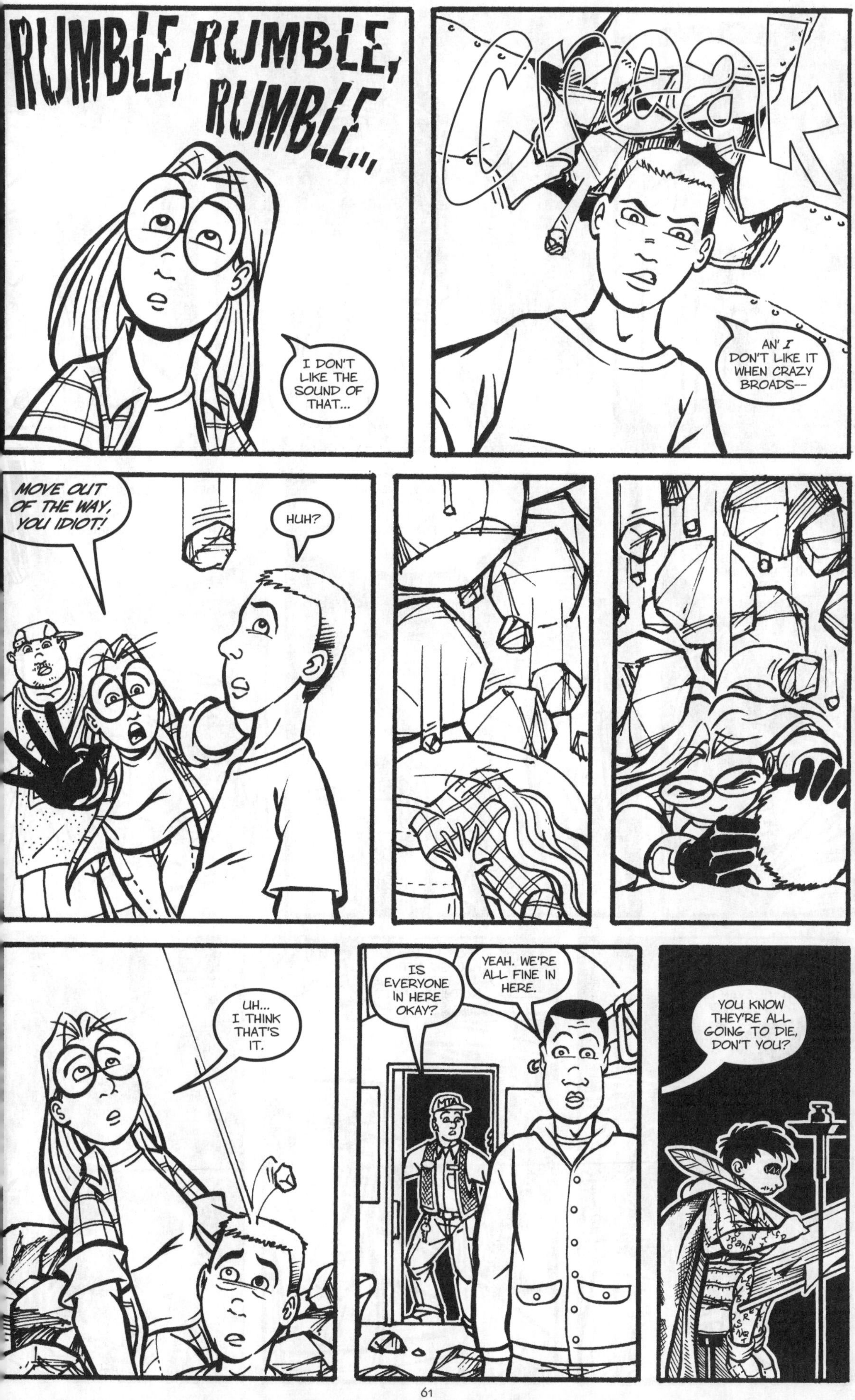
RUMBLE, RUMBLE, RUMBLE...
I DON'T LIKE THE SOUND OF THAT...
creak
AN' I DON'T LIKE IT WHEN CRAZY BROADS--
MOVE OUT OF THE WAY, YOU IDIOT!
HUH?
UH... I THINK THAT'S IT.
IS EVERYONE IN HERE OKAY?
YEAH. WE'RE ALL FINE IN HERE.
MTA
YOU KNOW THEY'RE ALL GOING TO DIE, DON'T YOU?

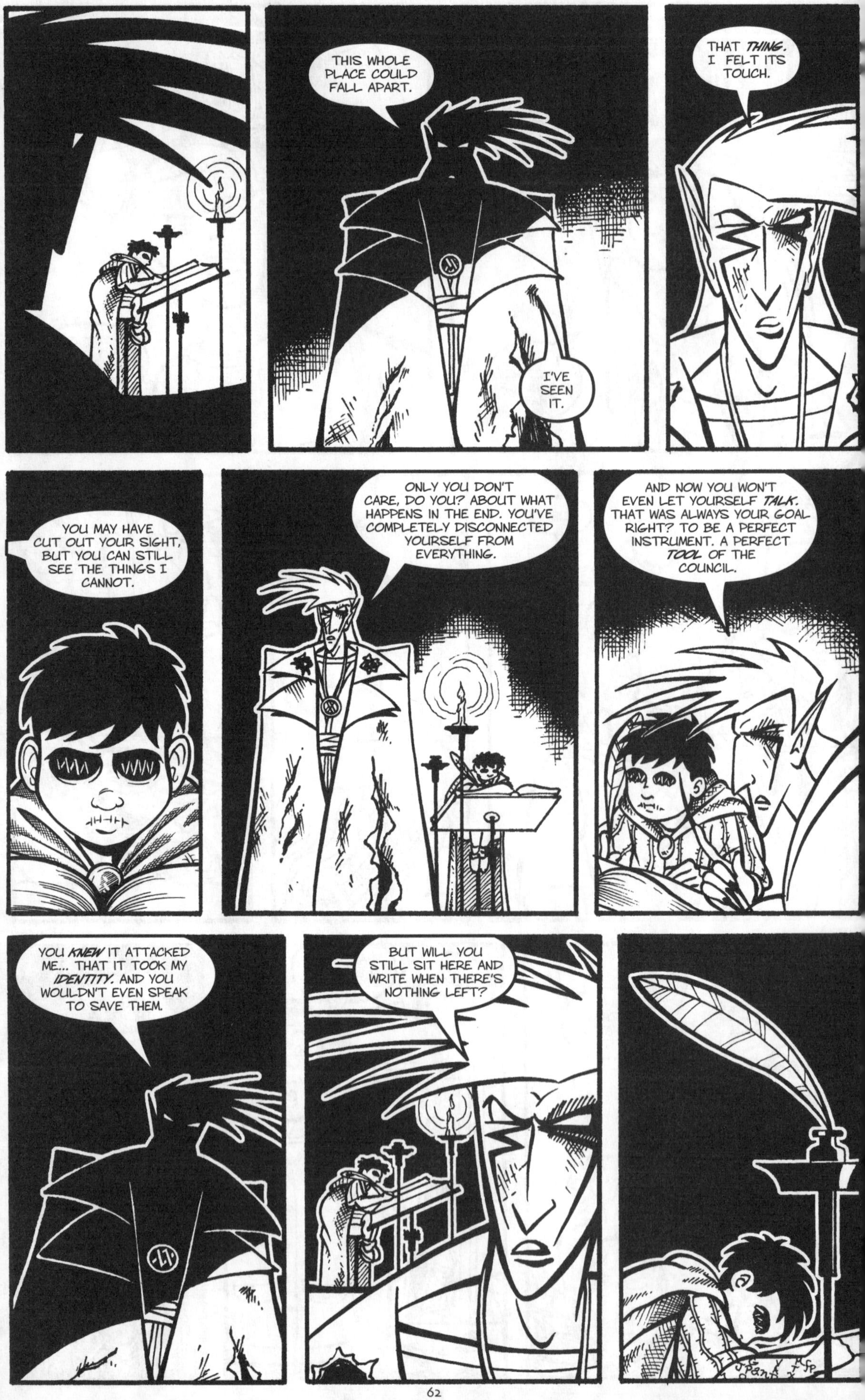
THIS WHOLE PLACE COULD FALL APART.
I'VE SEEN IT.
THAT THING. I FELT ITS TOUCH.
YOU MAY HAVE CUT OUT YOUR SIGHT, BUT YOU CAN STILL SEE THE THINGS I CANNOT.
ONLY YOU DON'T CARE, DO YOU? ABOUT WHAT HAPPENS IN THE END. YOU'VE COMPLETELY DISCONNECTED YOURSELF FROM EVERYTHING.
AND NOW YOU WON'T EVEN LET YOURSELF TALK. THAT WAS ALWAYS YOUR GOAL RIGHT? TO BE A PERFECT INSTRUMENT. A PERFECT TOOL OF THE COUNCIL.
YOU KNEW IT ATTACKED ME... THAT IT TOOK MY IDENTITY. AND YOU WOULDN'T EVEN SPEAK TO SAVE THEM.
BUT WILL YOU STILL SIT HERE AND WRITE WHEN THERE'S NOTHING LEFT?

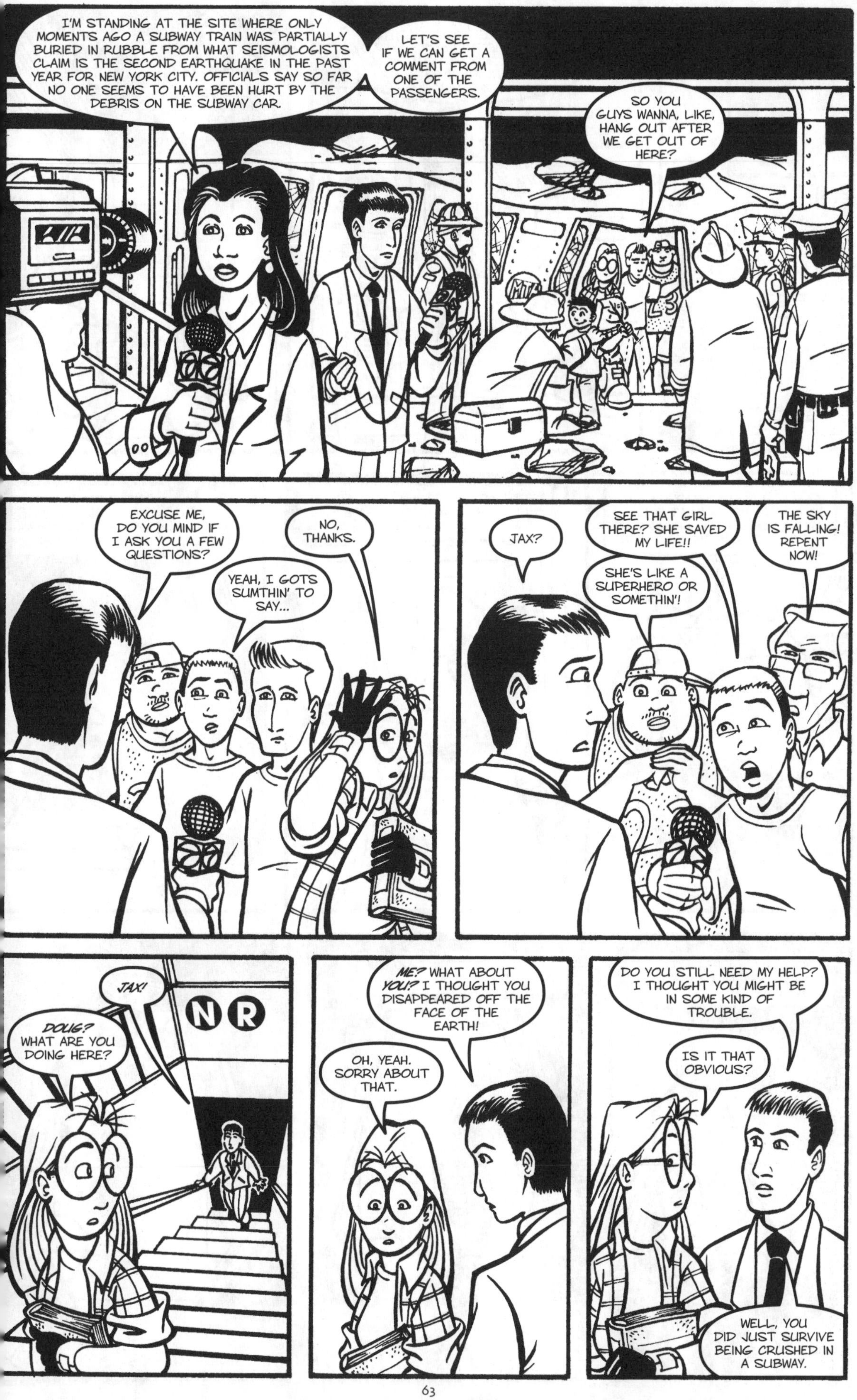
I'M STANDING AT THE SITE WHERE ONLY MOMENTS AGO A SUBWAY TRAIN WAS PARTIALLY BURIED IN RUBBLE FROM WHAT SEISMOLOGISTS CLAIM IS THE SECOND EARTHQUAKE IN THE PAST YEAR FOR NEW YORK CITY. OFFICIALS SAY SO FAR NO ONE SEEMS TO HAVE BEEN HURT BY THE DEBRIS ON THE SUBWAY CAR.
LET'S SEE IF WE CAN GET A COMMENT FROM ONE OF THE PASSENGERS.
SO YOU GUYS WANNA, LIKE, HANG OUT AFTER WE GET OUT OF HERE?
EXCUSE ME, DO YOU MIND IF I ASK YOU A FEW QUESTIONS?
NO, THANKS.
YEAH, I GOTS SUMTHIN' TO SAY...
JAX?
SEE THAT GIRL THERE? SHE SAVED MY LIFE!!
SHE'S LIKE A SUPERHERO OR SOMETHIN'!
THE SKY IS FALLING! REPENT NOW!
JAX!
DOUG? WHAT ARE YOU DOING HERE?
N R
ME? WHAT ABOUT YOU? I THOUGHT YOU DISAPPEARED OFF THE FACE OF THE EARTH!
OH, YEAH. SORRY ABOUT THAT.
DO YOU STILL NEED MY HELP? I THOUGHT YOU MIGHT BE IN SOME KIND OF TROUBLE.
IS IT THAT OBVIOUS?
WELL, YOU DID JUST SURVIVE BEING CRUSHED IN A SUBWAY.

DOWNTOWN NEW YORK...

WHEN THE PHONE GOT DISCONNECTED THAT NIGHT I THOUGHT I HEARD POLICE SHOWING UP AND SOMEONE MENTIONING HIDING YOUR JOURNAL OR SOMETHING.

HMM... I GUESS YOU DON'T WANT ANY COFFEE.

"I FELL ASLEEP ON DOUG'S COUCH, AFRAID OF WHAT ELSE COULD POSSIBLY HAPPEN TO ME IF I STAYED AWAKE ANY LONGER."

"I DREAMT THAT I WAS IN A PRISON CELL WITH ONLY A TELEVISION FULL OF STATIC TO KEEP ME COMPANY..."

"AND I KEPT WATCHING RERUNS OF THE SAME SHOW, OVER AND OVER."

"EVENTUALLY, I REALIZED I COULD JUST GET UP AND LEAVE..."

"BECAUSE THERE WAS NO ONE THERE TO STOP ME."

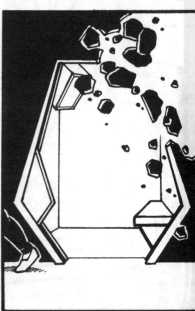

"I BEGAN TO NOTICE SOME PEOPLE WERE STILL LEFT THERE... BUT THEY WEREN'T PEOPLE... AND THEY WEREN'T BREATHING."

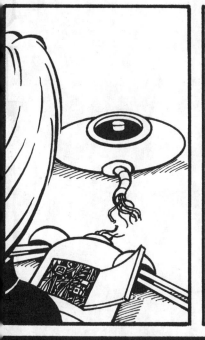

"I SIFTED THROUGH THEM AS IF THEY WERE OLD FRIENDS... EVEN THOUGH THEY DIDN'T SEEM FAMILIAR TO ME AT THE TIME."

Every word is for the sole purpose of documentation, guided by the perspective of those who cannot participate, nor interfere in such events.

I write these reports as I write any of my text, and although as Scribe I may pass judgement, I do not pretend I can persuade the opinion of those eternal.

ANXIETY
disorder

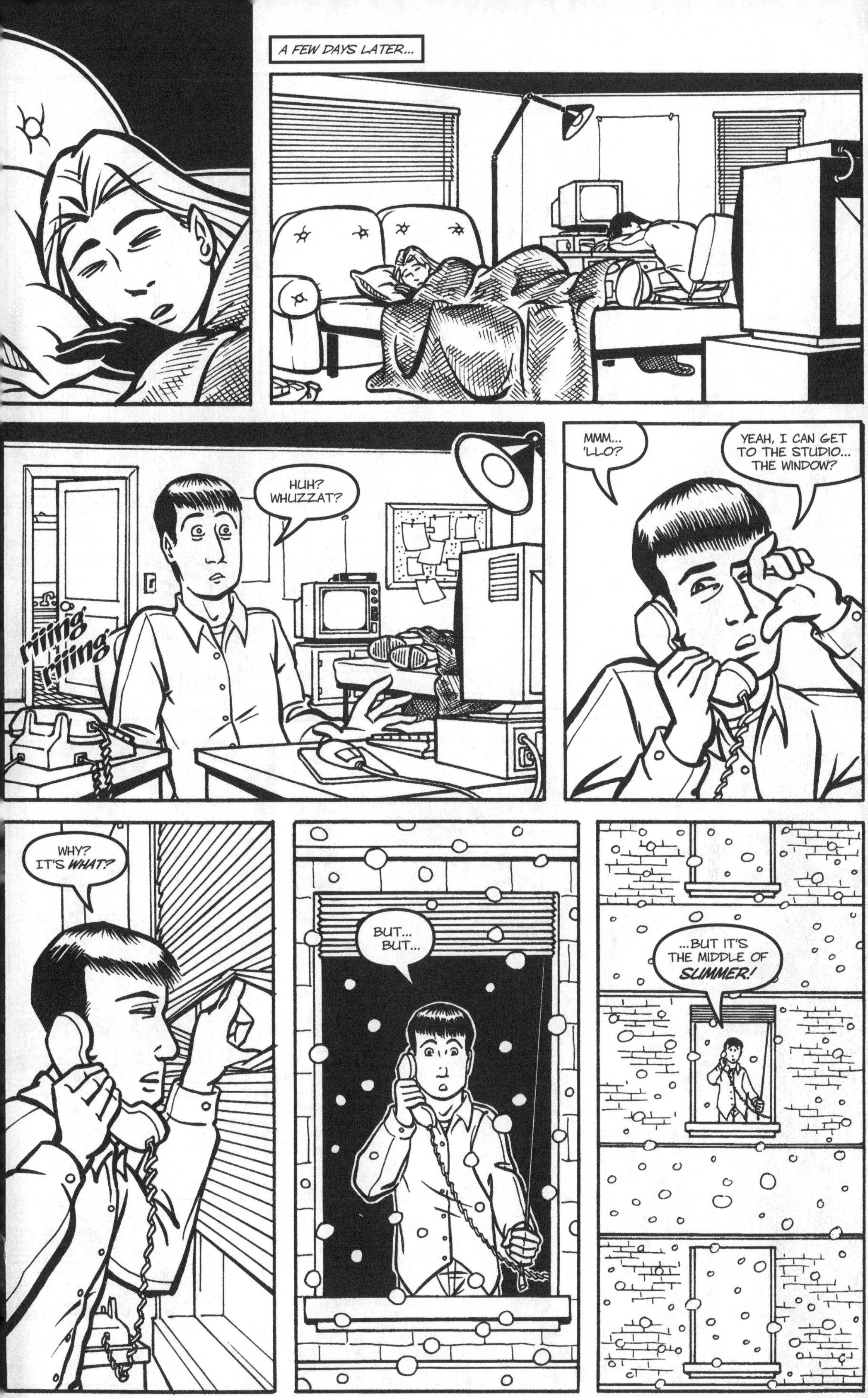
A FEW DAYS LATER...
riiing riiing
HUH? WHUZZAT?
MMM... 'LLO?
YEAH, I CAN GET TO THE STUDIO... THE WINDOW?
WHY? IT'S WHAT?
BUT... BUT...
...BUT IT'S THE MIDDLE OF SUMMER!

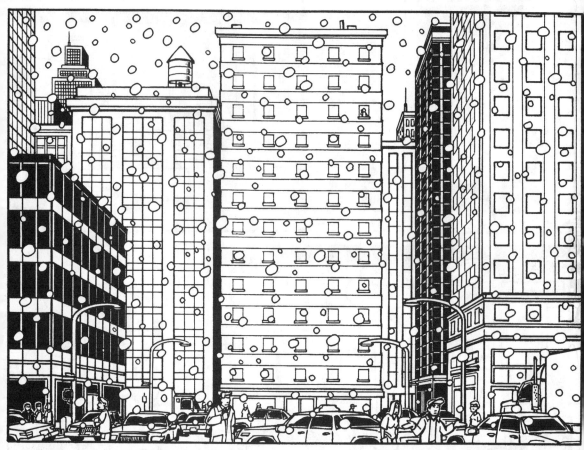

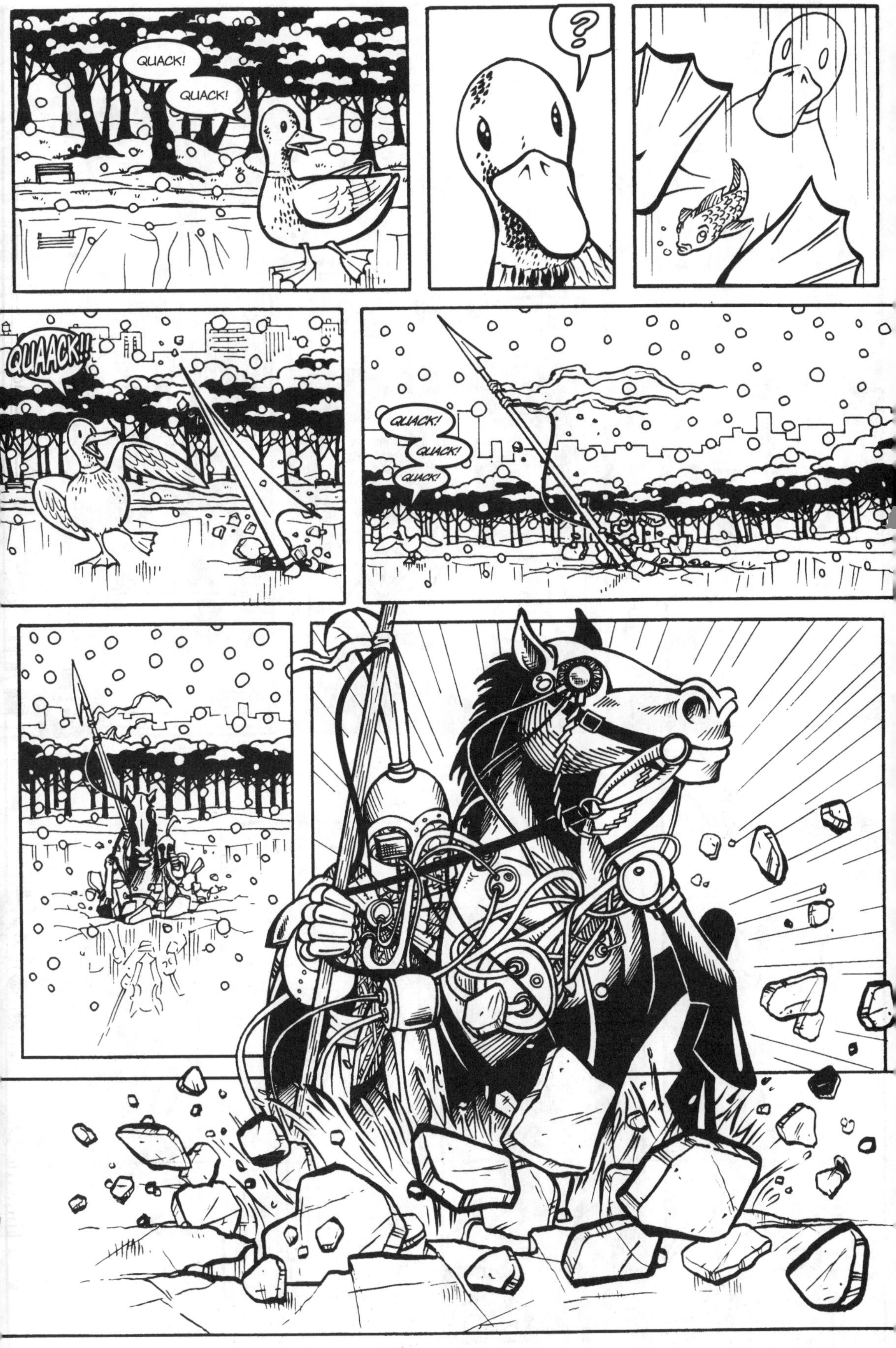
QUACK!
QUACK!
?
QUAACK!!
QUACK!
QUACK!
QUACK!

WHATSAMATTA? YOU PEOPLES NEVER SEEN *SNOW* BEFORE? COME ON, *LET'S GO!*

WHAT? WHAT IS THAT?

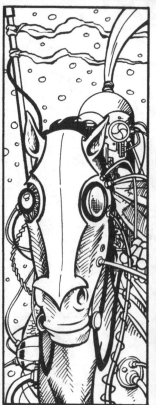

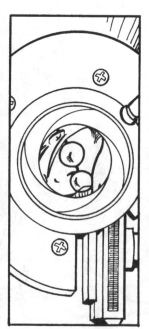

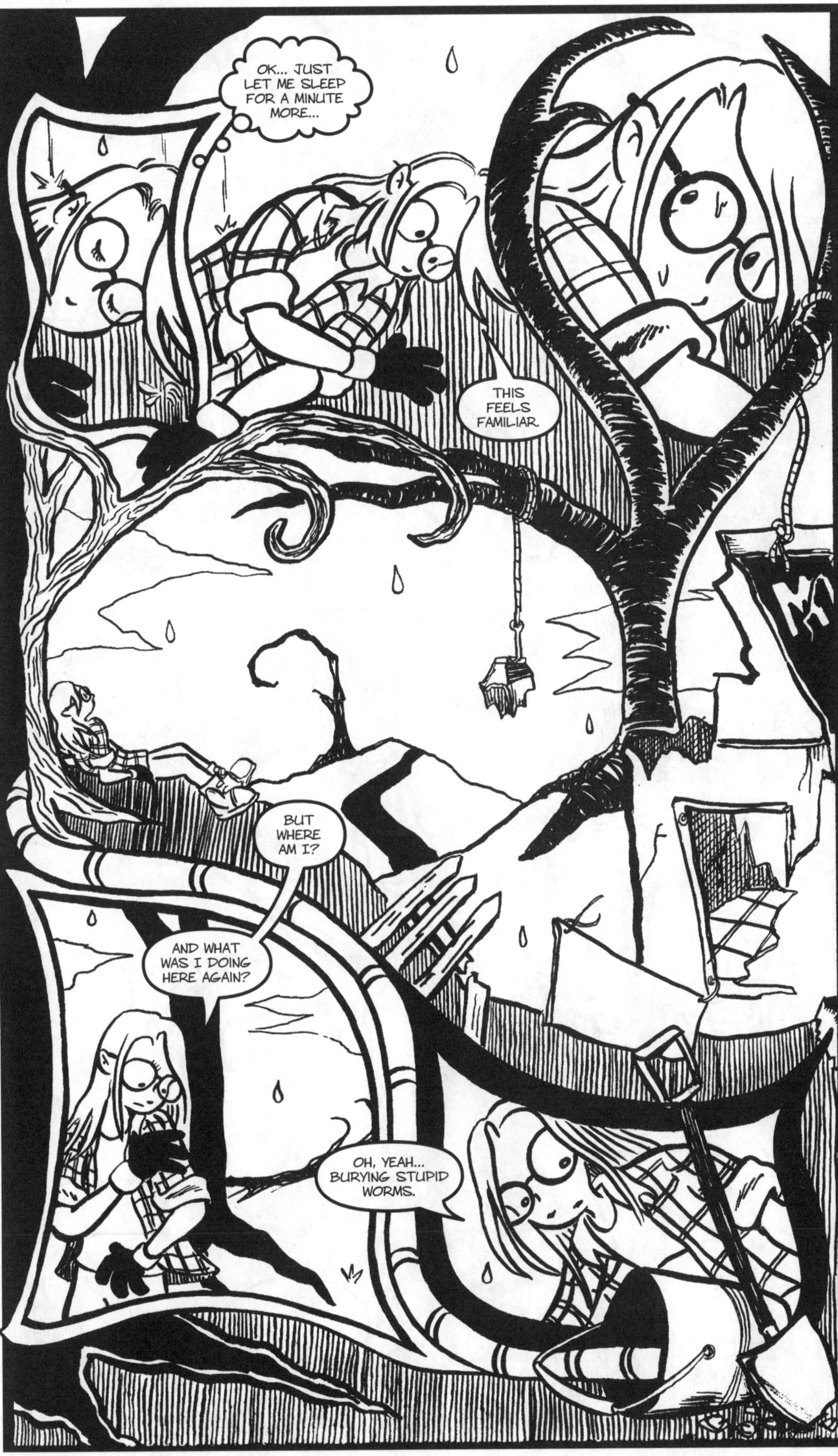
OK... JUST LET ME SLEEP FOR A MINUTE MORE...
THIS FEELS FAMILIAR.
BUT WHERE AM I?
AND WHAT WAS I DOING HERE AGAIN?
OH, YEAH... BURYING STUPID WORMS.

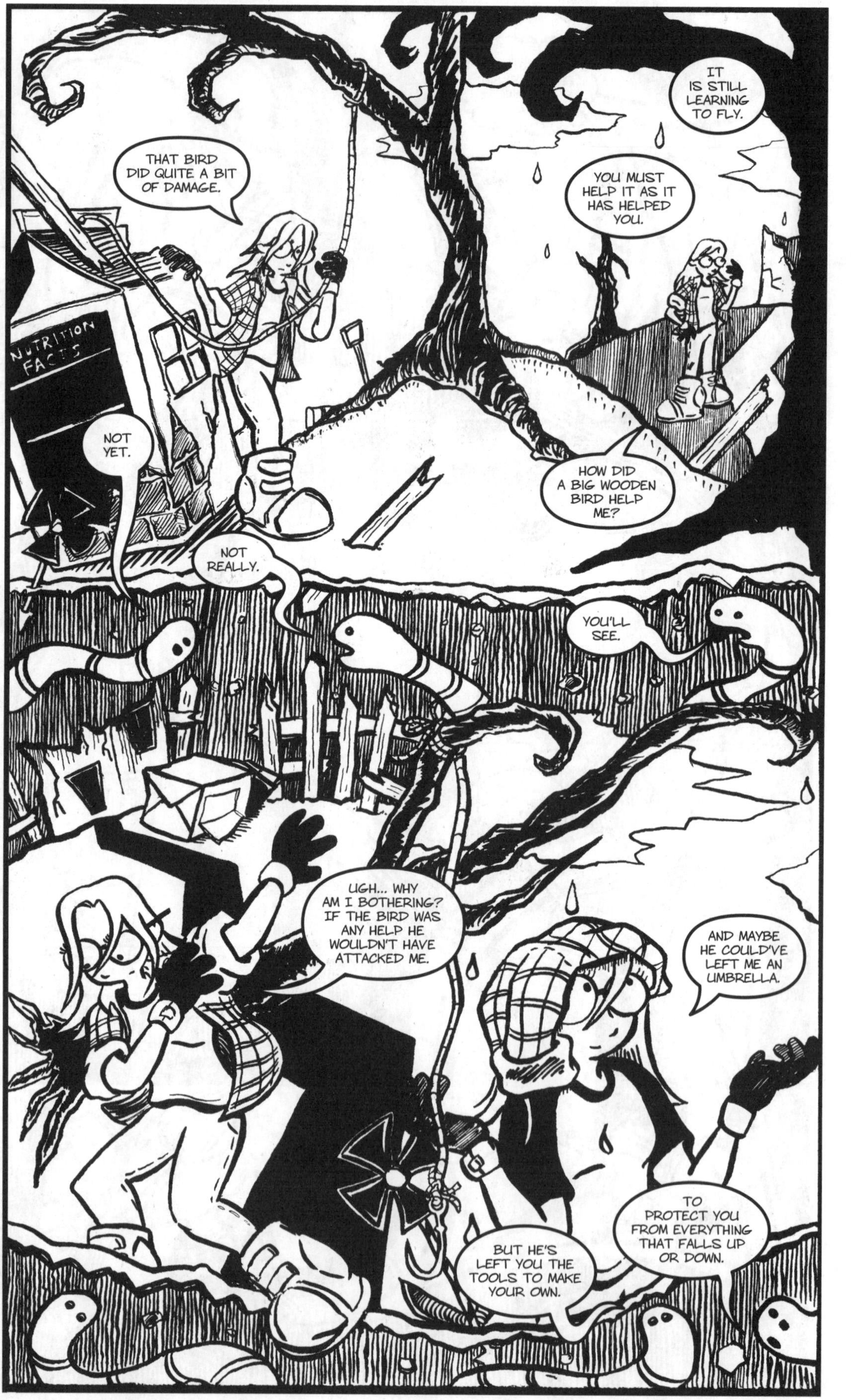
THAT BIRD DID QUITE A BIT OF DAMAGE.
IT IS STILL LEARNING TO FLY.
YOU MUST HELP IT AS IT HAS HELPED YOU.
NUTRITION FACTS
NOT YET.
HOW DID A BIG WOODEN BIRD HELP ME?
NOT REALLY.
YOU'LL SEE.
UGH... WHY AM I BOTHERING? IF THE BIRD WAS ANY HELP HE WOULDN'T HAVE ATTACKED ME.
AND MAYBE HE COULD'VE LEFT ME AN UMBRELLA.
BUT HE'S LEFT YOU THE TOOLS TO MAKE YOUR OWN.
TO PROTECT YOU FROM EVERYTHING THAT FALLS UP OR DOWN.

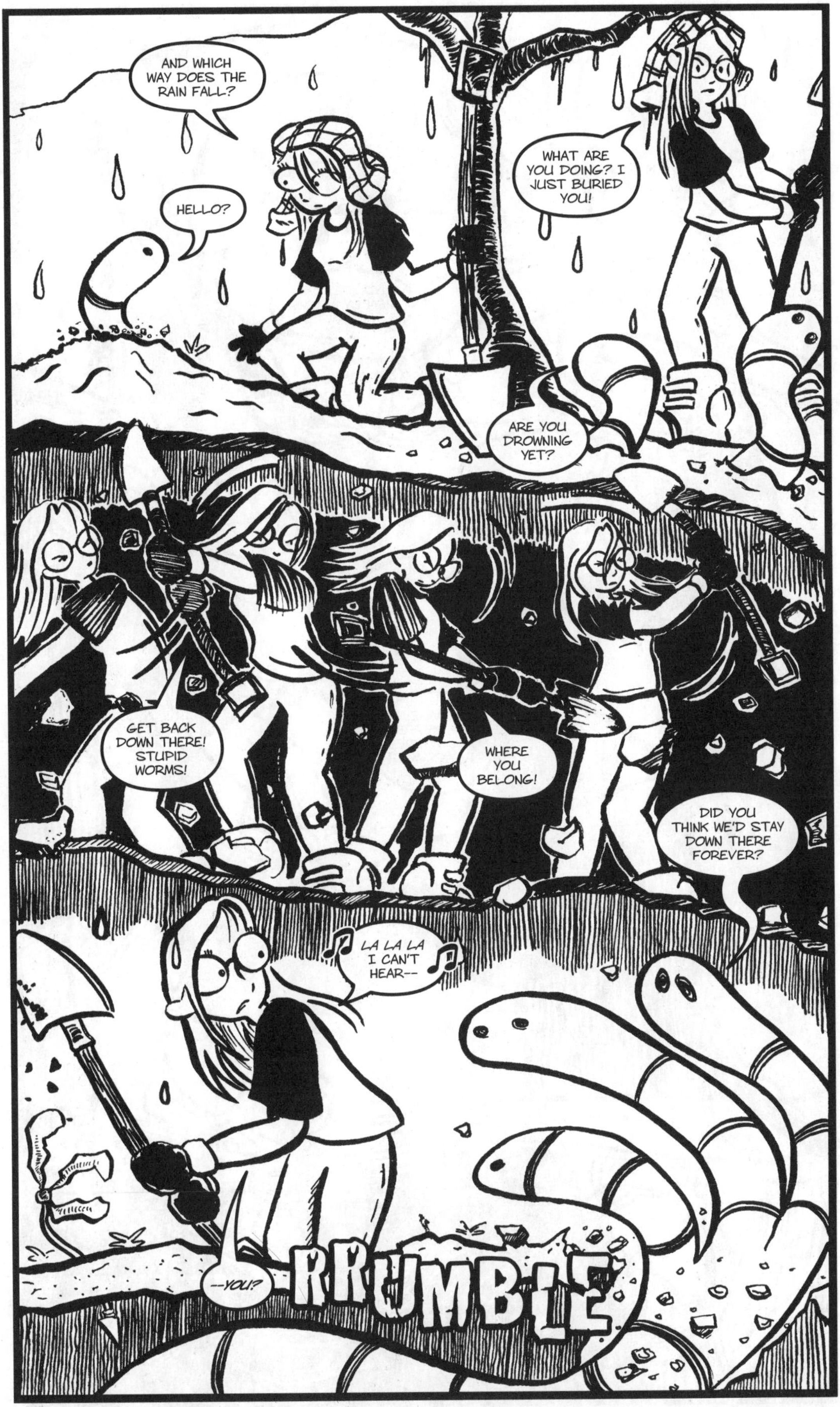
AND WHICH WAY DOES THE RAIN FALL?
HELLO?
WHAT ARE YOU DOING? I JUST BURIED YOU!
ARE YOU DROWNING YET?
GET BACK DOWN THERE! STUPID WORMS!
WHERE YOU BELONG!
DID YOU THINK WE'D STAY DOWN THERE FOREVER?
LA LA LA I CAN'T HEAR--
--YOU!?
RRUMBLE

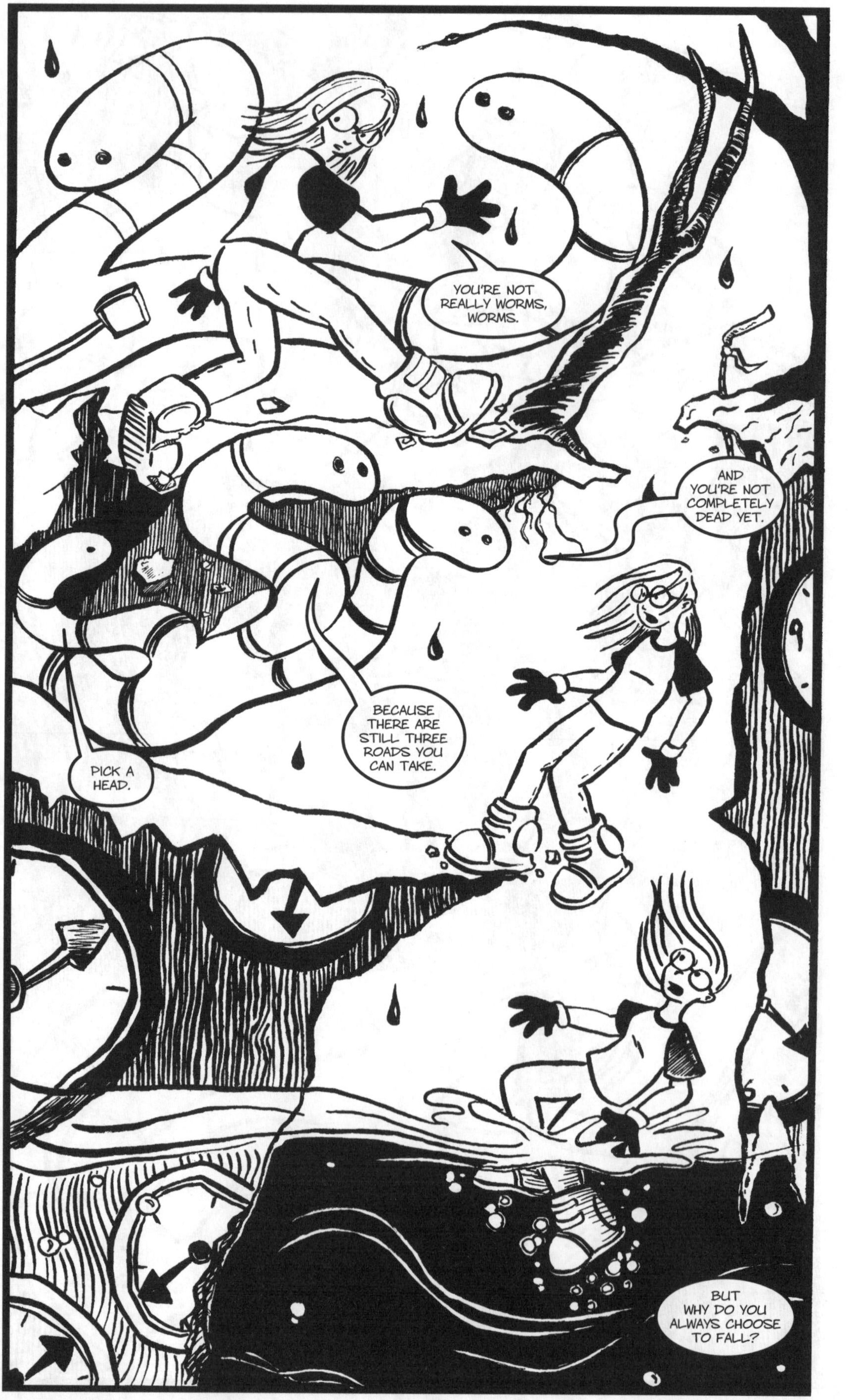
YOU'RE NOT REALLY WORMS, WORMS.
AND YOU'RE NOT COMPLETELY DEAD YET.
BECAUSE THERE ARE STILL THREE ROADS YOU CAN TAKE.
PICK A HEAD.
BUT WHY DO YOU ALWAYS CHOOSE TO FALL?

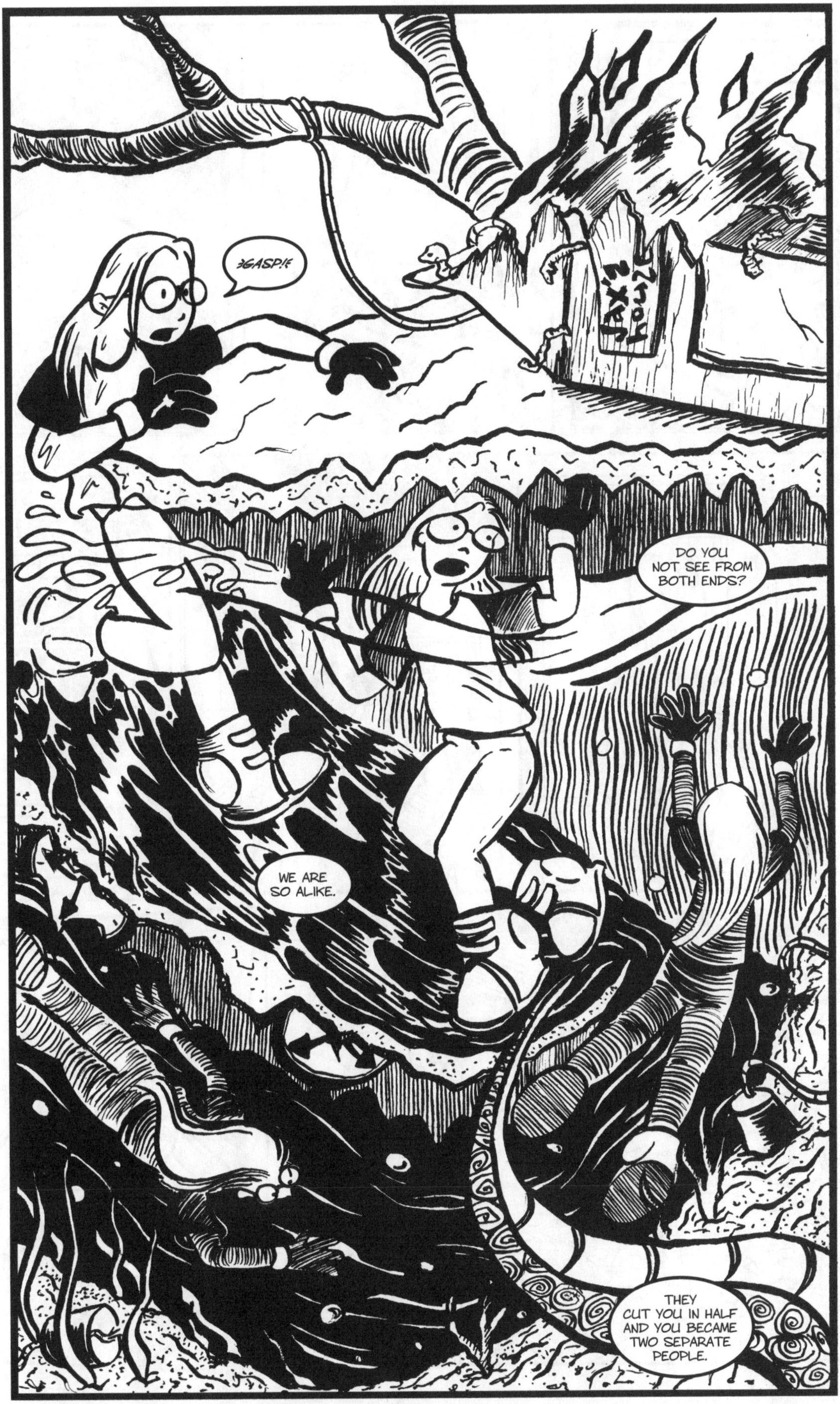
GASP!
DO YOU NOT SEE FROM BOTH ENDS?
WE ARE SO ALIKE.
THEY CUT YOU IN HALF AND YOU BECAME TWO SEPARATE PEOPLE.

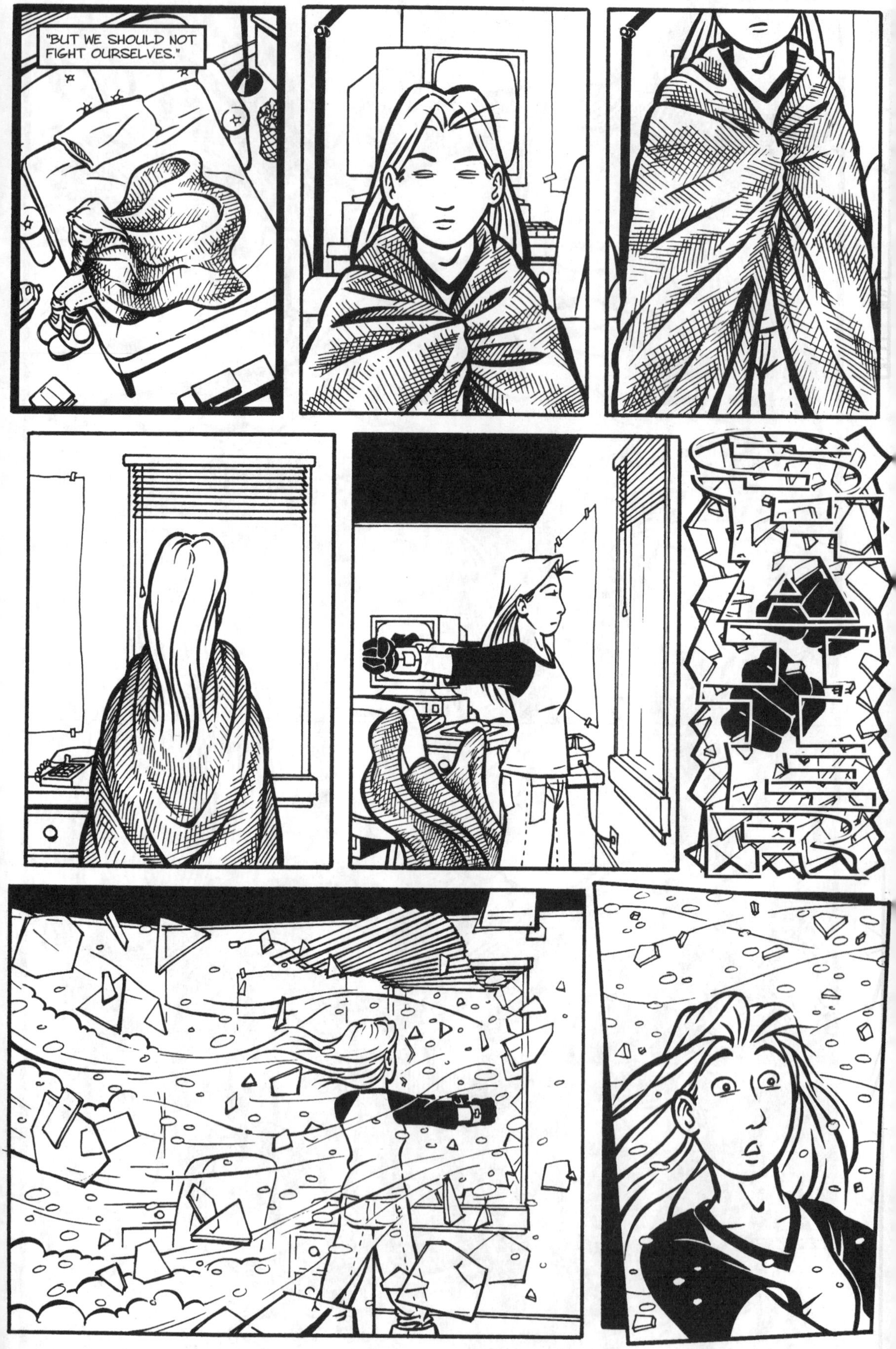
"BUT WE SHOULD NOT FIGHT OURSELVES."

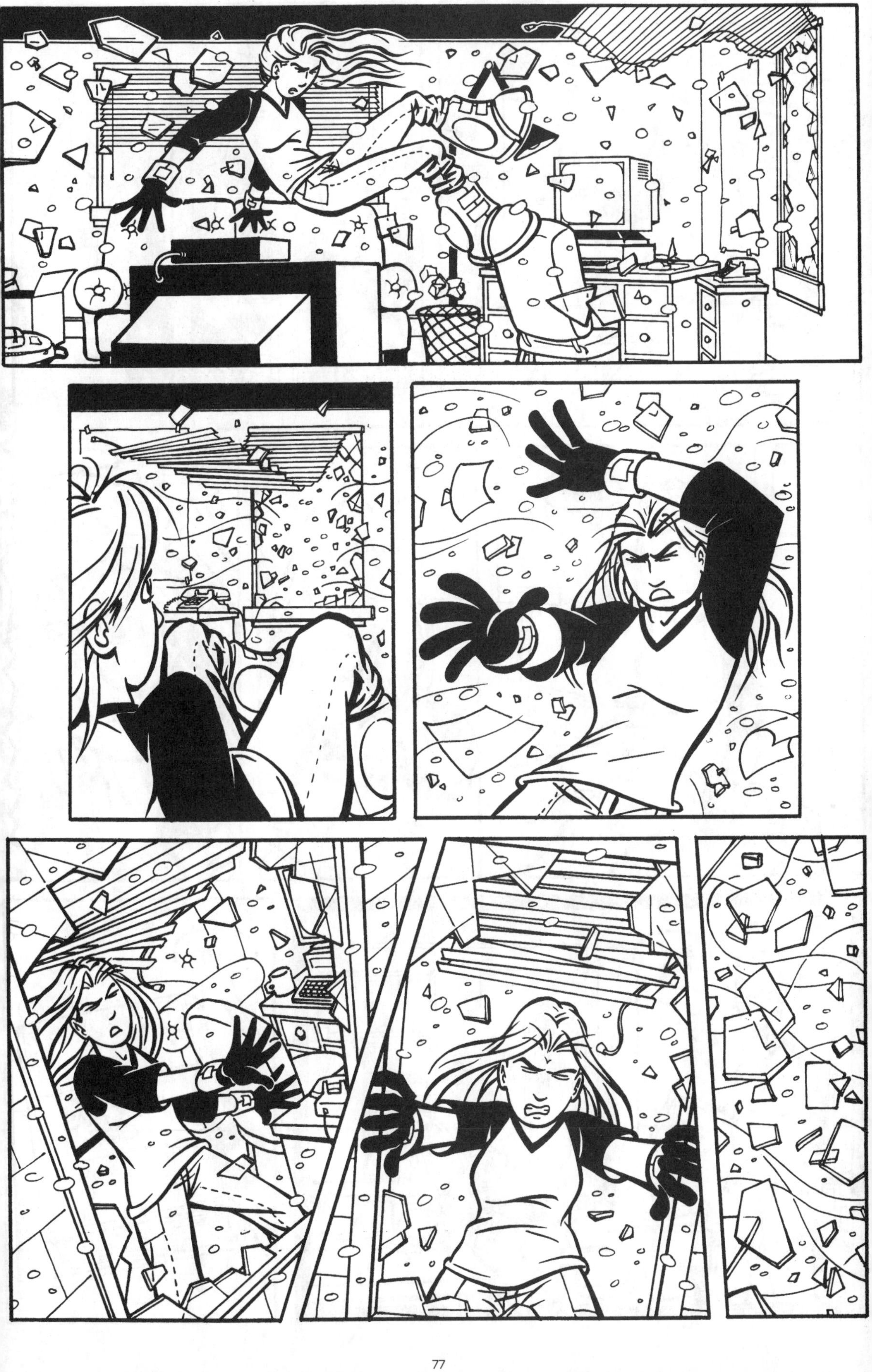

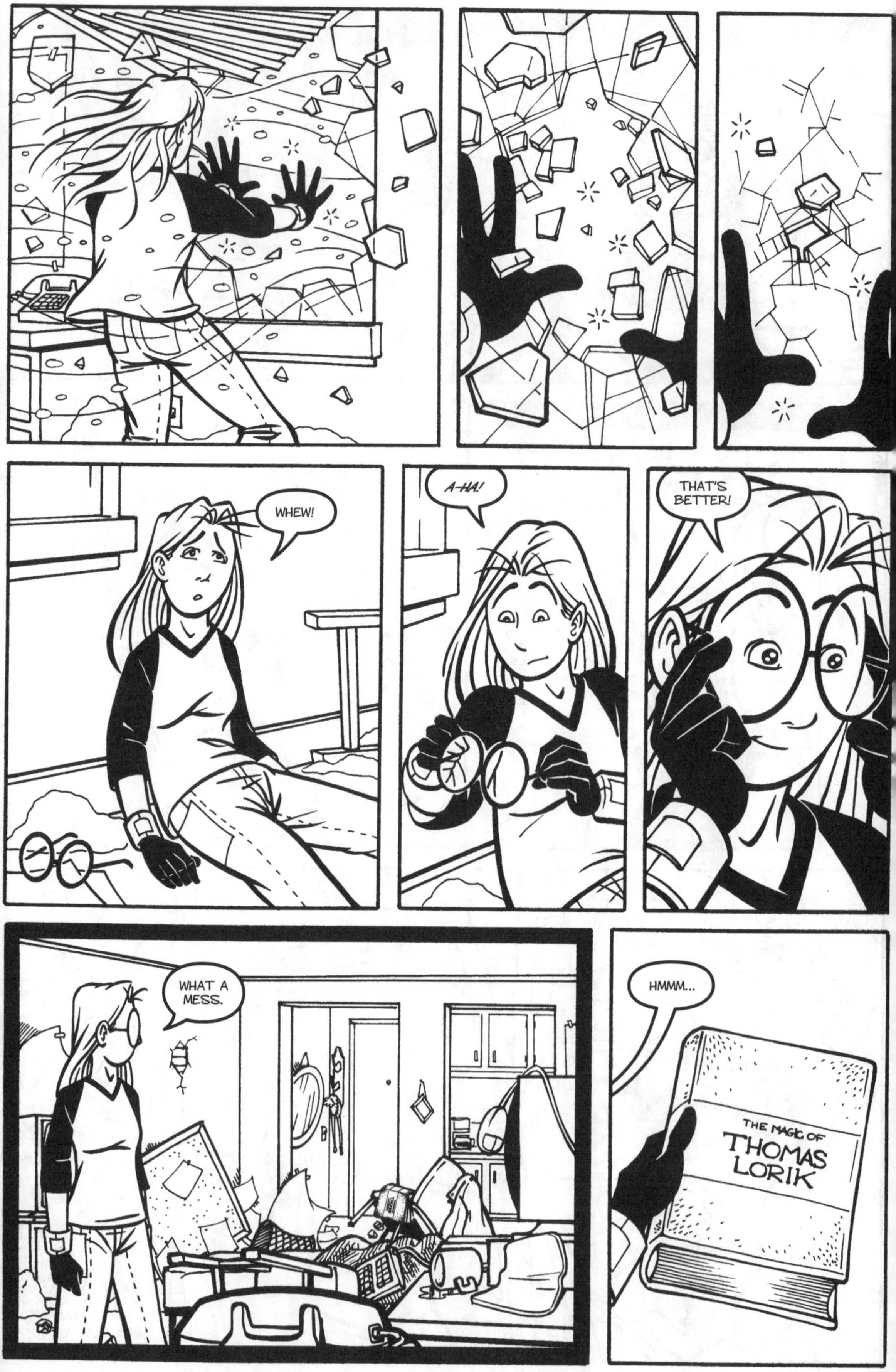
WHEW!
A-HA!
THAT'S BETTER!
WHAT A MESS.
HMMM...
THE MAGIC OF THOMAS LORIK

AFTER ALMOST KILLING MYSELF WHILE WALKING IN MY SLEEP I GOT IT IN MY HEAD TO FINALLY GO SEE THOMAS LORIK. UNLIKE EVERYTHING ELSE IN MY LIFE, IT ALMOST MADE SENSE.

DOUG WON'T MIND IF I BORROW SOME OF HIS STUFF.

THOMAS LORIK WAS LIKE AN IMAGINARY FIGURE TO ME IN THE FORM OF A REAL PERSON... AND IT'S NOT LIKE I DIDN'T ALREADY KNOW WHERE HE LIVED.

NICE DOORBELL.

I GREW UP READING HIS FAIRYTALES AND LATER, HIS ESSAYS ON THE REALITY OF MAGIC, WHICH PROBABLY RUINED HIS CAREER BUT CONFIRMED MY LOYALTY TO HIM.

OOPS.

creak

MR. LORIK?

I HAD SO MANY ROMANTIC IDEAS ABOUT WHO THOMAS LORIK *REALLY* WAS AND HOW HE COULD WRITE ABOUT THE THINGS HE DID.

YOUR DOOR WAS OPEN...

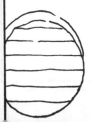

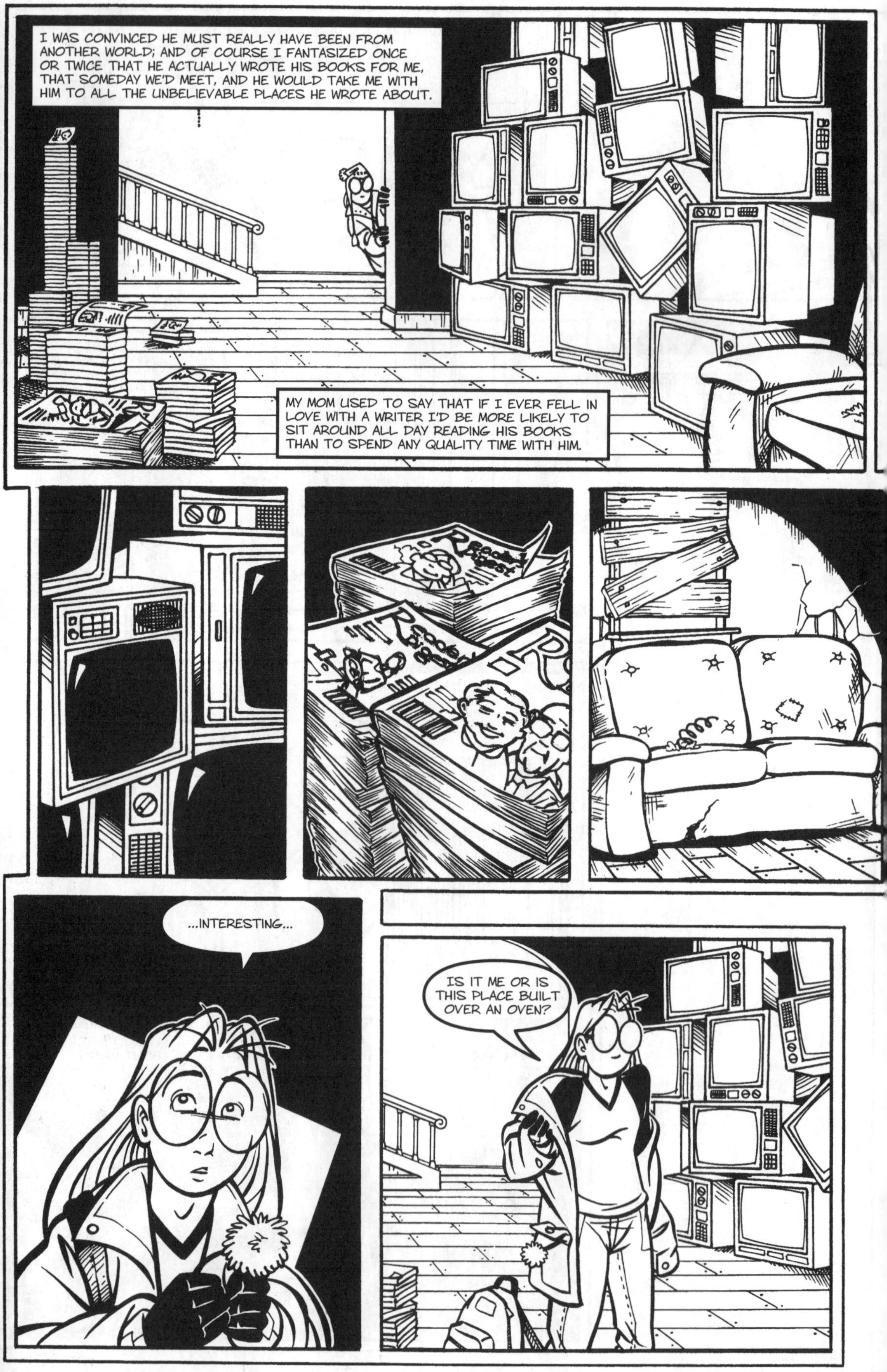
I WAS CONVINCED HE MUST REALLY HAVE BEEN FROM ANOTHER WORLD; AND OF COURSE I FANTASIZED ONCE OR TWICE THAT HE ACTUALLY WROTE HIS BOOKS FOR ME, THAT SOMEDAY WE'D MEET, AND HE WOULD TAKE ME WITH HIM TO ALL THE UNBELIEVABLE PLACES HE WROTE ABOUT.
MY MOM USED TO SAY THAT IF I EVER FELL IN LOVE WITH A WRITER I'D BE MORE LIKELY TO SIT AROUND ALL DAY READING HIS BOOKS THAN TO SPEND ANY QUALITY TIME WITH HIM.
...INTERESTING...
IS IT ME OR IS THIS PLACE BUILT OVER AN OVEN?

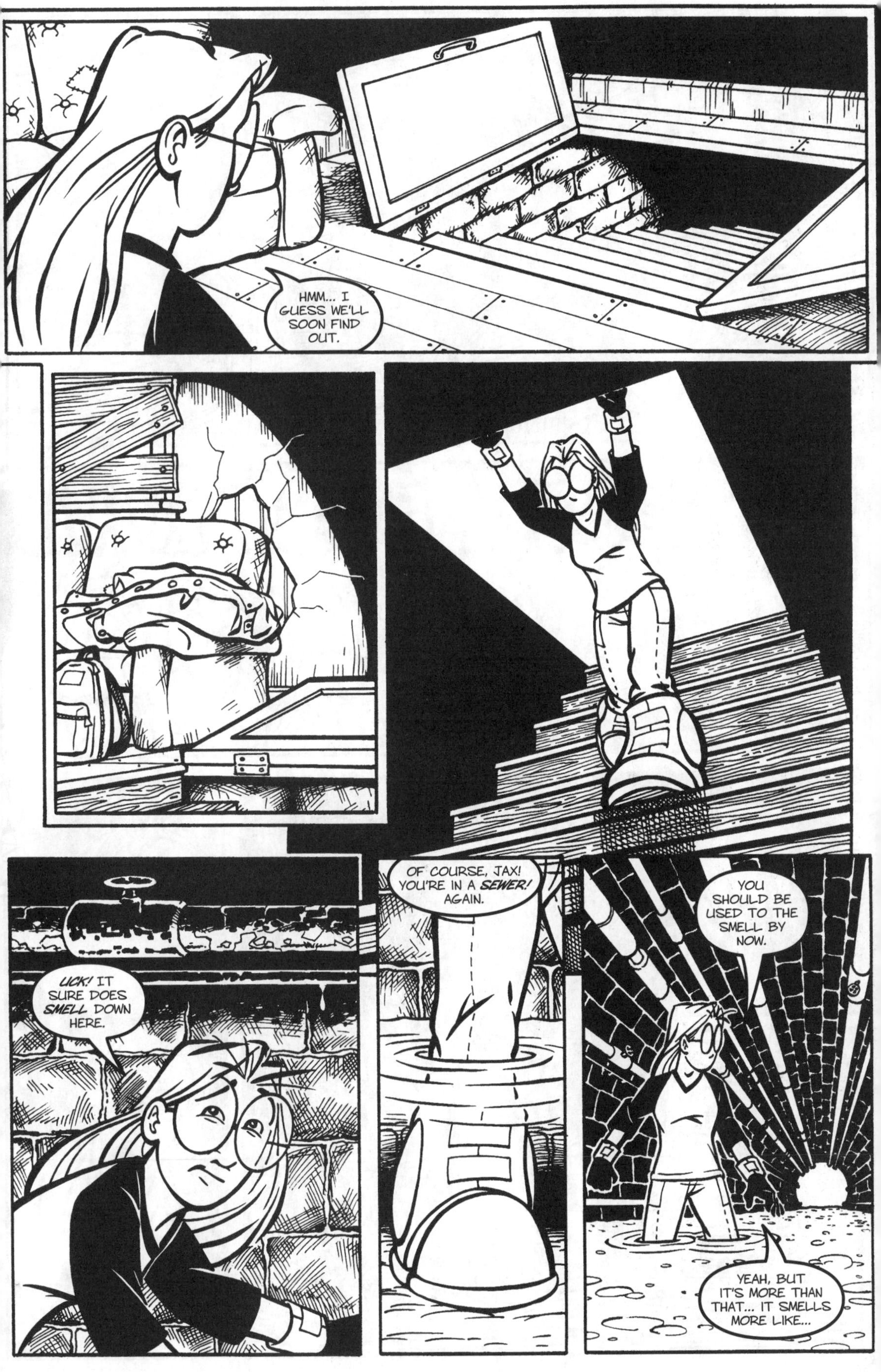
HMM... I GUESS WE'LL SOON FIND OUT.
UCK! IT SURE DOES SMELL DOWN HERE.
OF COURSE, JAX! YOU'RE IN A SEWER! AGAIN.
YOU SHOULD BE USED TO THE SMELL BY NOW.
YEAH, BUT IT'S MORE THAN THAT... IT SMELLS MORE LIKE...

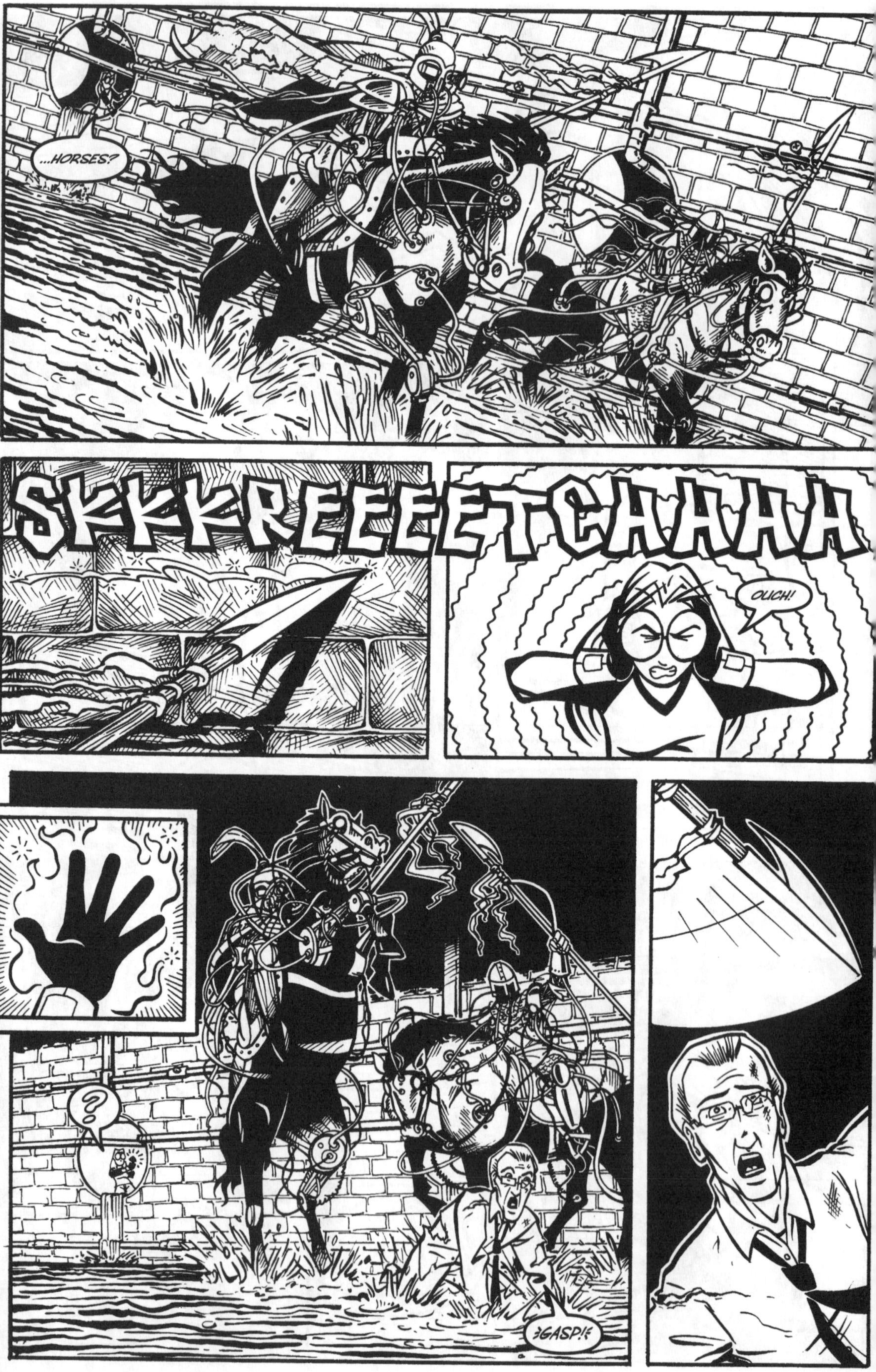
...HORSES?
SKKKREEEEETCHHHHH
OUCH!
?
}GASP!{

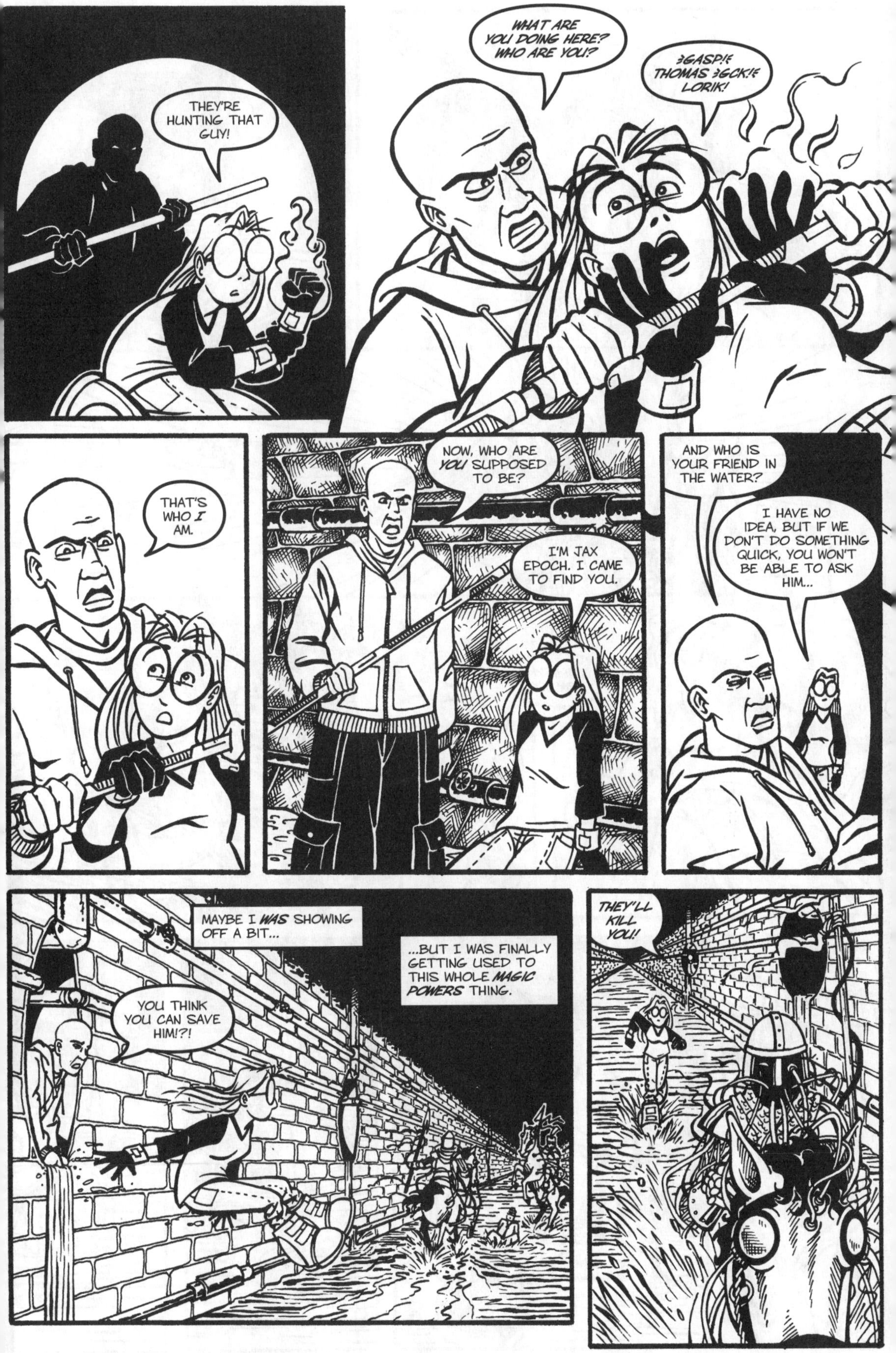
THEY'RE HUNTING THAT GUY!
WHAT ARE YOU DOING HERE? WHO ARE YOU?
GASP! THOMAS GCK! LORIK!
THAT'S WHO I AM.
NOW, WHO ARE YOU SUPPOSED TO BE?
I'M JAX EPOCH. I CAME TO FIND YOU.
AND WHO IS YOUR FRIEND IN THE WATER?
I HAVE NO IDEA, BUT IF WE DON'T DO SOMETHING QUICK, YOU WON'T BE ABLE TO ASK HIM...
MAYBE I WAS SHOWING OFF A BIT...
...BUT I WAS FINALLY GETTING USED TO THIS WHOLE MAGIC POWERS THING.
YOU THINK YOU CAN SAVE HIM!?!
THEY'LL KILL YOU!

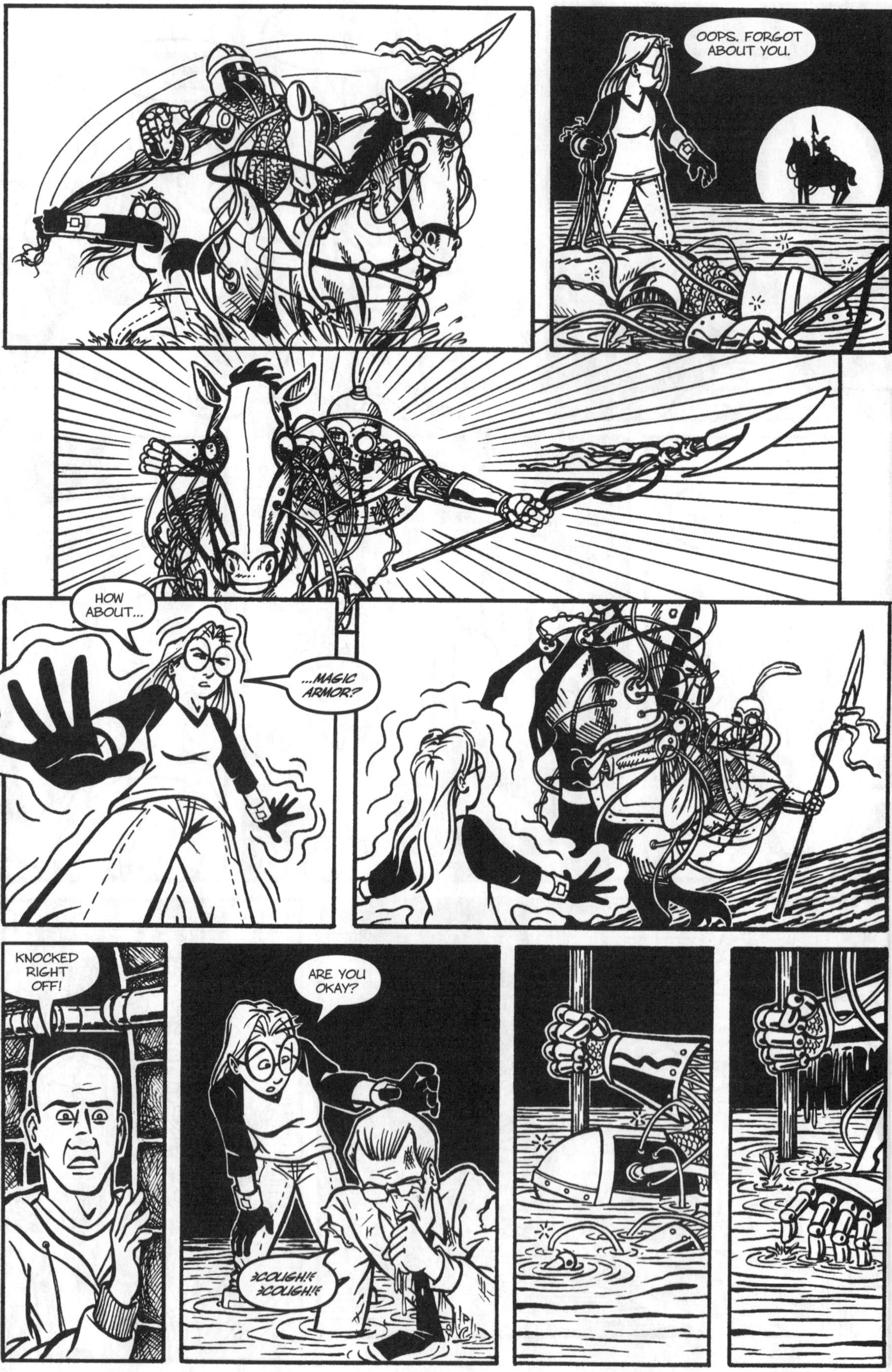
OOPS. FORGOT ABOUT YOU.
HOW ABOUT...
...MAGIC ARMOR?
KNOCKED RIGHT OFF!
ARE YOU OKAY?
COUGH! COUGH!

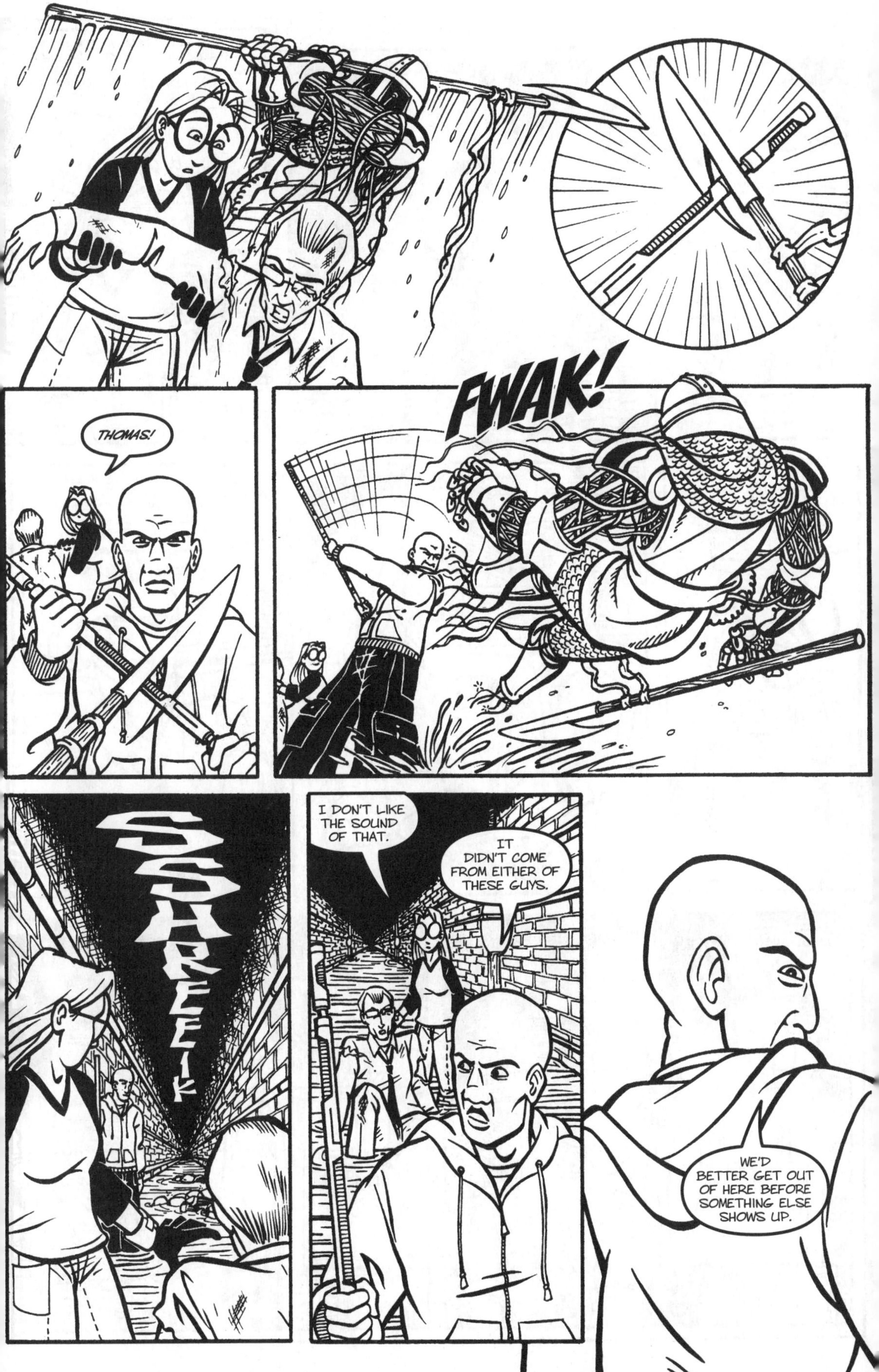
THOMAS!
FWAK!
SSHREEEIK
I DON'T LIKE THE SOUND OF THAT.
IT DIDN'T COME FROM EITHER OF THESE GUYS.
WE'D BETTER GET OUT OF HERE BEFORE SOMETHING ELSE SHOWS UP.

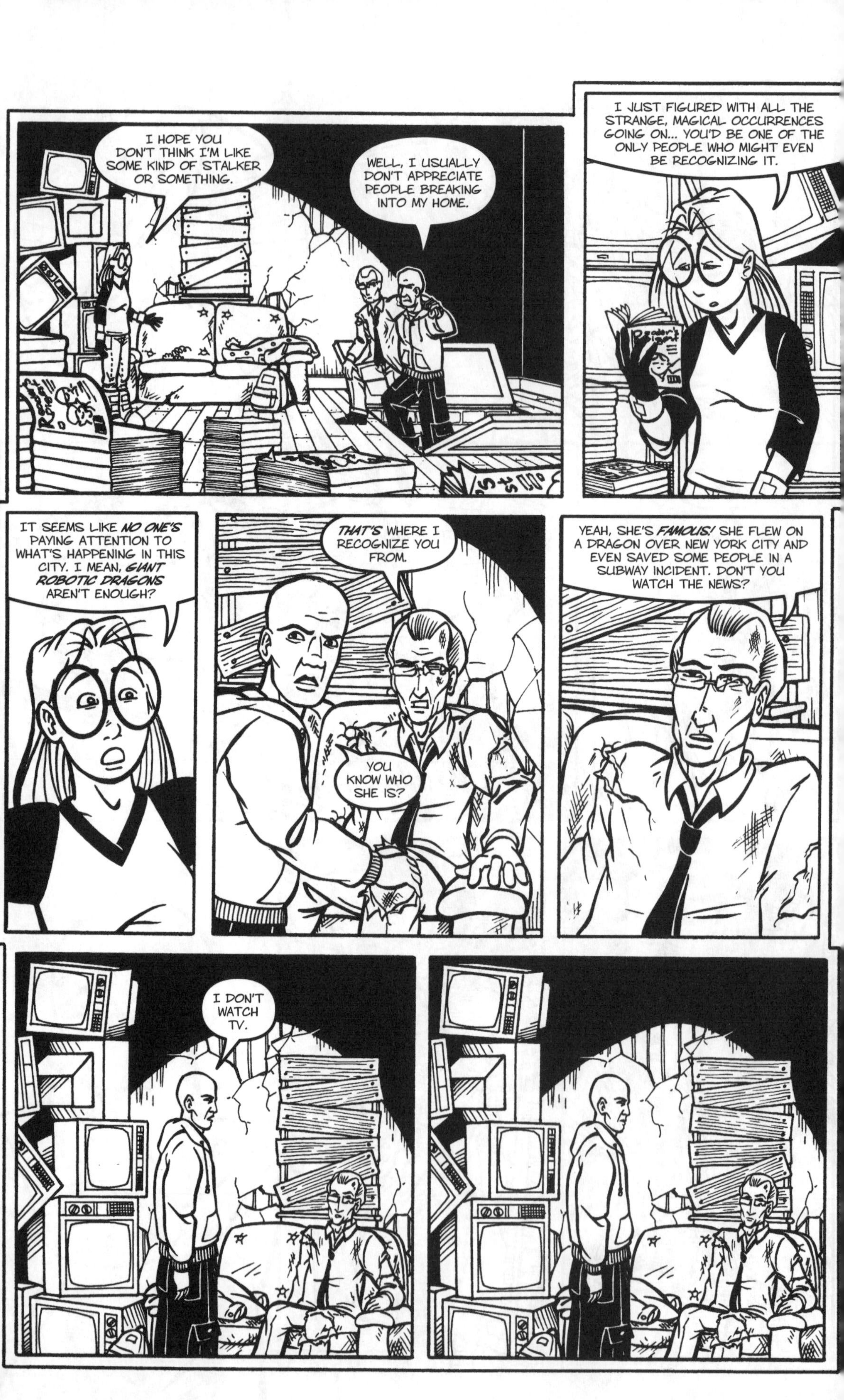
I HOPE YOU DON'T THINK I'M LIKE SOME KIND OF STALKER OR SOMETHING.
WELL, I USUALLY DON'T APPRECIATE PEOPLE BREAKING INTO MY HOME.
I JUST FIGURED WITH ALL THE STRANGE, MAGICAL OCCURRENCES GOING ON... YOU'D BE ONE OF THE ONLY PEOPLE WHO MIGHT EVEN BE RECOGNIZING IT.
IT SEEMS LIKE NO ONE'S PAYING ATTENTION TO WHAT'S HAPPENING IN THIS CITY. I MEAN, GIANT ROBOTIC DRAGONS AREN'T ENOUGH?
THAT'S WHERE I RECOGNIZE YOU FROM.
YOU KNOW WHO SHE IS?
YEAH, SHE'S FAMOUS! SHE FLEW ON A DRAGON OVER NEW YORK CITY AND EVEN SAVED SOME PEOPLE IN A SUBWAY INCIDENT. DON'T YOU WATCH THE NEWS?
I DON'T WATCH TV.

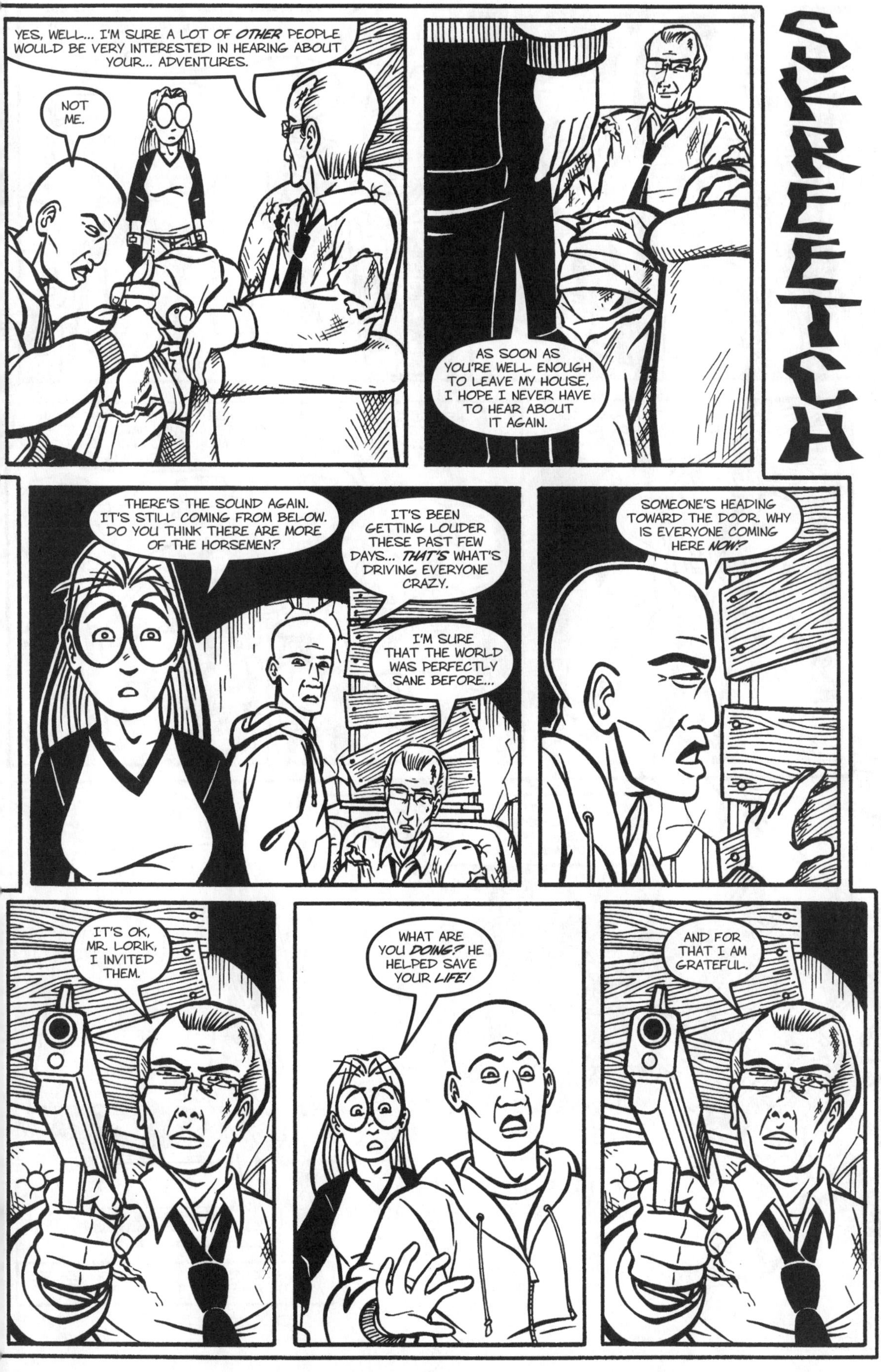

YES, WELL... I'M SURE A LOT OF OTHER PEOPLE WOULD BE VERY INTERESTED IN HEARING ABOUT YOUR... ADVENTURES.
NOT ME.
AS SOON AS YOU'RE WELL ENOUGH TO LEAVE MY HOUSE, I HOPE I NEVER HAVE TO HEAR ABOUT IT AGAIN.
SKREETCH
THERE'S THE SOUND AGAIN. IT'S STILL COMING FROM BELOW. DO YOU THINK THERE ARE MORE OF THE HORSEMEN?
IT'S BEEN GETTING LOUDER THESE PAST FEW DAYS... THAT'S WHAT'S DRIVING EVERYONE CRAZY.
I'M SURE THAT THE WORLD WAS PERFECTLY SANE BEFORE...
SOMEONE'S HEADING TOWARD THE DOOR. WHY IS EVERYONE COMING HERE NOW?
IT'S OK, MR. LORIK, I INVITED THEM.
WHAT ARE YOU DOING? HE HELPED SAVE YOUR LIFE!
AND FOR THAT I AM GRATEFUL.

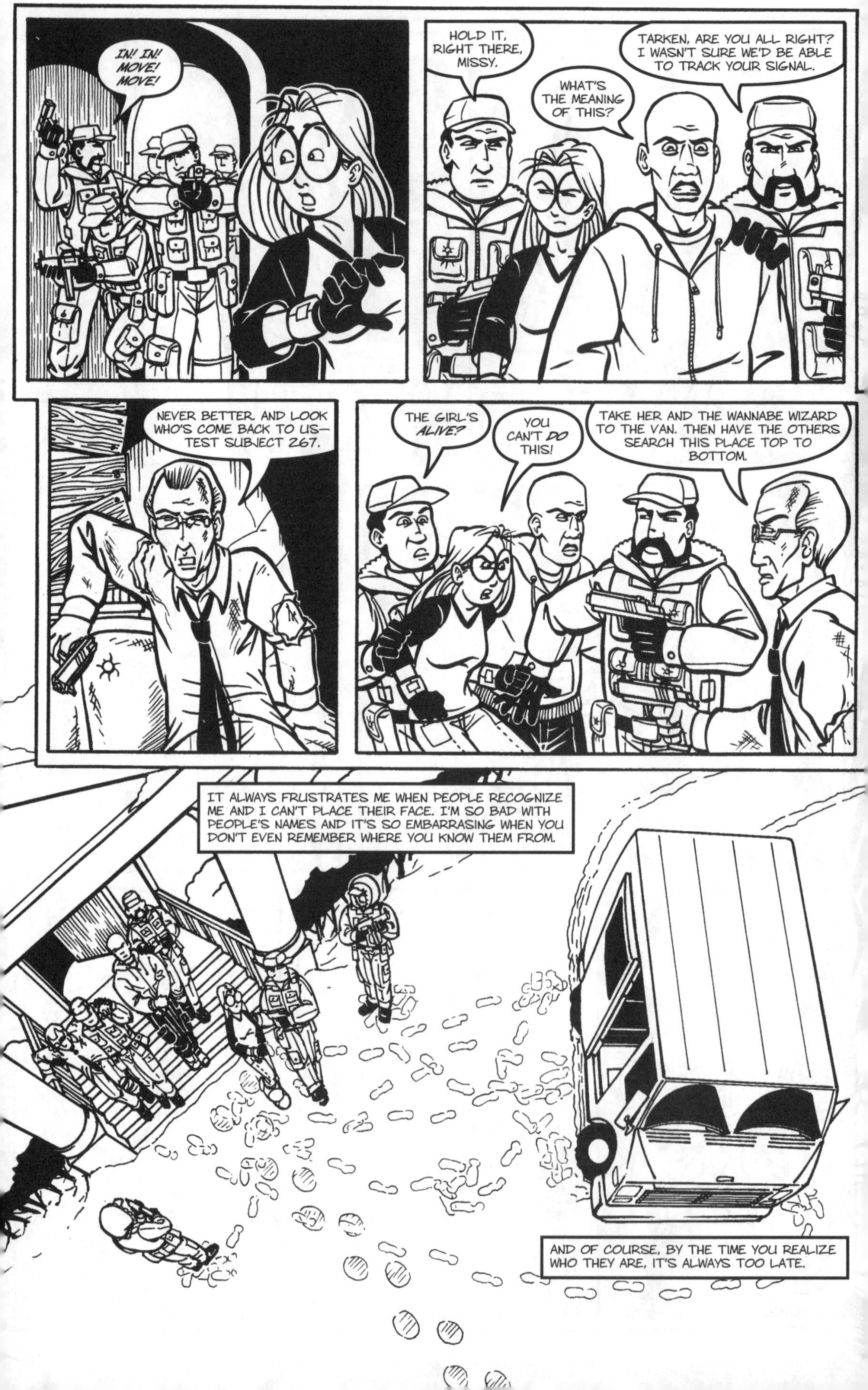
IN! IN! MOVE! MOVE!
HOLD IT, RIGHT THERE, MISSY.
WHAT'S THE MEANING OF THIS?
TARKEN, ARE YOU ALL RIGHT? I WASN'T SURE WE'D BE ABLE TO TRACK YOUR SIGNAL.
NEVER BETTER AND LOOK WHO'S COME BACK TO US— TEST SUBJECT 267.
THE GIRL'S *ALIVE?*
YOU CAN'T *DO* THIS!
TAKE HER AND THE WANNABE WIZARD TO THE VAN. THEN HAVE THE OTHERS SEARCH THIS PLACE TOP TO BOTTOM.
IT ALWAYS FRUSTRATES ME WHEN PEOPLE RECOGNIZE ME AND I CAN'T PLACE THEIR FACE. I'M SO BAD WITH PEOPLE'S NAMES AND IT'S SO EMBARRASING WHEN YOU DON'T EVEN REMEMBER WHERE YOU KNOW THEM FROM.
AND OF COURSE, BY THE TIME YOU REALIZE WHO THEY ARE, IT'S ALWAYS TOO LATE.

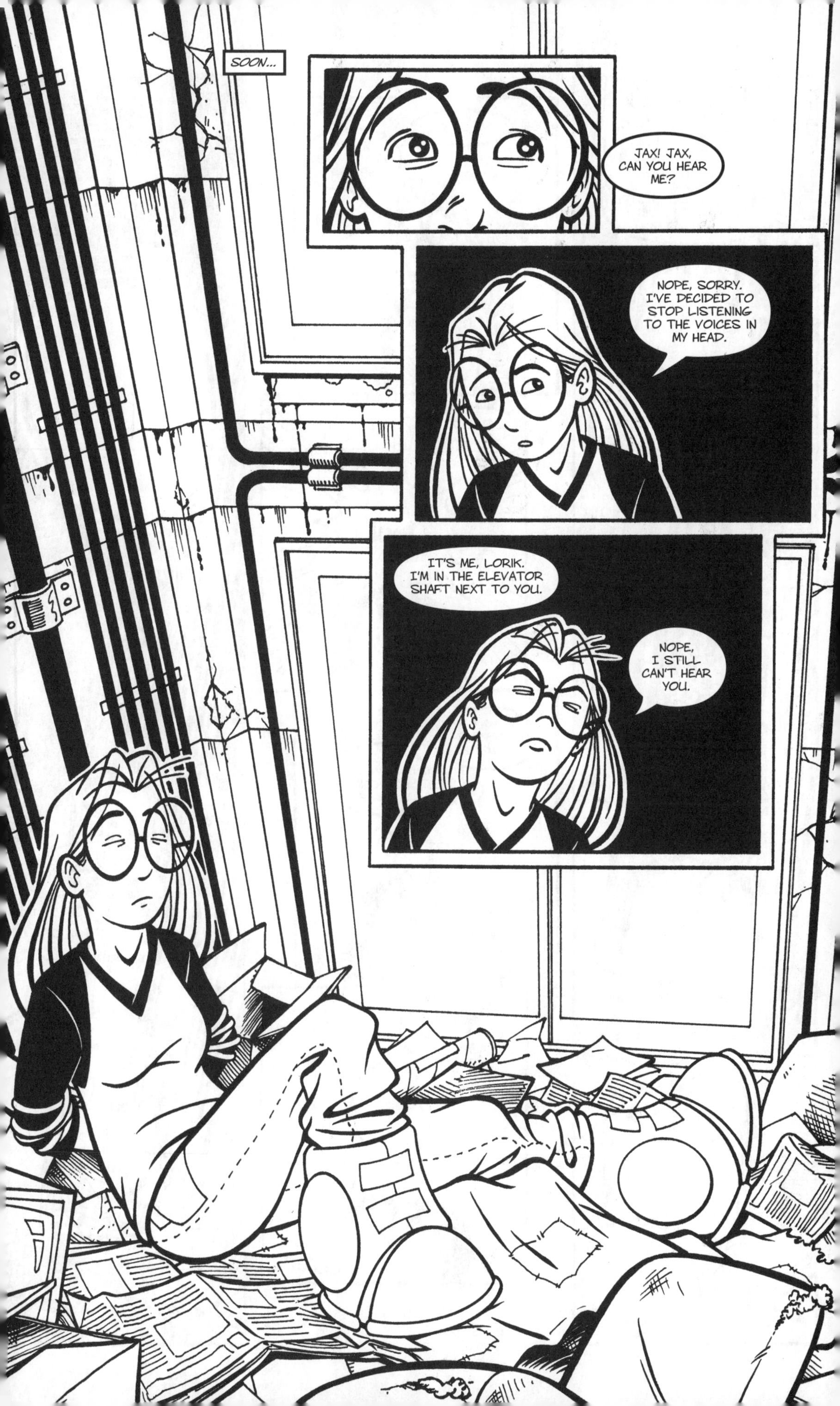
SOON...
JAX! JAX, CAN YOU HEAR ME?
NOPE, SORRY. I'VE DECIDED TO STOP LISTENING TO THE VOICES IN MY HEAD.
IT'S ME, LORIK. I'M IN THE ELEVATOR SHAFT NEXT TO YOU.
NOPE, I STILL CAN'T HEAR YOU.

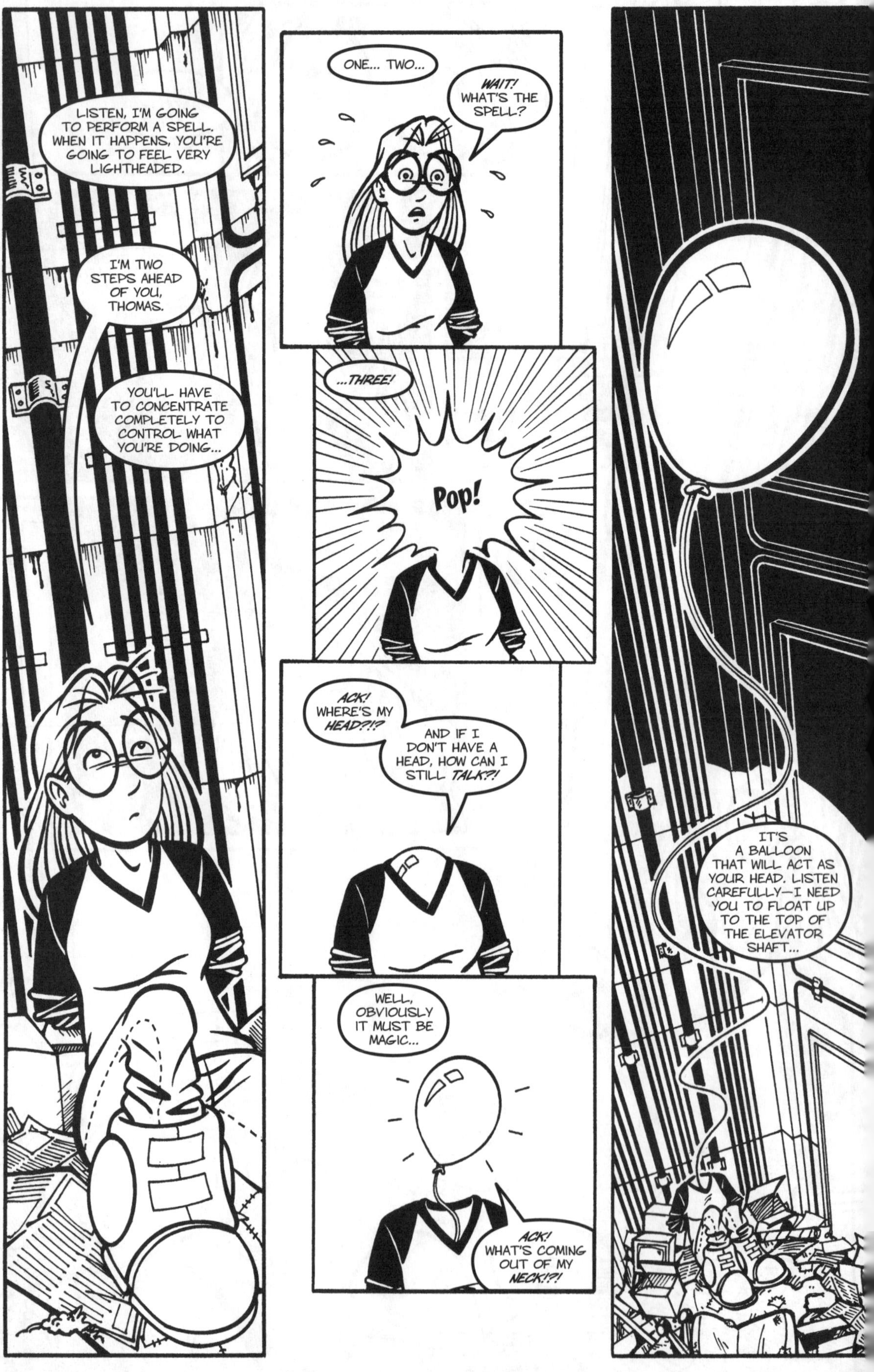
LISTEN, I'M GOING TO PERFORM A SPELL. WHEN IT HAPPENS, YOU'RE GOING TO FEEL VERY LIGHTHEADED.
I'M TWO STEPS AHEAD OF YOU, THOMAS.
YOU'LL HAVE TO CONCENTRATE COMPLETELY TO CONTROL WHAT YOU'RE DOING...
ONE... TWO...
WAIT! WHAT'S THE SPELL?
...THREE!
Pop!
ACK! WHERE'S MY HEAD?!?
AND IF I DON'T HAVE A HEAD, HOW CAN I STILL TALK?!
WELL, OBVIOUSLY IT MUST BE MAGIC...
ACK! WHAT'S COMING OUT OF MY NECK!?!
IT'S A BALLOON THAT WILL ACT AS YOUR HEAD. LISTEN CAREFULLY—I NEED YOU TO FLOAT UP TO THE TOP OF THE ELEVATOR SHAFT...

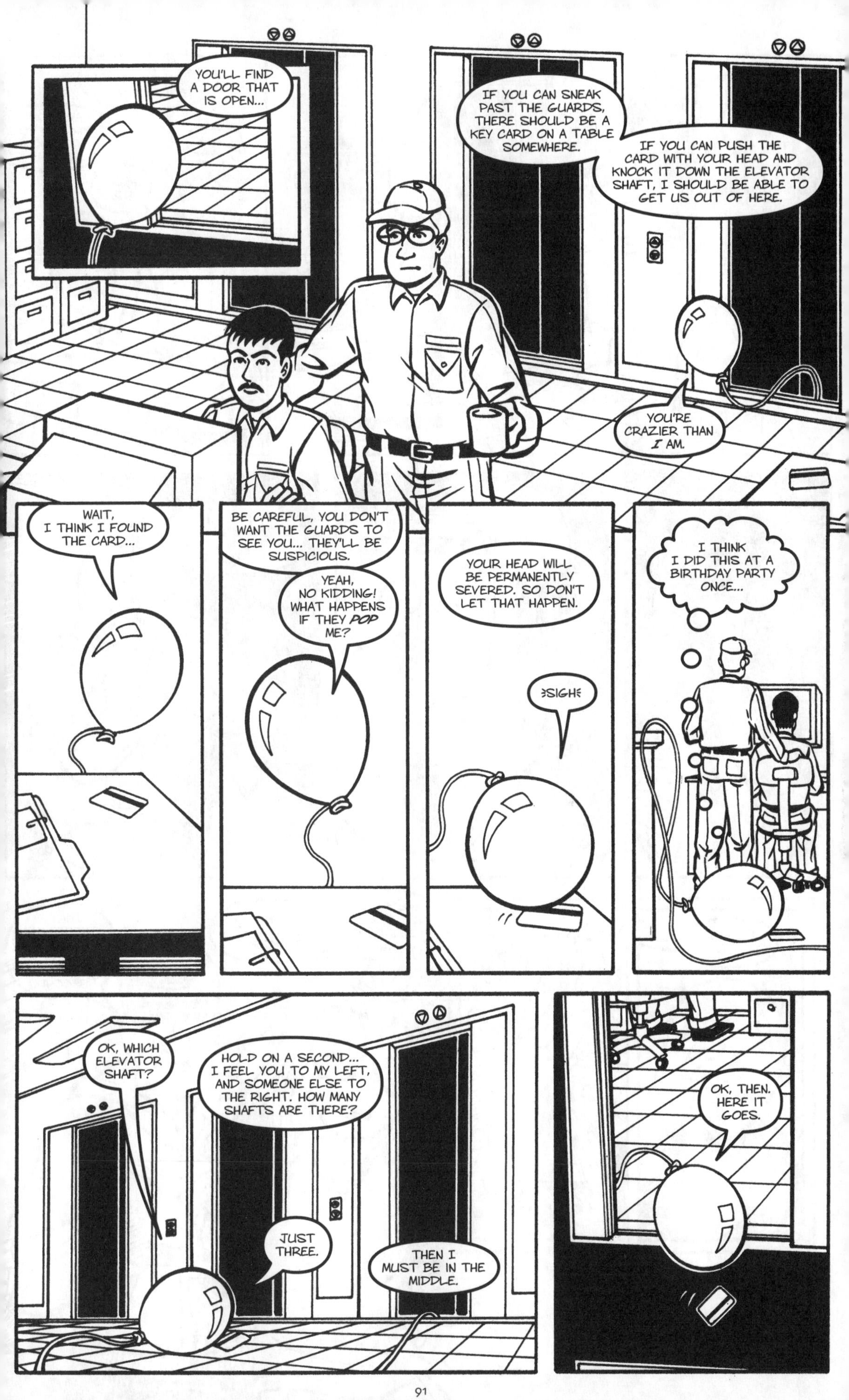
YOU'LL FIND A DOOR THAT IS OPEN...
IF YOU CAN SNEAK PAST THE GUARDS, THERE SHOULD BE A KEY CARD ON A TABLE SOMEWHERE.
IF YOU CAN PUSH THE CARD WITH YOUR HEAD AND KNOCK IT DOWN THE ELEVATOR SHAFT, I SHOULD BE ABLE TO GET US OUT OF HERE.
YOU'RE CRAZIER THAN I AM.
WAIT, I THINK I FOUND THE CARD...
BE CAREFUL, YOU DON'T WANT THE GUARDS TO SEE YOU... THEY'LL BE SUSPICIOUS.
YEAH, NO KIDDING! WHAT HAPPENS IF THEY POP ME?
YOUR HEAD WILL BE PERMANENTLY SEVERED. SO DON'T LET THAT HAPPEN.
SIGH
I THINK I DID THIS AT A BIRTHDAY PARTY ONCE...
OK, WHICH ELEVATOR SHAFT?
HOLD ON A SECOND... I FEEL YOU TO MY LEFT, AND SOMEONE ELSE TO THE RIGHT. HOW MANY SHAFTS ARE THERE?
JUST THREE.
THEN I MUST BE IN THE MIDDLE.
OK, THEN. HERE IT GOES.

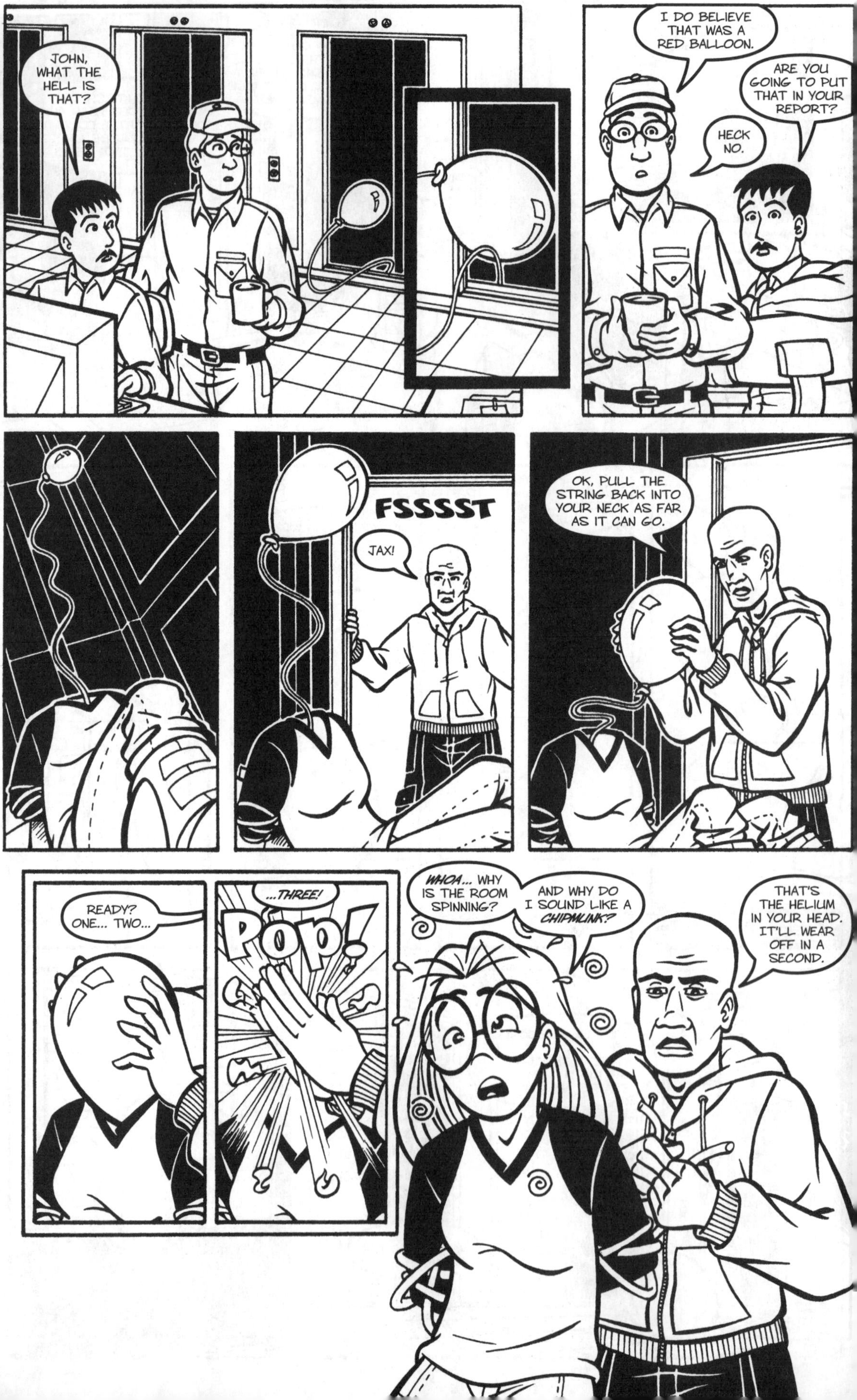
JOHN, WHAT THE HELL IS THAT?
I DO BELIEVE THAT WAS A RED BALLOON.
ARE YOU GOING TO PUT THAT IN YOUR REPORT?
HECK NO.
FSSSST
JAX!
OK, PULL THE STRING BACK INTO YOUR NECK AS FAR AS IT CAN GO.
READY? ONE... TWO...
...THREE!
POP!
WHOA... WHY IS THE ROOM SPINNING?
AND WHY DO I SOUND LIKE A CHIPMUNK?
THAT'S THE HELIUM IN YOUR HEAD. IT'LL WEAR OFF IN A SECOND.

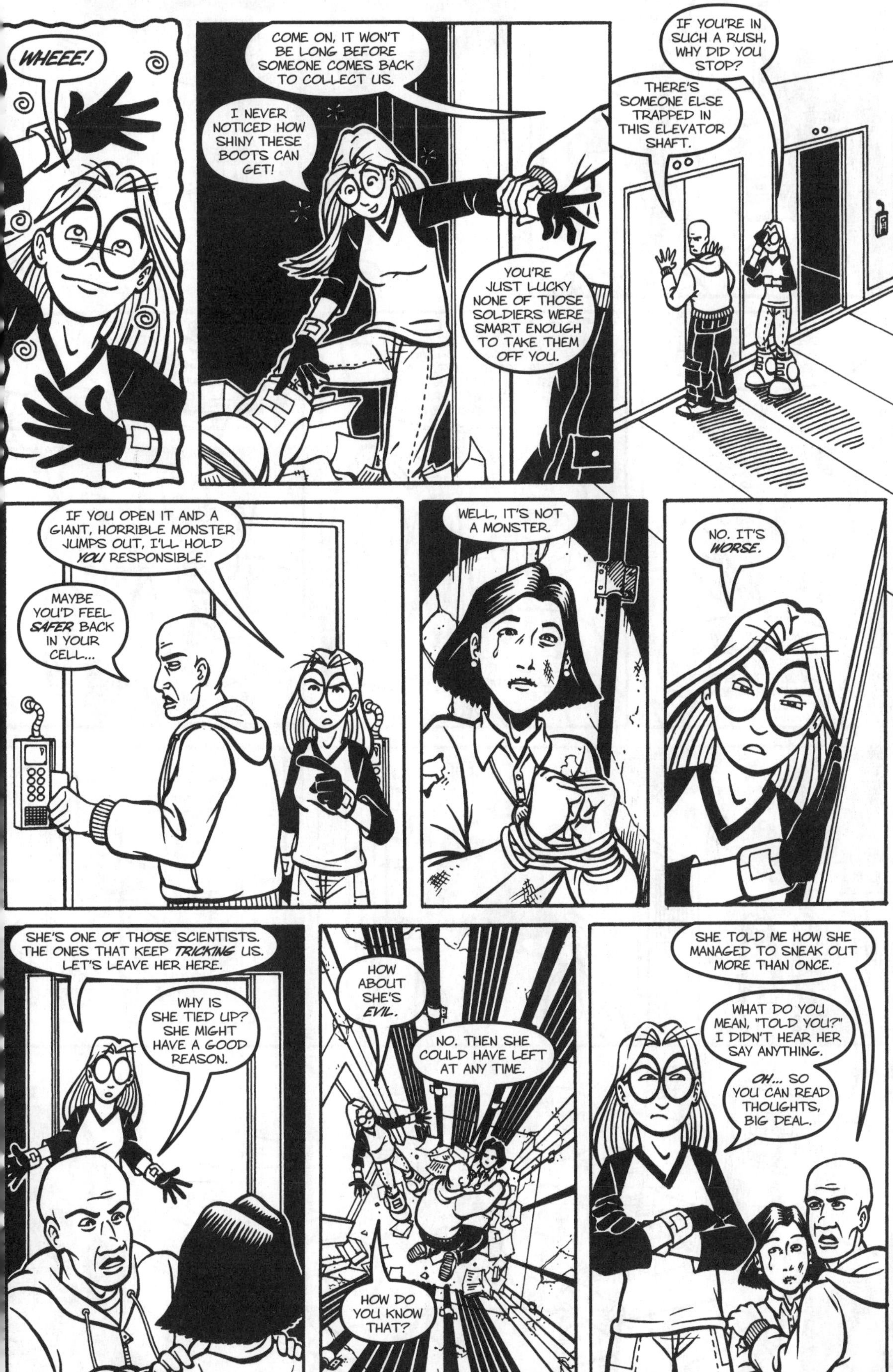
WHEEE!
COME ON, IT WON'T BE LONG BEFORE SOMEONE COMES BACK TO COLLECT US.
I NEVER NOTICED HOW SHINY THESE BOOTS CAN GET!
YOU'RE JUST LUCKY NONE OF THOSE SOLDIERS WERE SMART ENOUGH TO TAKE THEM OFF YOU.
IF YOU'RE IN SUCH A RUSH, WHY DID YOU STOP?
THERE'S SOMEONE ELSE TRAPPED IN THIS ELEVATOR SHAFT.
IF YOU OPEN IT AND A GIANT, HORRIBLE MONSTER JUMPS OUT, I'LL HOLD YOU RESPONSIBLE.
MAYBE YOU'D FEEL SAFER BACK IN YOUR CELL...
WELL, IT'S NOT A MONSTER.
NO. IT'S WORSE.
SHE'S ONE OF THOSE SCIENTISTS. THE ONES THAT KEEP TRICKING US. LET'S LEAVE HER HERE.
WHY IS SHE TIED UP? SHE MIGHT HAVE A GOOD REASON.
HOW ABOUT SHE'S EVIL.
NO. THEN SHE COULD HAVE LEFT AT ANY TIME.
HOW DO YOU KNOW THAT?
SHE TOLD ME HOW SHE MANAGED TO SNEAK OUT MORE THAN ONCE.
WHAT DO YOU MEAN, "TOLD YOU?" I DIDN'T HEAR HER SAY ANYTHING.
OH... SO YOU CAN READ THOUGHTS, BIG DEAL.

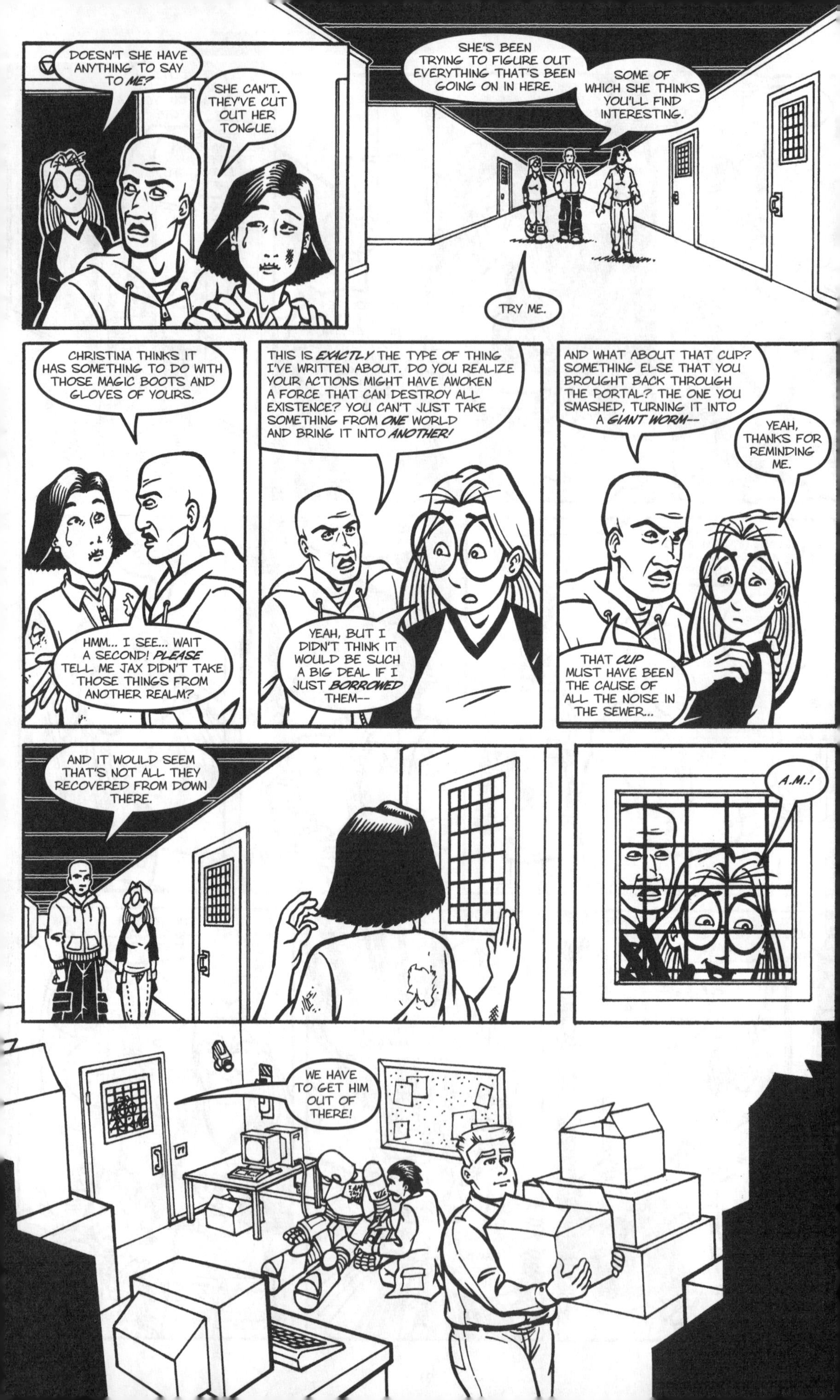
DOESN'T SHE HAVE ANYTHING TO SAY TO *ME?*
SHE CAN'T. THEY'VE CUT OUT HER TONGUE.
SHE'S BEEN TRYING TO FIGURE OUT EVERYTHING THAT'S BEEN GOING ON IN HERE.
SOME OF WHICH SHE THINKS YOU'LL FIND INTERESTING.
TRY ME.
CHRISTINA THINKS IT HAS SOMETHING TO DO WITH THOSE MAGIC BOOTS AND GLOVES OF YOURS.
HMM... I SEE... WAIT A SECOND! *PLEASE* TELL ME JAX DIDN'T TAKE THOSE THINGS FROM ANOTHER REALM?
THIS IS *EXACTLY* THE TYPE OF THING I'VE WRITTEN ABOUT. DO YOU REALIZE YOUR ACTIONS MIGHT HAVE AWOKEN A FORCE THAT CAN DESTROY ALL EXISTENCE? YOU CAN'T JUST TAKE SOMETHING FROM *ONE* WORLD AND BRING IT INTO *ANOTHER!*
YEAH, BUT I DIDN'T THINK IT WOULD BE SUCH A BIG DEAL IF I JUST *BORROWED* THEM--
AND WHAT ABOUT THAT CUP? SOMETHING ELSE THAT YOU BROUGHT BACK THROUGH THE PORTAL? THE ONE YOU SMASHED, TURNING IT INTO A *GIANT WORM*--
YEAH, THANKS FOR REMINDING ME.
THAT *CUP* MUST HAVE BEEN THE CAUSE OF ALL THE NOISE IN THE SEWER...
AND IT WOULD SEEM THAT'S NOT ALL THEY RECOVERED FROM DOWN THERE.
A.M.!
WE HAVE TO GET HIM OUT OF THERE!

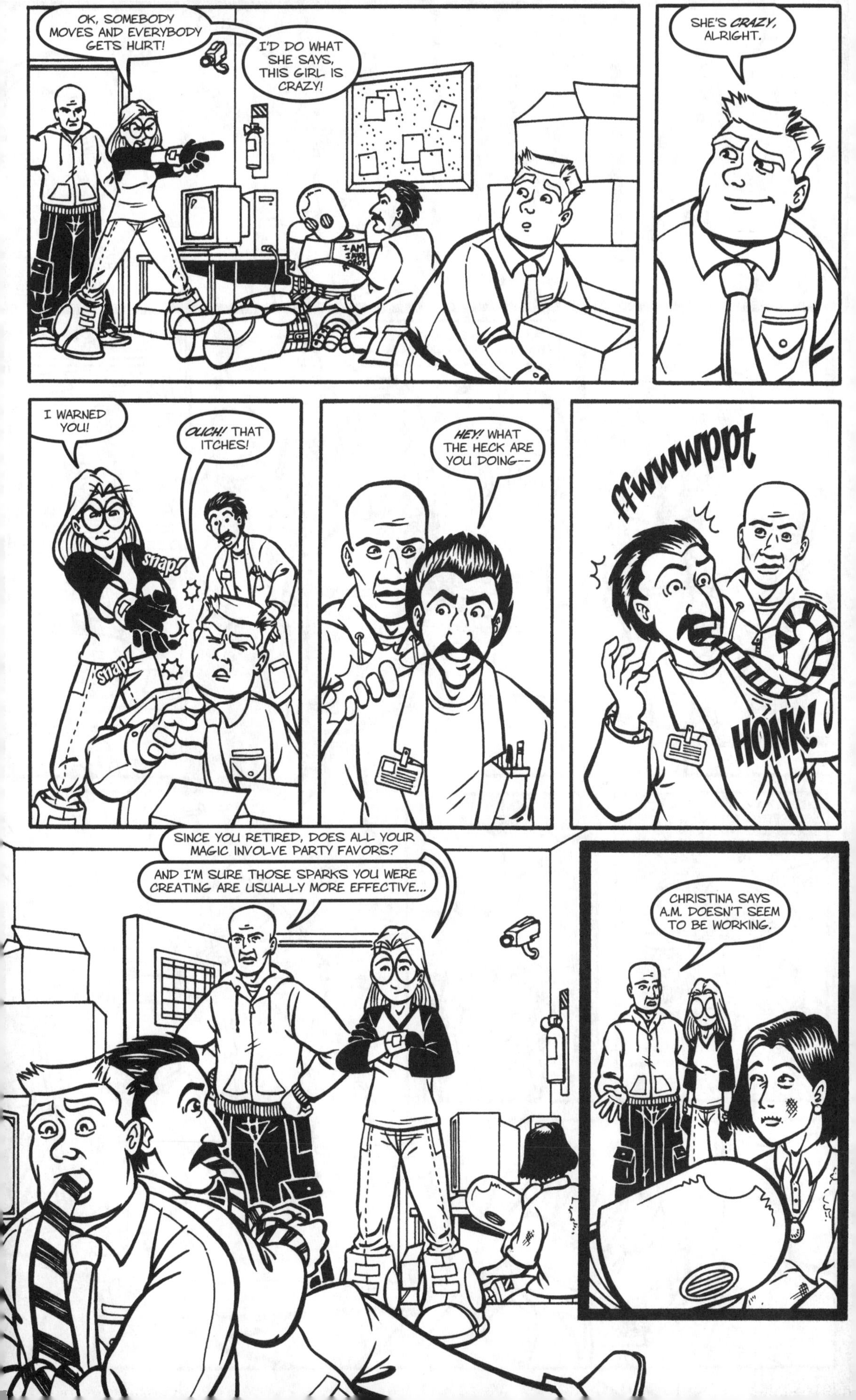

OK, SOMEBODY MOVES AND EVERYBODY GETS HURT!
I'D DO WHAT SHE SAYS, THIS GIRL IS CRAZY!
I AM 3PIO ROBOT
SHE'S CRAZY, ALRIGHT.
I WARNED YOU!
OUCH! THAT ITCHES!
snap!
snap!
HEY! WHAT THE HECK ARE YOU DOING--
ffwwwppt
HONK!
SINCE YOU RETIRED, DOES ALL YOUR MAGIC INVOLVE PARTY FAVORS?
AND I'M SURE THOSE SPARKS YOU WERE CREATING ARE USUALLY MORE EFFECTIVE...
CHRISTINA SAYS A.M. DOESN'T SEEM TO BE WORKING.

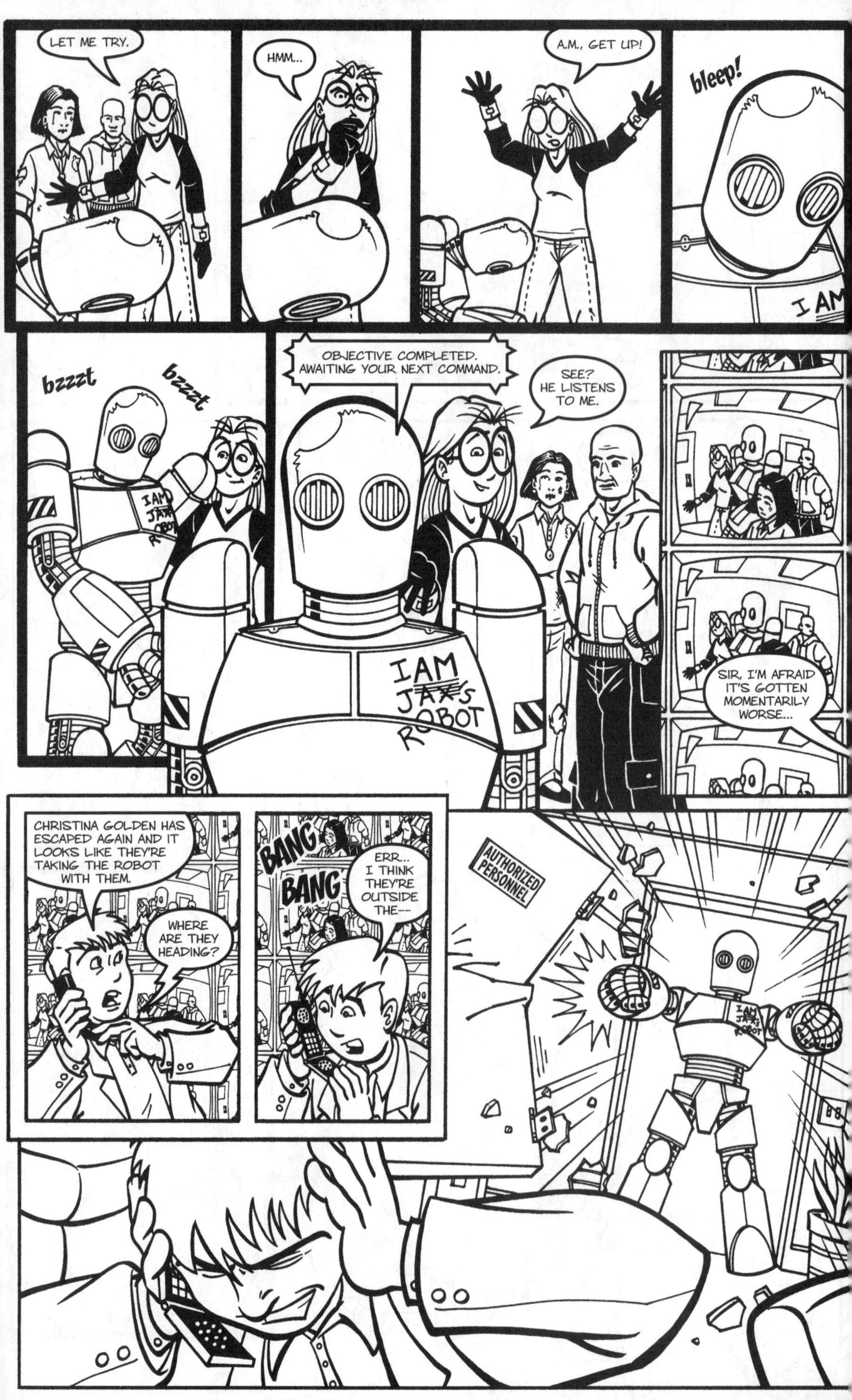
LET ME TRY.
HMM...
A.M., GET UP!
bleep!
I AM
bzzzt
bzzzt
I AM JAX'S ROBOT
OBJECTIVE COMPLETED. AWAITING YOUR NEXT COMMAND.
SEE? HE LISTENS TO ME.
I AM JAX'S ROBOT
SIR, I'M AFRAID IT'S GOTTEN MOMENTARILY WORSE...
CHRISTINA GOLDEN HAS ESCAPED AGAIN AND IT LOOKS LIKE THEY'RE TAKING THE ROBOT WITH THEM.
WHERE ARE THEY HEADING?
BANG
BANG
ERR... I THINK THEY'RE OUTSIDE THE--
AUTHORIZED PERSONNEL
I AM JAX'S ROBOT

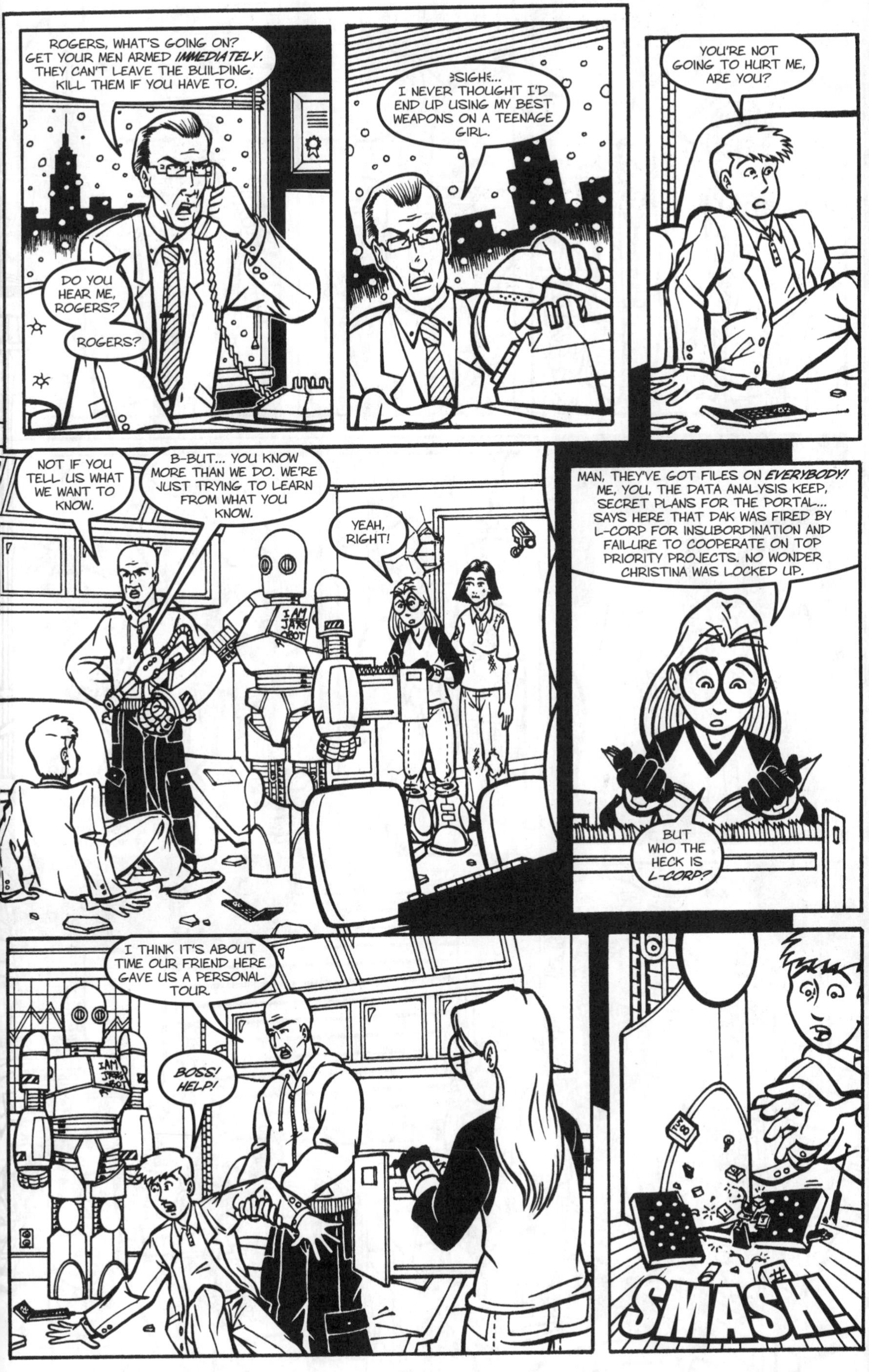
ROGERS, WHAT'S GOING ON? GET YOUR MEN ARMED *IMMEDIATELY.* THEY CAN'T LEAVE THE BUILDING. KILL THEM IF YOU HAVE TO.
DO YOU HEAR ME, ROGERS?
ROGERS?
SIGH... I NEVER THOUGHT I'D END UP USING MY BEST WEAPONS ON A TEENAGE GIRL.
YOU'RE NOT GOING TO HURT ME, ARE YOU?
NOT IF YOU TELL US WHAT WE WANT TO KNOW.
B-BUT... YOU KNOW MORE THAN WE DO. WE'RE JUST TRYING TO LEARN FROM WHAT YOU KNOW.
YEAH, RIGHT!
MAN, THEY'VE GOT FILES ON *EVERYBODY!* ME, YOU, THE DATA ANALYSIS KEEP, SECRET PLANS FOR THE PORTAL... SAYS HERE THAT DAK WAS FIRED BY L-CORP FOR INSUBORDINATION AND FAILURE TO COOPERATE ON TOP PRIORITY PROJECTS. NO WONDER CHRISTINA WAS LOCKED UP.
BUT WHO THE HECK IS *L-CORP?*
I THINK IT'S ABOUT TIME OUR FRIEND HERE GAVE US A PERSONAL TOUR.
BOSS! HELP!
SMASH!

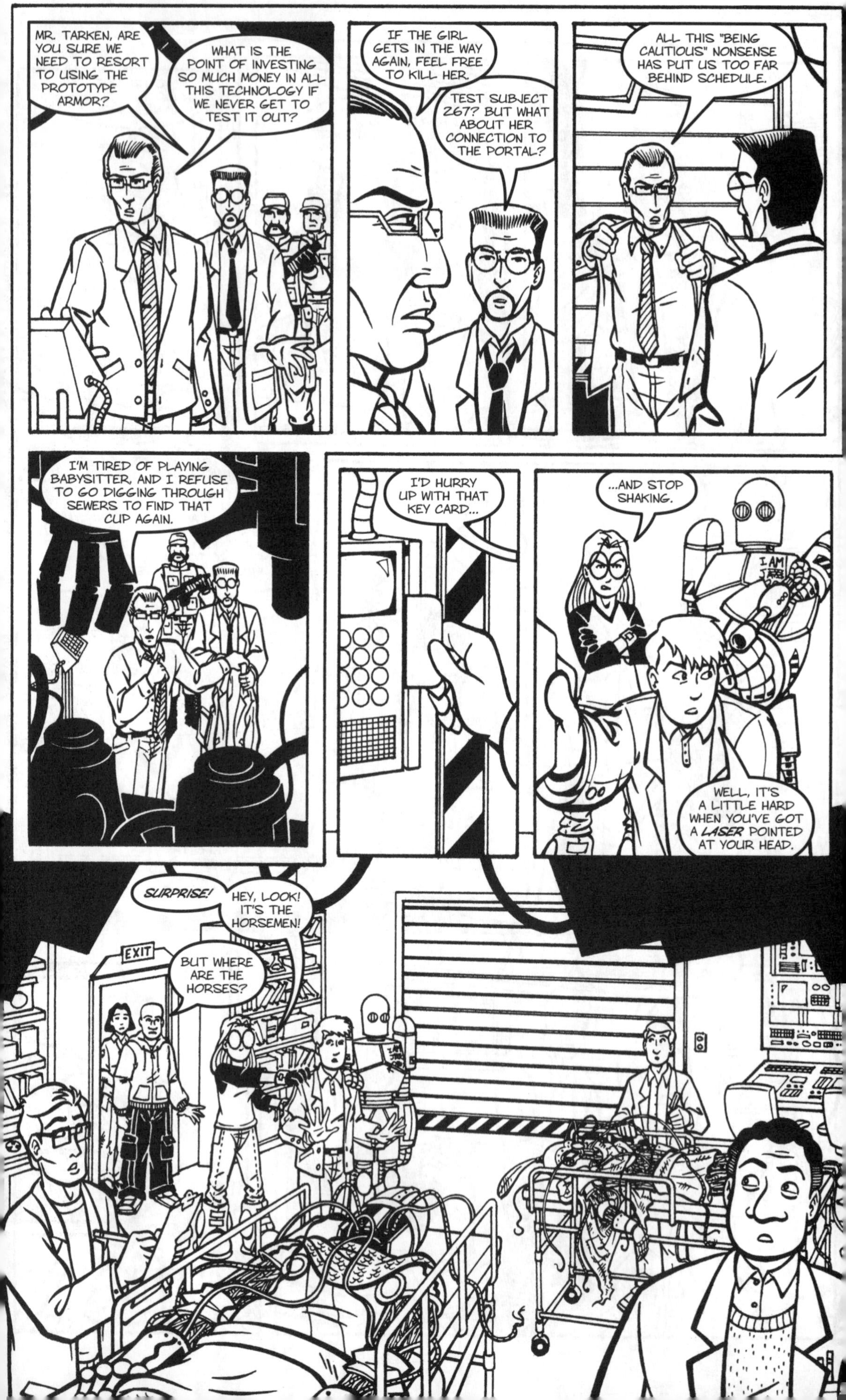
MR. TARKEN, ARE YOU SURE WE NEED TO RESORT TO USING THE PROTOTYPE ARMOR?
WHAT IS THE POINT OF INVESTING SO MUCH MONEY IN ALL THIS TECHNOLOGY IF WE NEVER GET TO TEST IT OUT?
IF THE GIRL GETS IN THE WAY AGAIN, FEEL FREE TO KILL HER.
TEST SUBJECT 267? BUT WHAT ABOUT HER CONNECTION TO THE PORTAL?
ALL THIS "BEING CAUTIOUS" NONSENSE HAS PUT US TOO FAR BEHIND SCHEDULE.
I'M TIRED OF PLAYING BABYSITTER, AND I REFUSE TO GO DIGGING THROUGH SEWERS TO FIND THAT CUP AGAIN.
I'D HURRY UP WITH THAT KEY CARD...
...AND STOP SHAKING.
I AM
WELL, IT'S A LITTLE HARD WHEN YOU'VE GOT A *LASER* POINTED AT YOUR HEAD.
SURPRISE!
HEY, LOOK! IT'S THE HORSEMEN!
EXIT
BUT WHERE ARE THE HORSES?

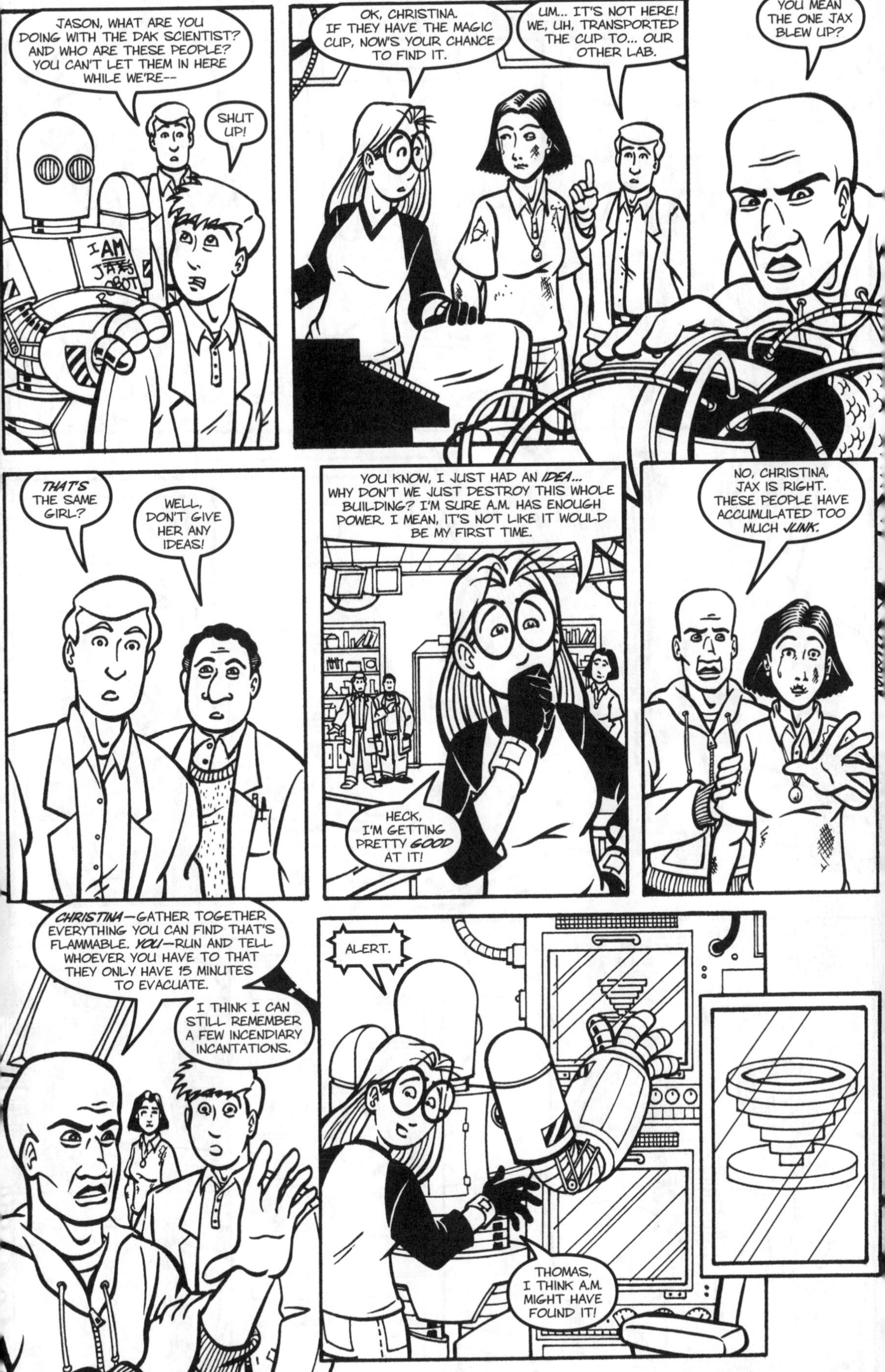

JASON, WHAT ARE YOU DOING WITH THE DAK SCIENTIST? AND WHO ARE THESE PEOPLE? YOU CAN'T LET THEM IN HERE WHILE WE'RE--
SHUT UP!
I AM JAXS ROBOT
OK, CHRISTINA. IF THEY HAVE THE MAGIC CUP, NOW'S YOUR CHANCE TO FIND IT.
UM... IT'S NOT HERE! WE, UH, TRANSPORTED THE CUP TO... OUR OTHER LAB.
YOU MEAN THE ONE JAX BLEW UP?
THAT'S THE SAME GIRL?
WELL, DON'T GIVE HER ANY IDEAS!
YOU KNOW, I JUST HAD AN IDEA... WHY DON'T WE JUST DESTROY THIS WHOLE BUILDING? I'M SURE A.M. HAS ENOUGH POWER. I MEAN, IT'S NOT LIKE IT WOULD BE MY FIRST TIME.
HECK, I'M GETTING PRETTY GOOD AT IT!
NO, CHRISTINA. JAX IS RIGHT. THESE PEOPLE HAVE ACCUMULATED TOO MUCH JUNK.
CHRISTINA—GATHER TOGETHER EVERYTHING YOU CAN FIND THAT'S FLAMMABLE. YOU—RUN AND TELL WHOEVER YOU HAVE TO THAT THEY ONLY HAVE 15 MINUTES TO EVACUATE.
I THINK I CAN STILL REMEMBER A FEW INCENDIARY INCANTATIONS.
ALERT.
THOMAS, I THINK A.M. MIGHT HAVE FOUND IT!

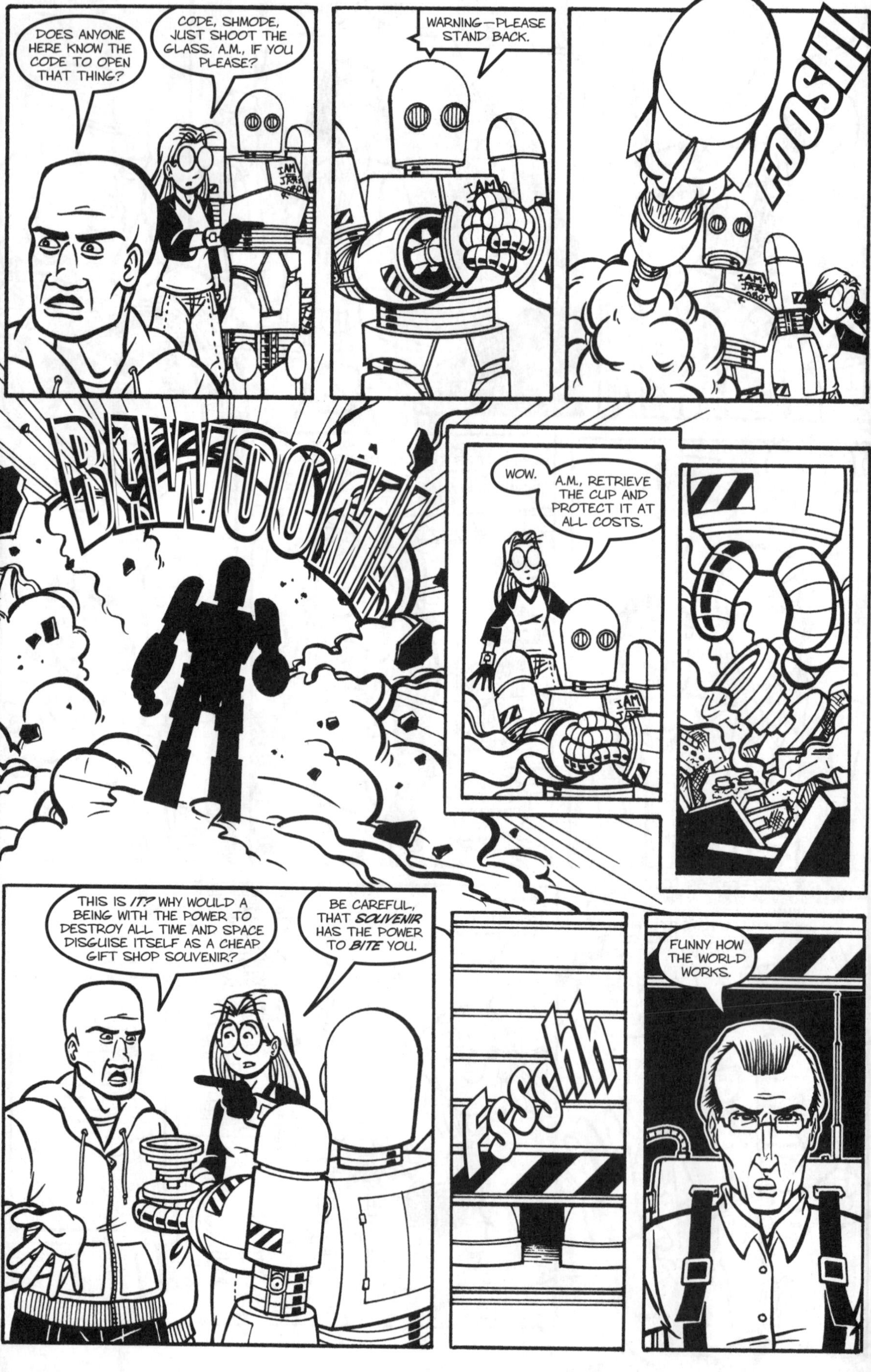
DOES ANYONE HERE KNOW THE CODE TO OPEN THAT THING?
CODE, SHMODE, JUST SHOOT THE GLASS. A.M., IF YOU PLEASE?
I AM JAMS ROBOT
WARNING—PLEASE STAND BACK.
I AM
FOOSH!
I AM JAMS ROBOT
BAWOOOM!
WOW.
A.M., RETRIEVE THE CUP AND PROTECT IT AT ALL COSTS.
I AM JA
THIS IS IT? WHY WOULD A BEING WITH THE POWER TO DESTROY ALL TIME AND SPACE DISGUISE ITSELF AS A CHEAP GIFT SHOP SOUVENIR?
BE CAREFUL, THAT SOUVENIR HAS THE POWER TO BITE YOU.
FSSSHH
FUNNY HOW THE WORLD WORKS.

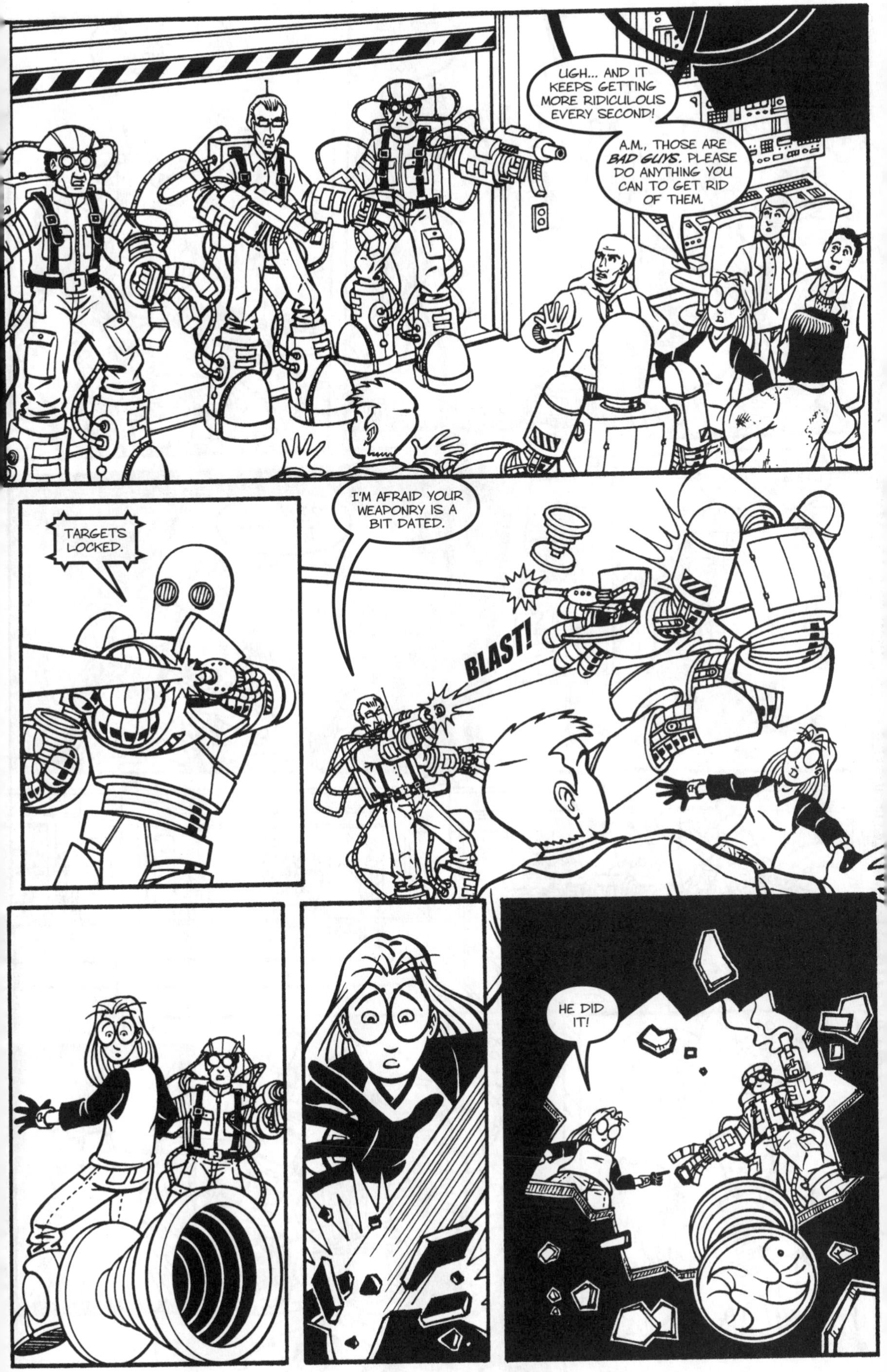
UGH... AND IT KEEPS GETTING MORE RIDICULOUS EVERY SECOND!
A.M., THOSE ARE BAD GUYS. PLEASE DO ANYTHING YOU CAN TO GET RID OF THEM.
TARGETS LOCKED.
I'M AFRAID YOUR WEAPONRY IS A BIT DATED.
BLAST!
HE DID IT!

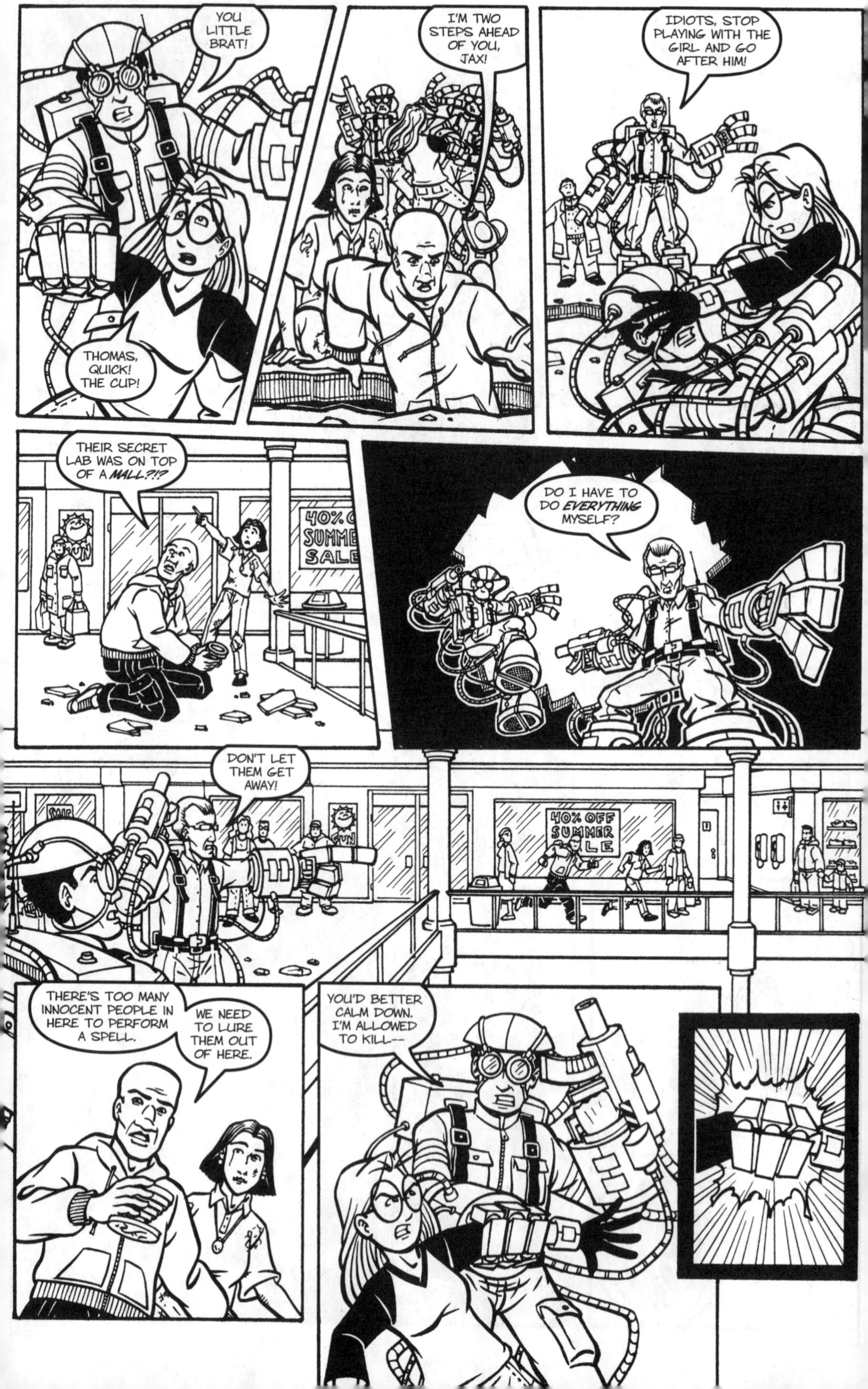

YOU LITTLE BRAT!
THOMAS, QUICK! THE CUP!
I'M TWO STEPS AHEAD OF YOU, JAX!
IDIOTS, STOP PLAYING WITH THE GIRL AND GO AFTER HIM!
THEIR SECRET LAB WAS ON TOP OF A *MALL?!?*
40% O
SUMME
SALE
DO I HAVE TO DO *EVERYTHING* MYSELF?
DON'T LET THEM GET AWAY!
40% OFF
SUMMER
LE
THERE'S TOO MANY INNOCENT PEOPLE IN HERE TO PERFORM A SPELL.
WE NEED TO LURE THEM OUT OF HERE.
YOU'D BETTER CALM DOWN. I'M ALLOWED TO KILL--

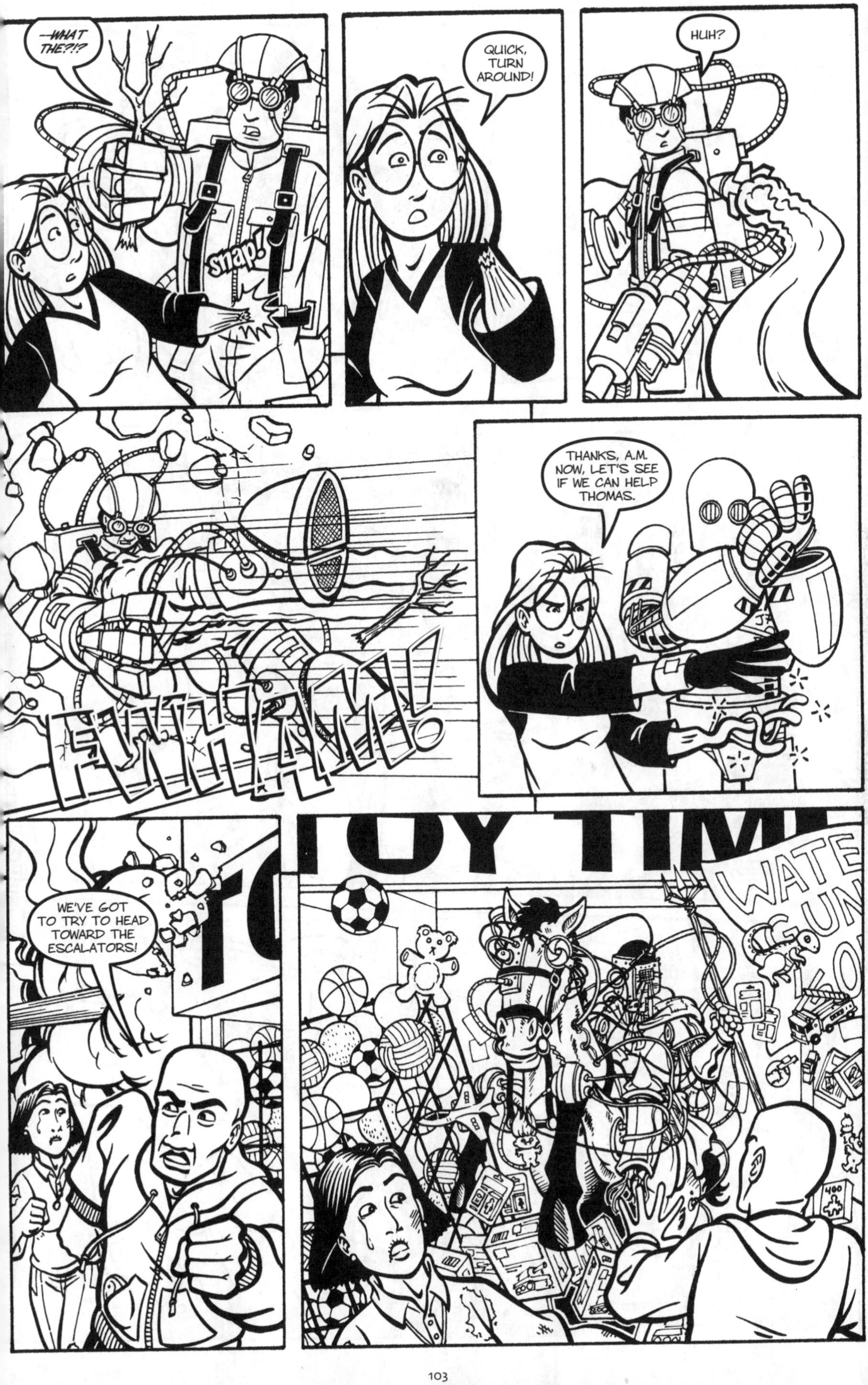
--WHAT THE?!?
SNAP!
QUICK, TURN AROUND!
HUH?
FWHAM!
THANKS, A.M. NOW, LET'S SEE IF WE CAN HELP THOMAS.
WE'VE GOT TO TRY TO HEAD TOWARD THE ESCALATORS!
TOY TIM
WATE
UN

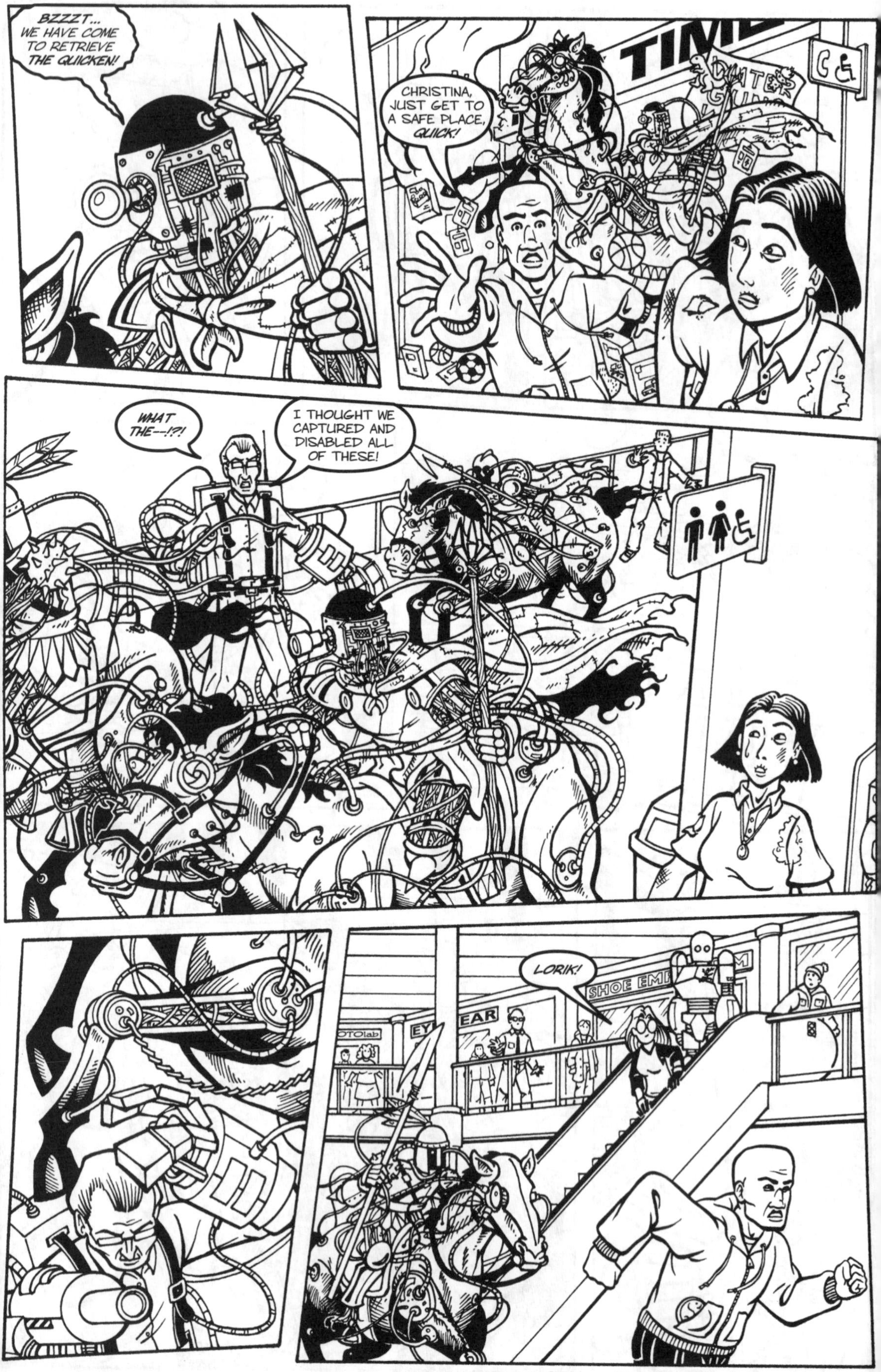
BZZZT... WE HAVE COME TO RETRIEVE THE QUICKEN!
CHRISTINA, JUST GET TO A SAFE PLACE, QUICK!
WHAT THE--!?!
I THOUGHT WE CAPTURED AND DISABLED ALL OF THESE!
LORIK!

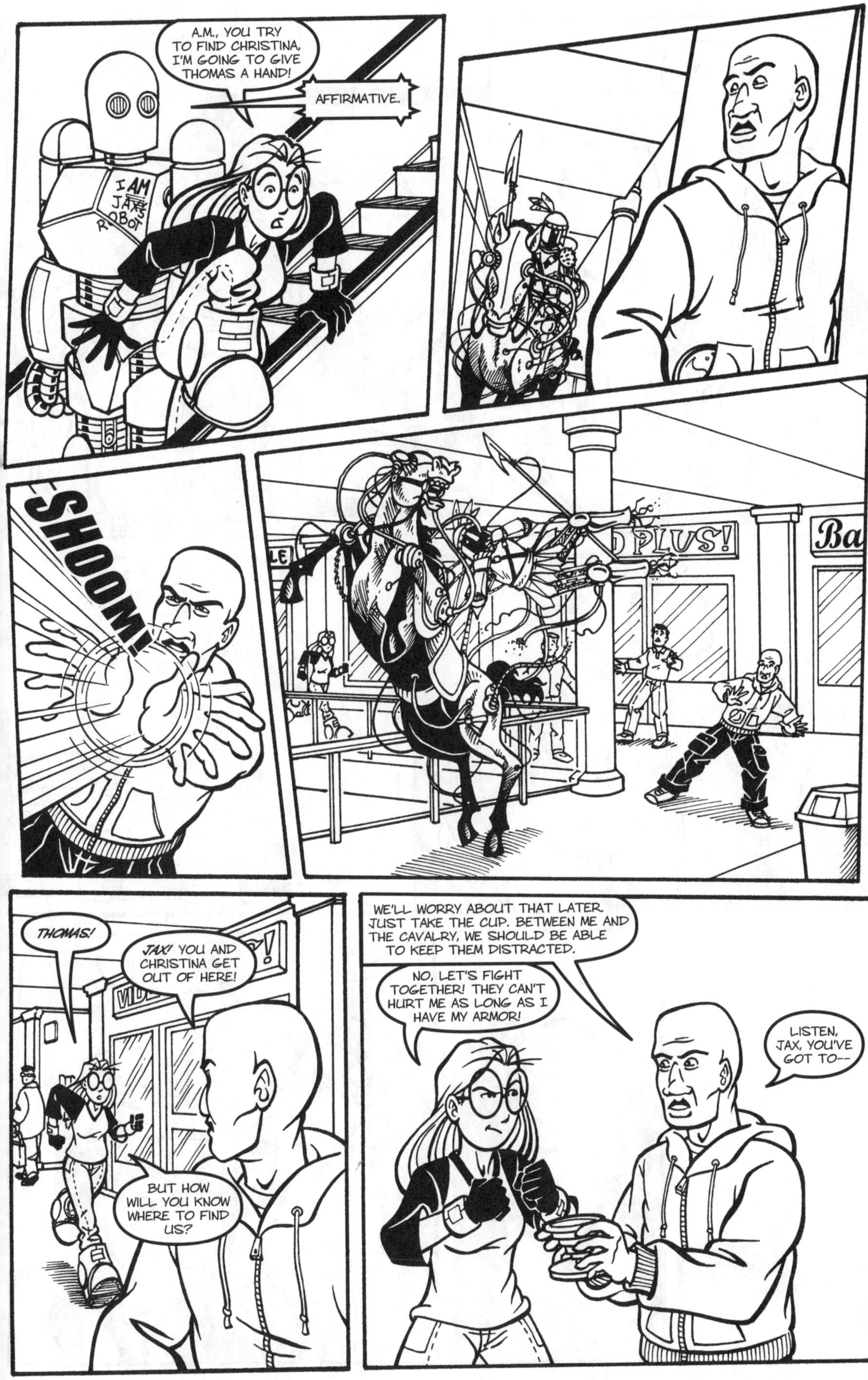
A.M., YOU TRY TO FIND CHRISTINA, I'M GOING TO GIVE THOMAS A HAND!
AFFIRMATIVE.
I AM JAX'S ROBOT
SHOOOM!
PLUS!
THOMAS!
JAX! YOU AND CHRISTINA GET OUT OF HERE!
BUT HOW WILL YOU KNOW WHERE TO FIND US?
WE'LL WORRY ABOUT THAT LATER. JUST TAKE THE CUP. BETWEEN ME AND THE CAVALRY, WE SHOULD BE ABLE TO KEEP THEM DISTRACTED.
NO, LET'S FIGHT TOGETHER! THEY CAN'T HURT ME AS LONG AS I HAVE MY ARMOR!
LISTEN, JAX, YOU'VE GOT TO--

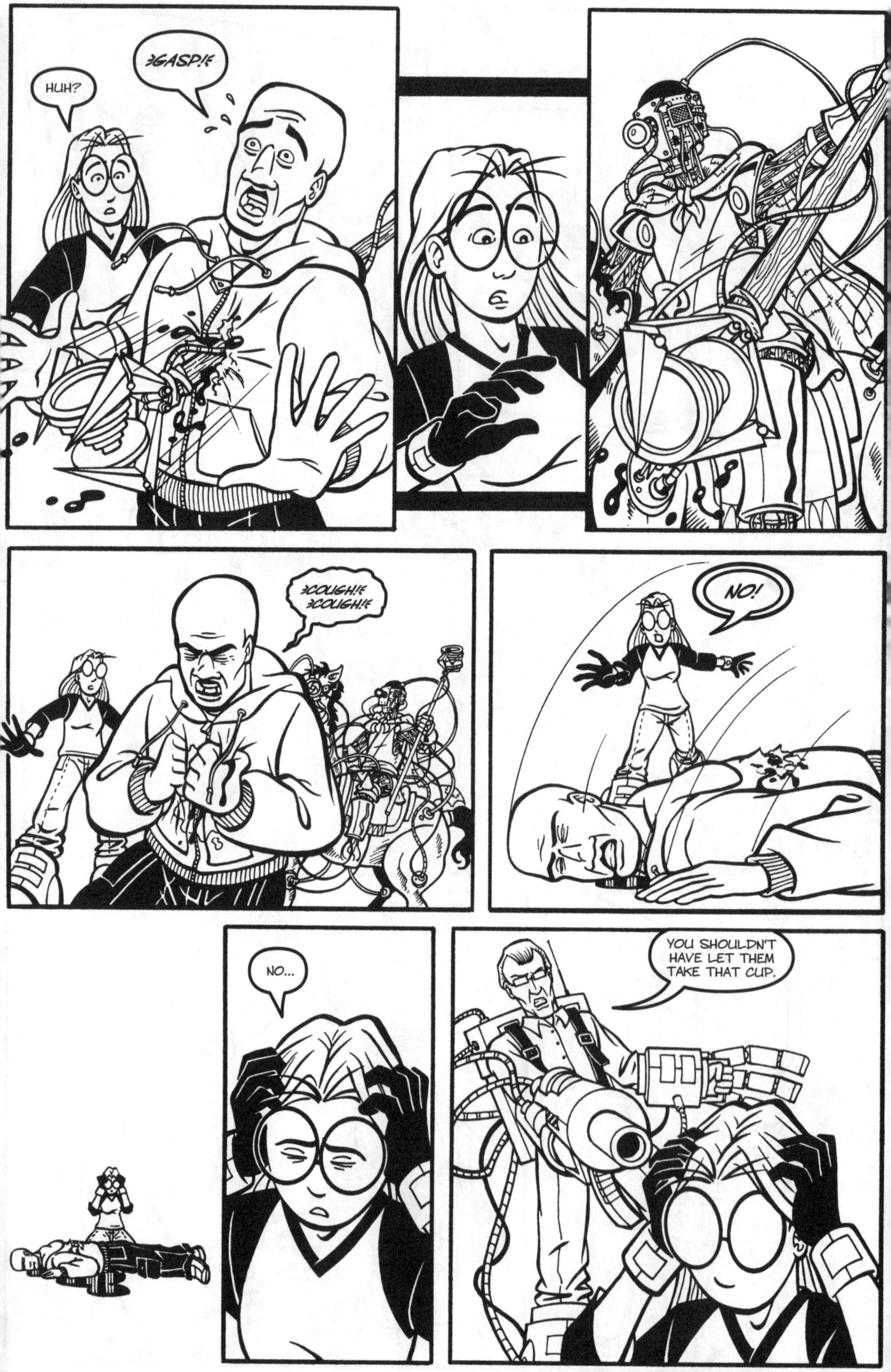
HUH?
GASP!
COUGH! COUGH!
NO!
NO...
YOU SHOULDN'T HAVE LET THEM TAKE THAT CUP.

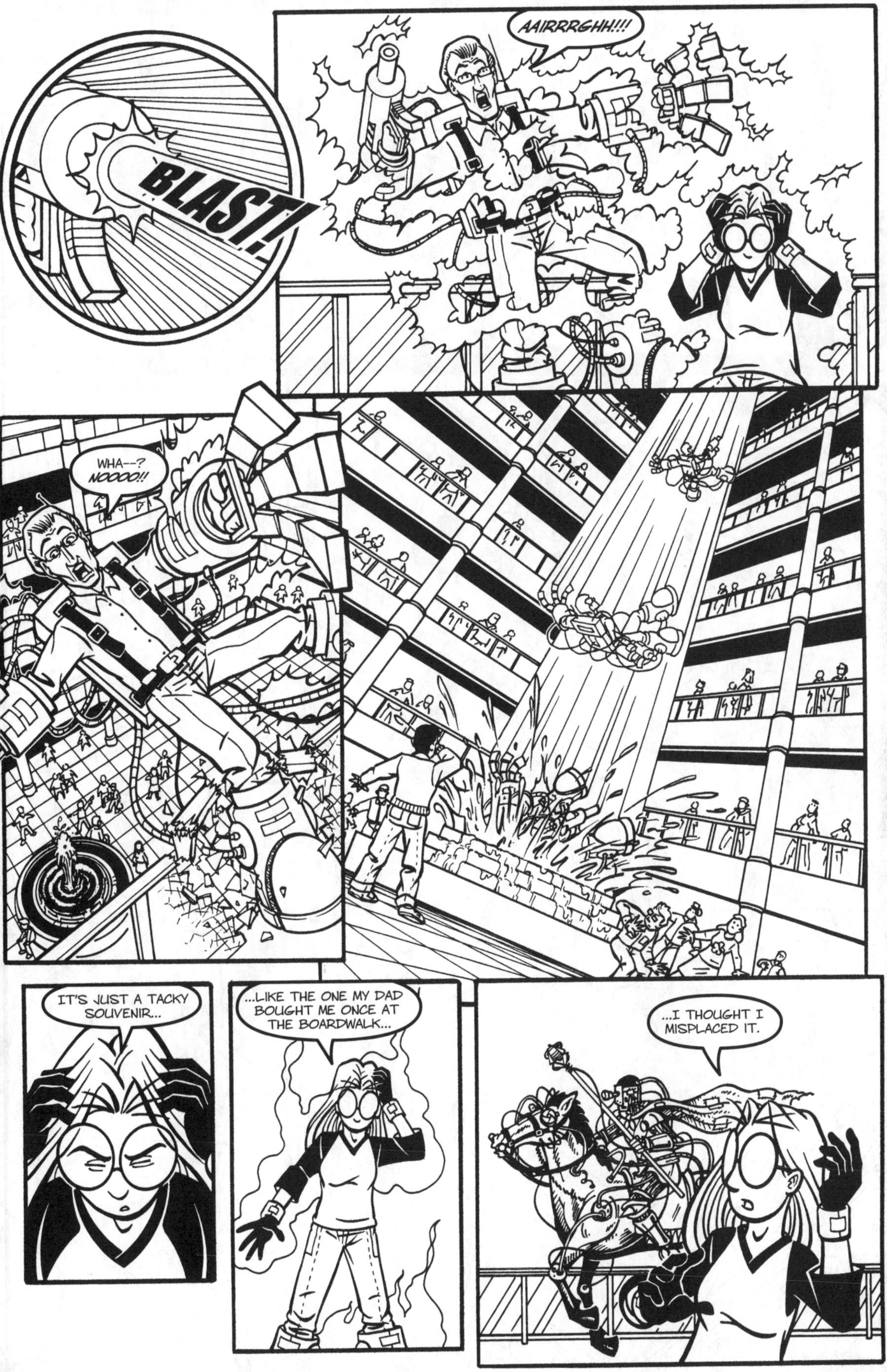
BLAST!
AAIRRRGHH!!!
WHA--? NOOOO!!
IT'S JUST A TACKY SOUVENIR...
...LIKE THE ONE MY DAD BOUGHT ME ONCE AT THE BOARDWALK...
...I THOUGHT I MISPLACED IT.

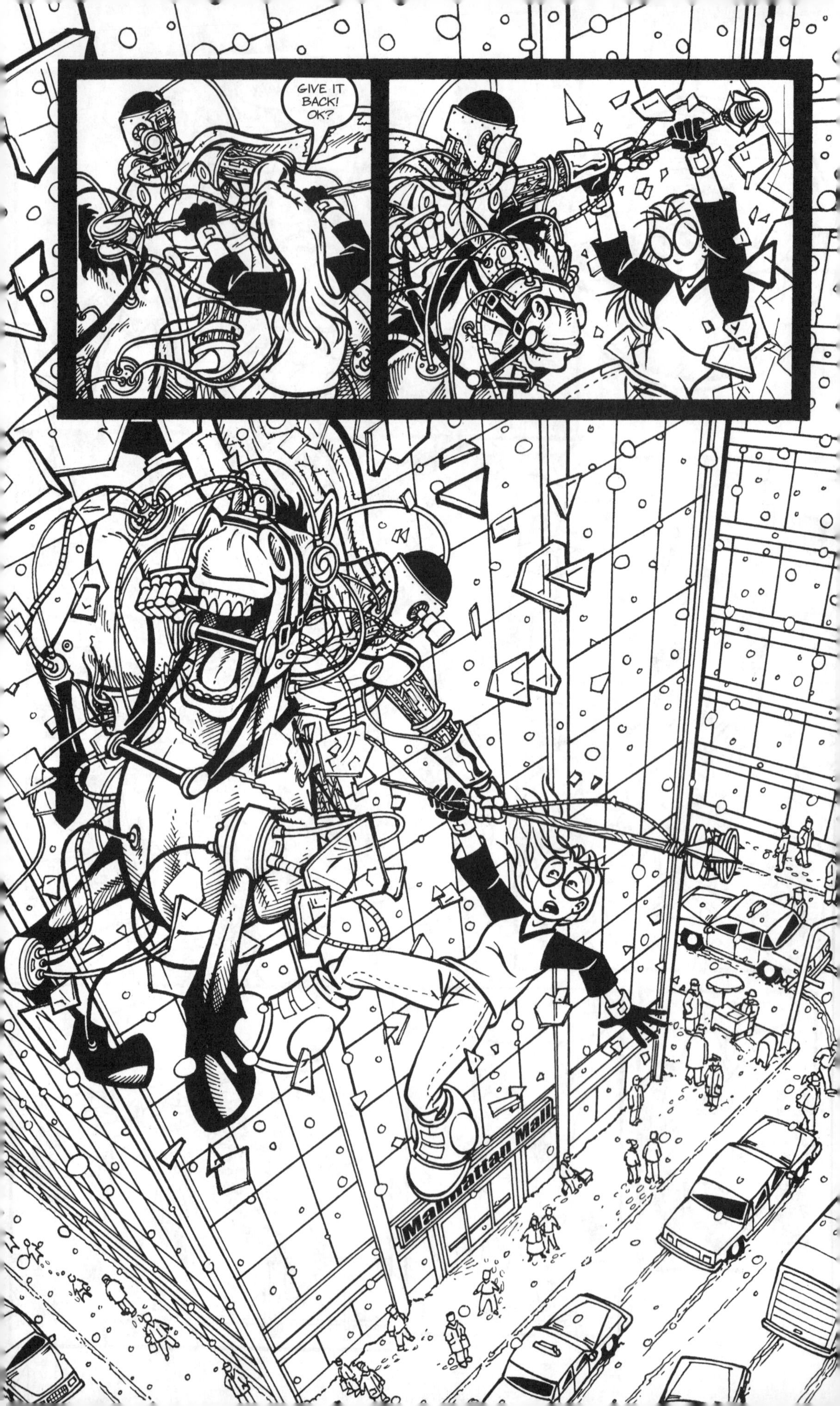
GIVE IT BACK! OK?
Manhattan Mall

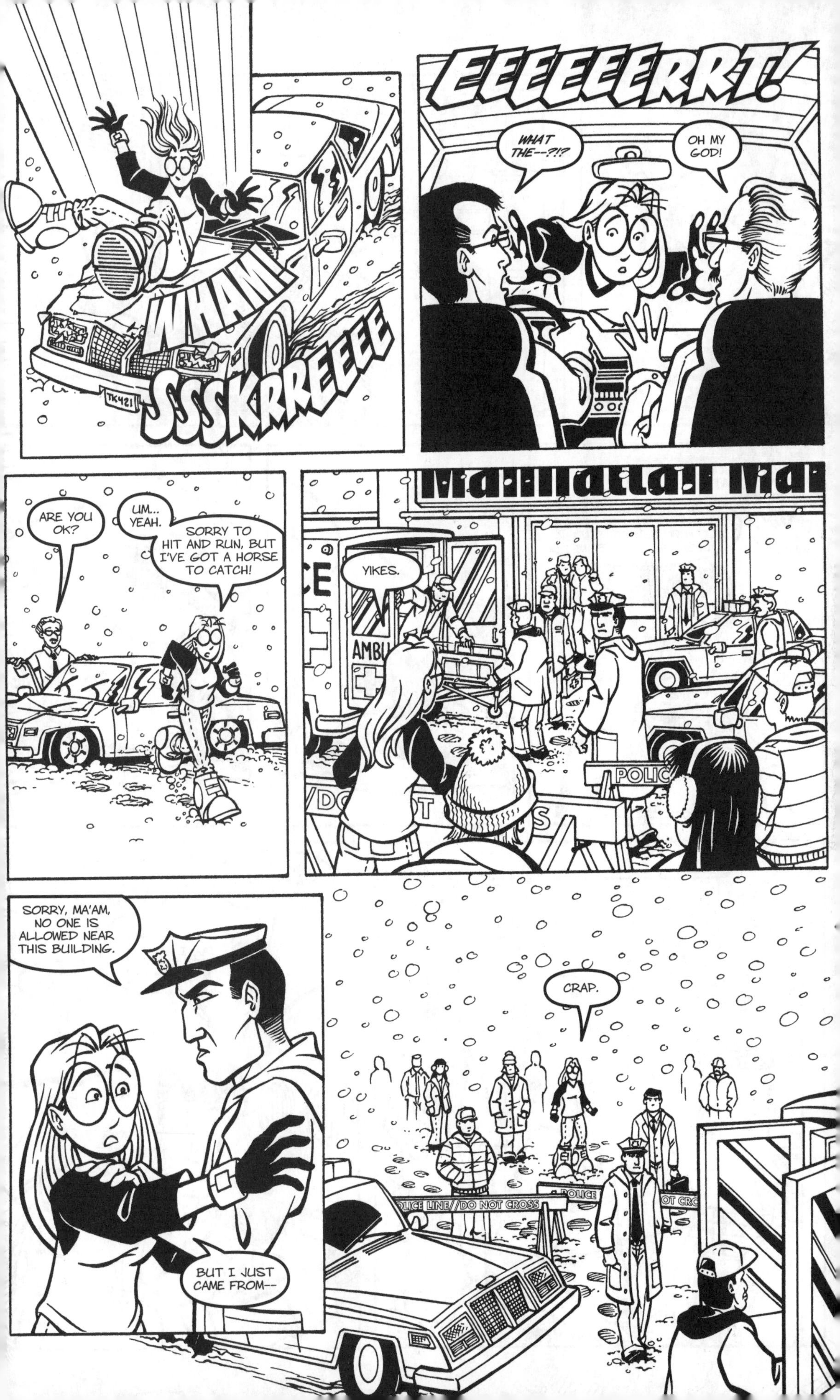
WHAM!
SSSKRREEEE
TK421
EEEEEERRRT!
WHAT THE--?!?
OH MY GOD!
ARE YOU OK?
UM... YEAH.
SORRY TO HIT AND RUN, BUT I'VE GOT A HORSE TO CATCH!
YIKES.
SORRY, MA'AM, NO ONE IS ALLOWED NEAR THIS BUILDING.
BUT I JUST CAME FROM--
POLICE LINE//DO NOT CROSS
CRAP.

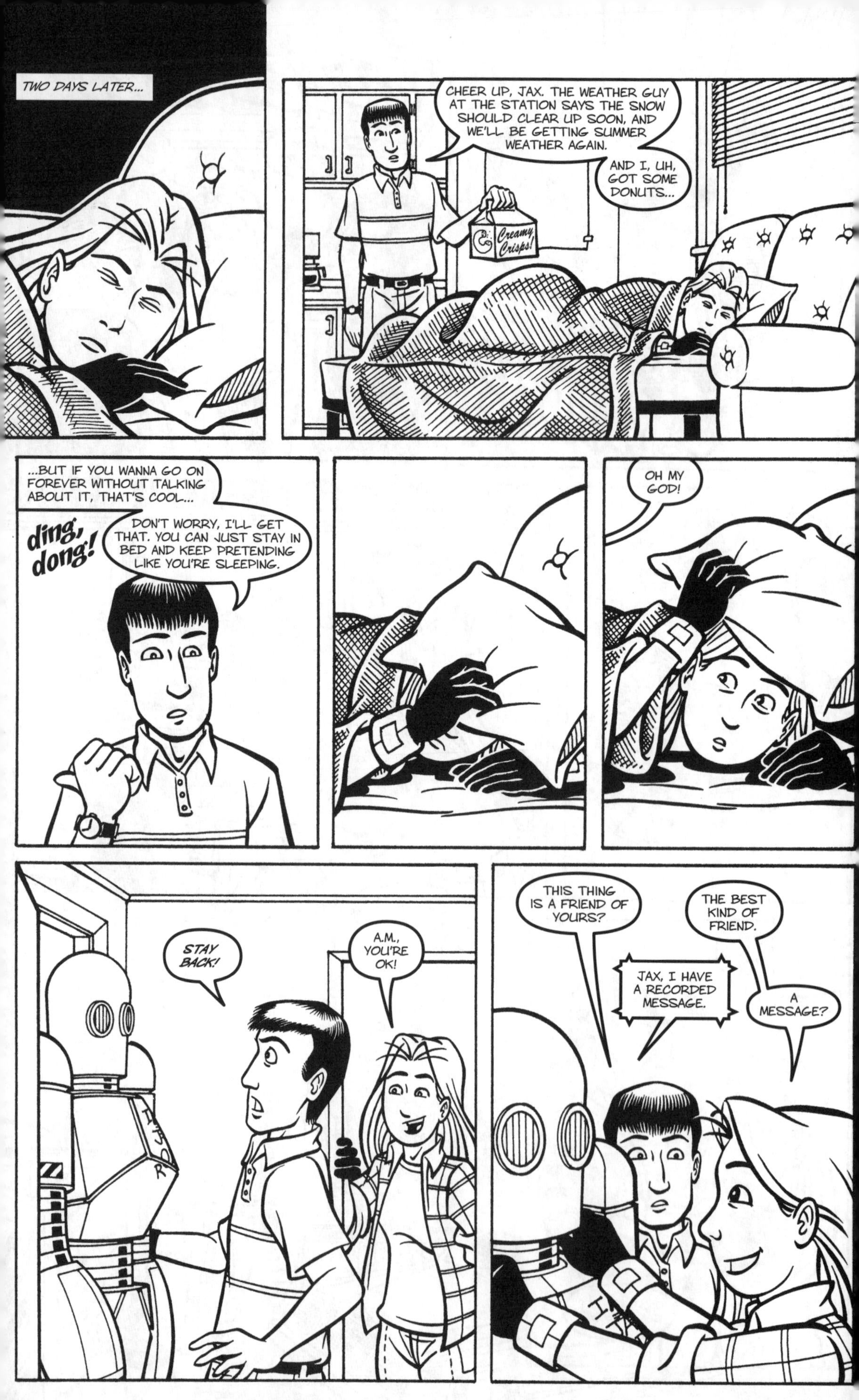
TWO DAYS LATER...
CHEER UP, JAX. THE WEATHER GUY AT THE STATION SAYS THE SNOW SHOULD CLEAR UP SOON, AND WE'LL BE GETTING SUMMER WEATHER AGAIN.
AND I, UH, GOT SOME DONUTS...
Creamy Crisps!
...BUT IF YOU WANNA GO ON FOREVER WITHOUT TALKING ABOUT IT, THAT'S COOL...
ding, dong!
DON'T WORRY, I'LL GET THAT. YOU CAN JUST STAY IN BED AND KEEP PRETENDING LIKE YOU'RE SLEEPING.
OH MY GOD!
STAY BACK!
A.M., YOU'RE OK!
THIS THING IS A FRIEND OF YOURS?
THE BEST KIND OF FRIEND.
JAX, I HAVE A RECORDED MESSAGE.
A MESSAGE?

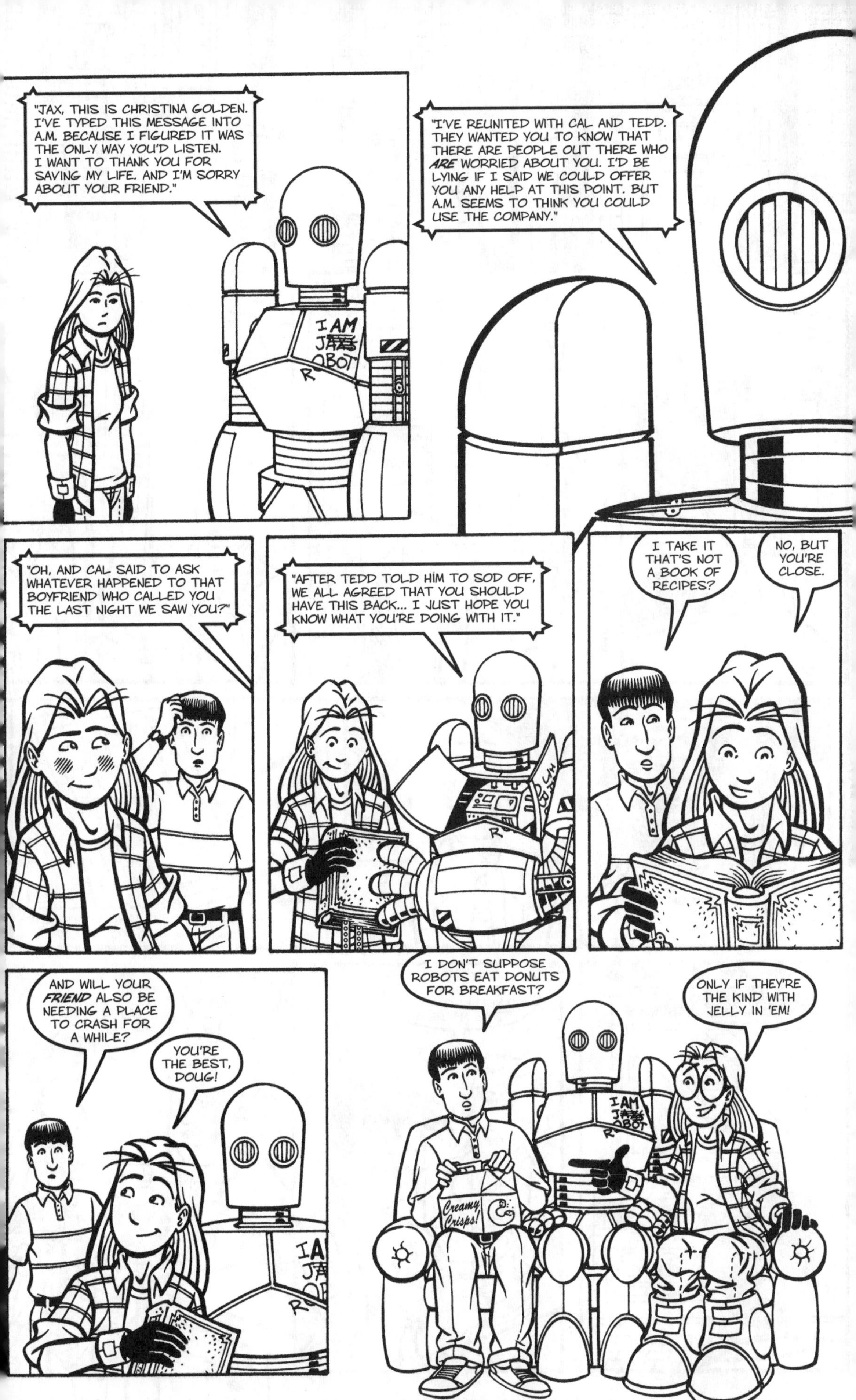
"JAX, THIS IS CHRISTINA GOLDEN. I'VE TYPED THIS MESSAGE INTO A.M. BECAUSE I FIGURED IT WAS THE ONLY WAY YOU'D LISTEN. I WANT TO THANK YOU FOR SAVING MY LIFE. AND I'M SORRY ABOUT YOUR FRIEND."
"I'VE REUNITED WITH CAL AND TEDD. THEY WANTED YOU TO KNOW THAT THERE ARE PEOPLE OUT THERE WHO *ARE* WORRIED ABOUT YOU. I'D BE LYING IF I SAID WE COULD OFFER YOU ANY HELP AT THIS POINT. BUT A.M. SEEMS TO THINK YOU COULD USE THE COMPANY."
"OH, AND CAL SAID TO ASK WHATEVER HAPPENED TO THAT BOYFRIEND WHO CALLED YOU THE LAST NIGHT WE SAW YOU?"
"AFTER TEDD TOLD HIM TO SOD OFF, WE ALL AGREED THAT YOU SHOULD HAVE THIS BACK... I JUST HOPE YOU KNOW WHAT YOU'RE DOING WITH IT."
I TAKE IT THAT'S NOT A BOOK OF RECIPES?
NO, BUT YOU'RE CLOSE.
AND WILL YOUR *FRIEND* ALSO BE NEEDING A PLACE TO CRASH FOR A WHILE?
YOU'RE THE BEST, DOUG!
I DON'T SUPPOSE ROBOTS EAT DONUTS FOR BREAKFAST?
ONLY IF THEY'RE THE KIND WITH JELLY IN 'EM!
Creamy Crisps!

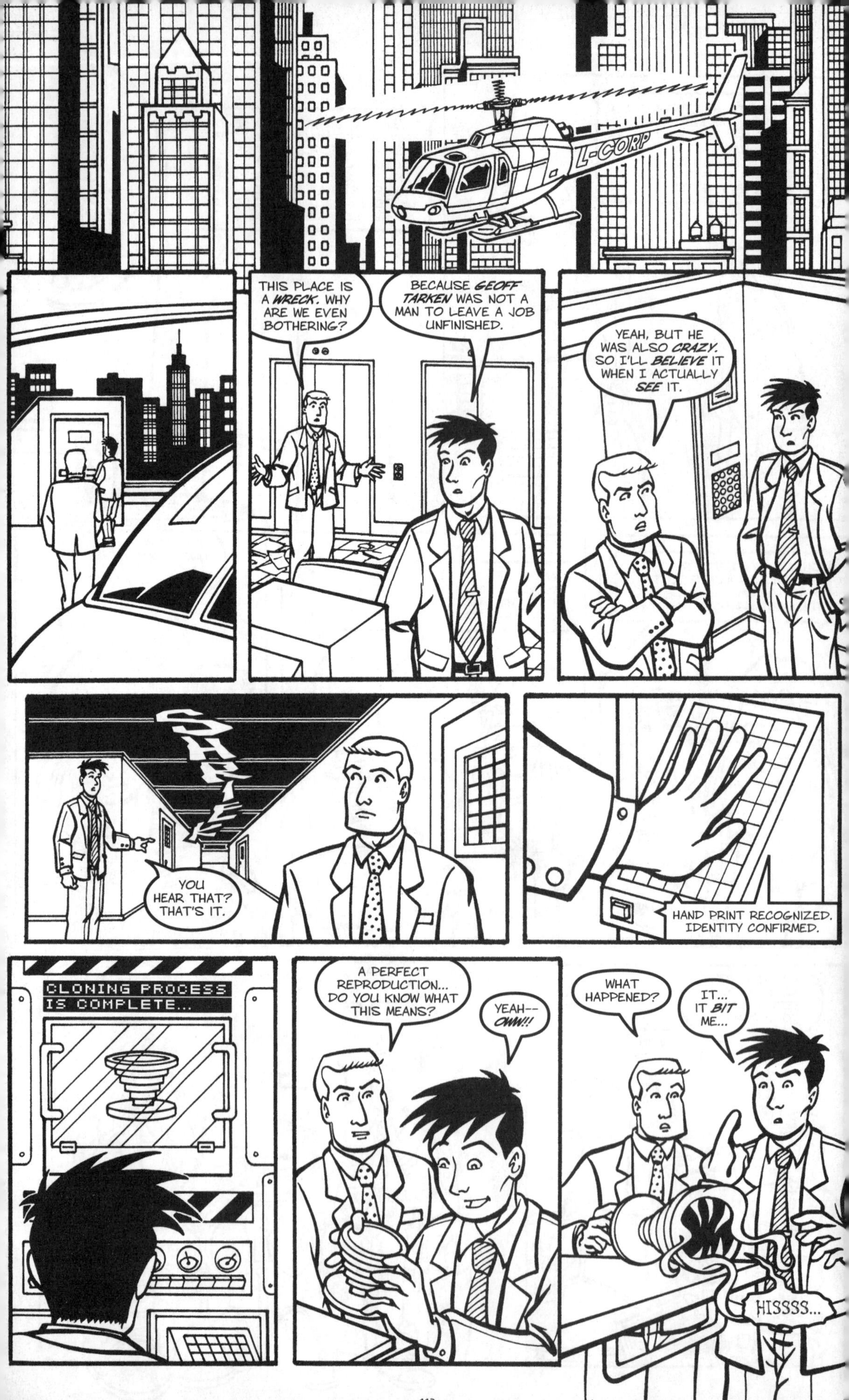
THIS PLACE IS A WRECK. WHY ARE WE EVEN BOTHERING?
BECAUSE GEOFF TARKEN WAS NOT A MAN TO LEAVE A JOB UNFINISHED.
YEAH, BUT HE WAS ALSO CRAZY. SO I'LL BELIEVE IT WHEN I ACTUALLY SEE IT.
SHRIEK
YOU HEAR THAT? THAT'S IT.
HAND PRINT RECOGNIZED. IDENTITY CONFIRMED.
CLONING PROCESS IS COMPLETE...
A PERFECT REPRODUCTION... DO YOU KNOW WHAT THIS MEANS?
YEAH-- OWW!!
WHAT HAPPENED?
IT... IT BIT ME...
HISSSS...

...for the birds

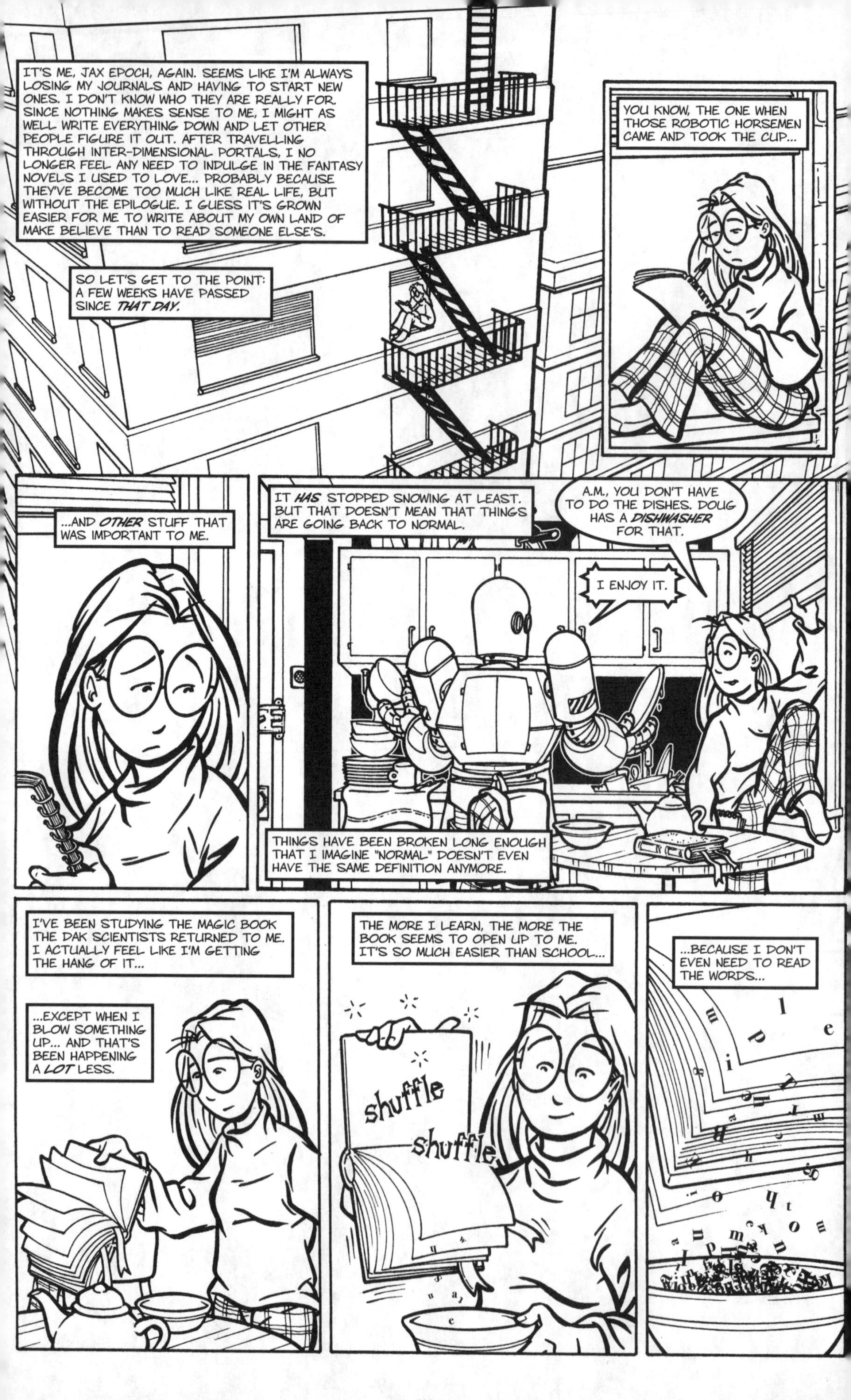

IT'S ME, JAX EPOCH, AGAIN. SEEMS LIKE I'M ALWAYS LOSING MY JOURNALS AND HAVING TO START NEW ONES. I DON'T KNOW WHO THEY ARE REALLY FOR. SINCE NOTHING MAKES SENSE TO ME, I MIGHT AS WELL WRITE EVERYTHING DOWN AND LET OTHER PEOPLE FIGURE IT OUT. AFTER TRAVELLING THROUGH INTER-DIMENSIONAL PORTALS, I NO LONGER FEEL ANY NEED TO INDULGE IN THE FANTASY NOVELS I USED TO LOVE... PROBABLY BECAUSE THEY'VE BECOME TOO MUCH LIKE REAL LIFE, BUT WITHOUT THE EPILOGUE. I GUESS IT'S GROWN EASIER FOR ME TO WRITE ABOUT MY OWN LAND OF MAKE BELIEVE THAN TO READ SOMEONE ELSE'S.
SO LET'S GET TO THE POINT: A FEW WEEKS HAVE PASSED SINCE *THAT DAY.*
YOU KNOW, THE ONE WHEN THOSE ROBOTIC HORSEMEN CAME AND TOOK THE CUP...
...AND *OTHER* STUFF THAT WAS IMPORTANT TO ME.
IT *HAS* STOPPED SNOWING AT LEAST. BUT THAT DOESN'T MEAN THAT THINGS ARE GOING BACK TO NORMAL.
A.M., YOU DON'T HAVE TO DO THE DISHES. DOUG HAS A *DISHWASHER* FOR THAT.
I ENJOY IT.
THINGS HAVE BEEN BROKEN LONG ENOUGH THAT I IMAGINE "NORMAL" DOESN'T EVEN HAVE THE SAME DEFINITION ANYMORE.
I'VE BEEN STUDYING THE MAGIC BOOK THE DAK SCIENTISTS RETURNED TO ME. I ACTUALLY FEEL LIKE I'M GETTING THE HANG OF IT...
...EXCEPT WHEN I BLOW SOMETHING UP... AND THAT'S BEEN HAPPENING A *LOT* LESS.
THE MORE I LEARN, THE MORE THE BOOK SEEMS TO OPEN UP TO ME. IT'S SO MUCH EASIER THAN SCHOOL...
shuffle
shuffle
...BECAUSE I DON'T EVEN NEED TO READ THE WORDS...

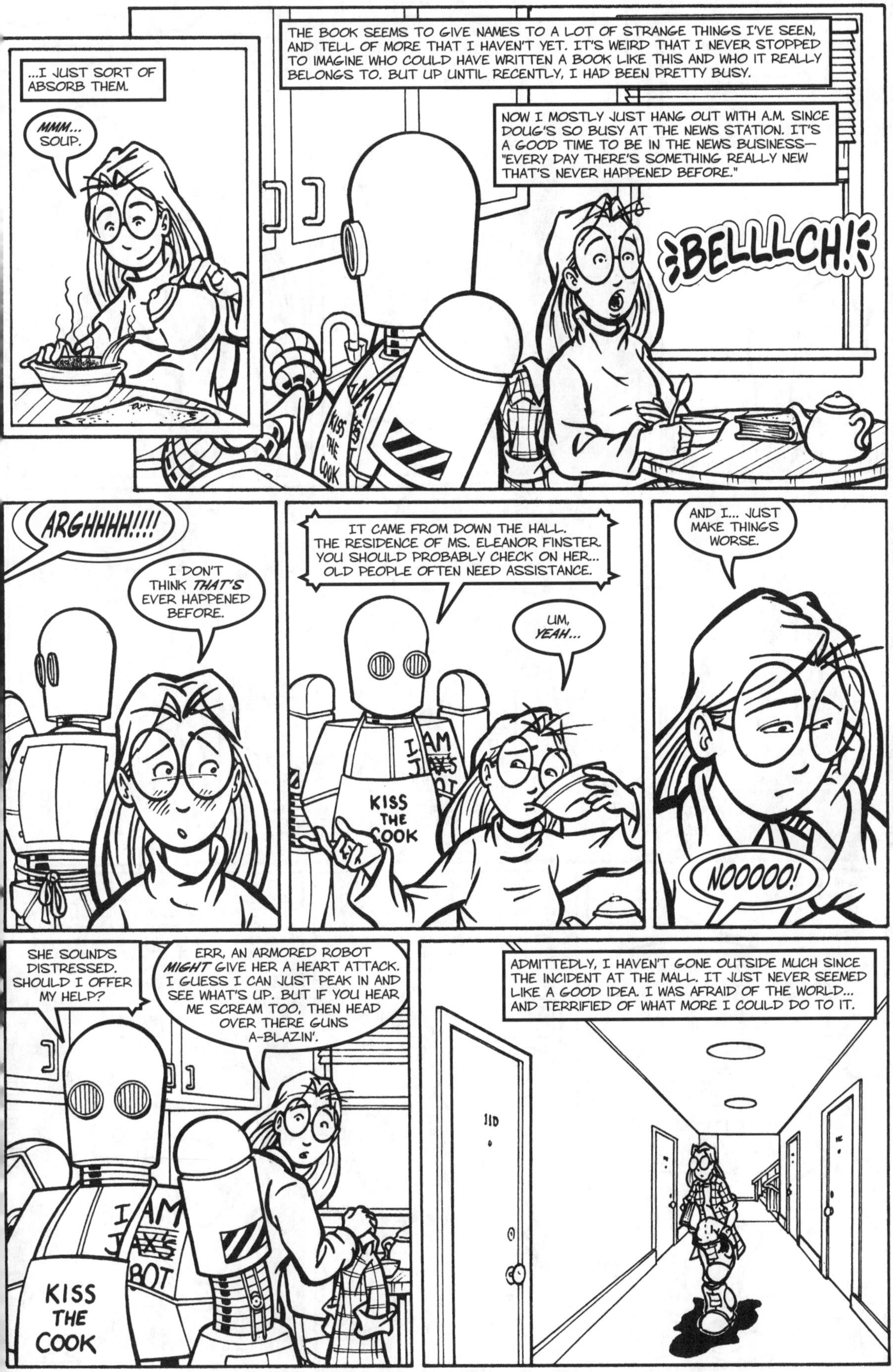

...I JUST SORT OF ABSORB THEM.
MMM... SOUP.
THE BOOK SEEMS TO GIVE NAMES TO A LOT OF STRANGE THINGS I'VE SEEN, AND TELL OF MORE THAT I HAVEN'T YET. IT'S WEIRD THAT I NEVER STOPPED TO IMAGINE WHO COULD HAVE WRITTEN A BOOK LIKE THIS AND WHO IT REALLY BELONGS TO. BUT UP UNTIL RECENTLY, I HAD BEEN PRETTY BUSY.
NOW I MOSTLY JUST HANG OUT WITH A.M. SINCE DOUG'S SO BUSY AT THE NEWS STATION. IT'S A GOOD TIME TO BE IN THE NEWS BUSINESS— "EVERY DAY THERE'S SOMETHING REALLY NEW THAT'S NEVER HAPPENED BEFORE."
BELLLCH!
KISS THE COOK
ARGHHHH!!!!
I DON'T THINK THAT'S EVER HAPPENED BEFORE.
IT CAME FROM DOWN THE HALL. THE RESIDENCE OF MS. ELEANOR FINSTER. YOU SHOULD PROBABLY CHECK ON HER... OLD PEOPLE OFTEN NEED ASSISTANCE.
UM, YEAH...
KISS THE COOK
AND I... JUST MAKE THINGS WORSE.
NOOOOO!
SHE SOUNDS DISTRESSED. SHOULD I OFFER MY HELP?
ERR, AN ARMORED ROBOT MIGHT GIVE HER A HEART ATTACK. I GUESS I CAN JUST PEAK IN AND SEE WHAT'S UP. BUT IF YOU HEAR ME SCREAM TOO, THEN HEAD OVER THERE GUNS A-BLAZIN'.
KISS THE COOK
ADMITTEDLY, I HAVEN'T GONE OUTSIDE MUCH SINCE THE INCIDENT AT THE MALL. IT JUST NEVER SEEMED LIKE A GOOD IDEA. I WAS AFRAID OF THE WORLD... AND TERRIFIED OF WHAT MORE I COULD DO TO IT.
11D

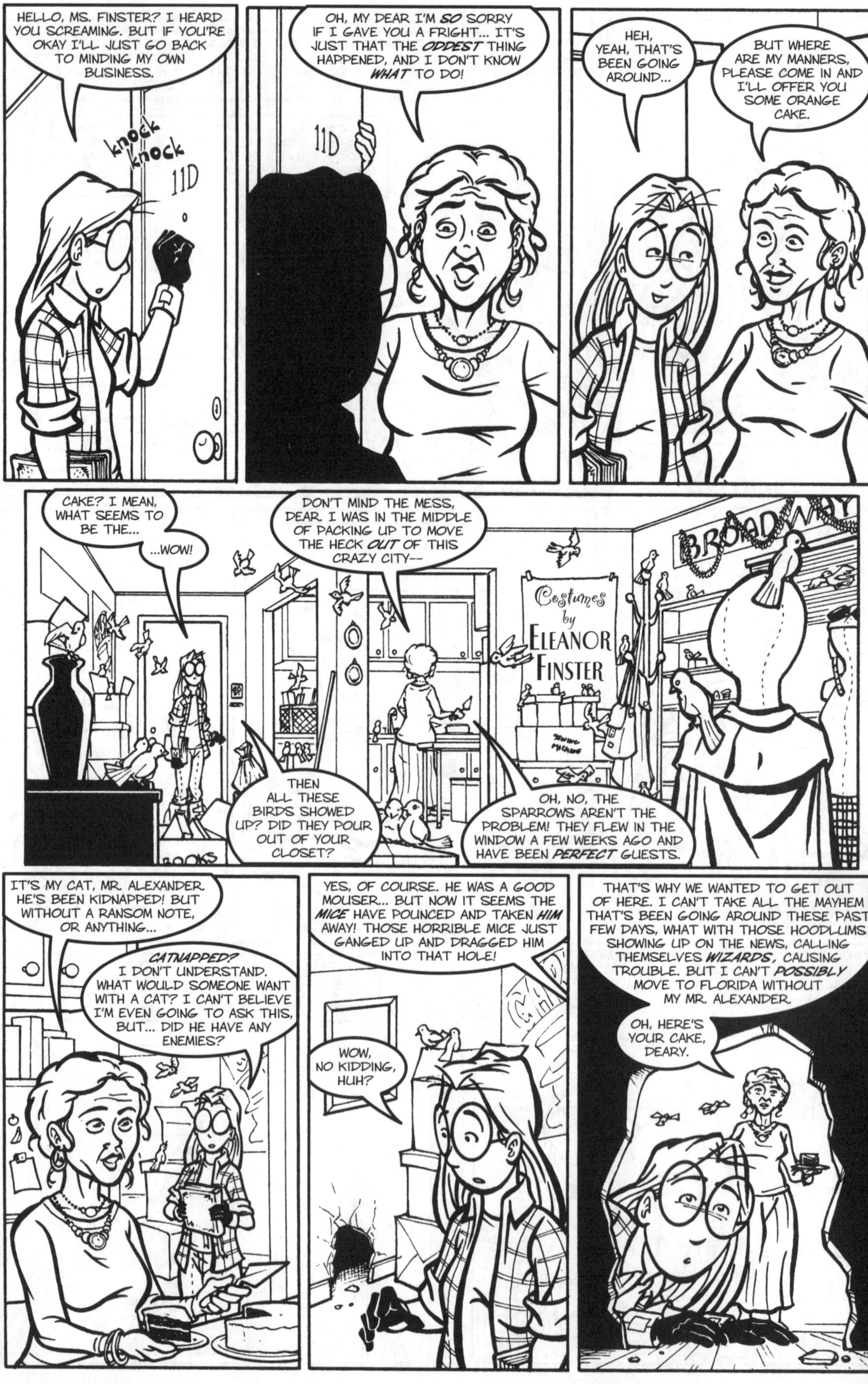
HELLO, MS. FINSTER? I HEARD YOU SCREAMING. BUT IF YOU'RE OKAY I'LL JUST GO BACK TO MINDING MY OWN BUSINESS.
knock knock
11D
OH, MY DEAR I'M SO SORRY IF I GAVE YOU A FRIGHT... IT'S JUST THAT THE ODDEST THING HAPPENED, AND I DON'T KNOW WHAT TO DO!
11D
HEH, YEAH, THAT'S BEEN GOING AROUND...
BUT WHERE ARE MY MANNERS, PLEASE COME IN AND I'LL OFFER YOU SOME ORANGE CAKE.
CAKE? I MEAN, WHAT SEEMS TO BE THE...
...WOW!
DON'T MIND THE MESS, DEAR. I WAS IN THE MIDDLE OF PACKING UP TO MOVE THE HECK OUT OF THIS CRAZY CITY--
BROADWAY
Costumes by ELEANOR FINSTER
THEN ALL THESE BIRDS SHOWED UP? DID THEY POUR OUT OF YOUR CLOSET?
OH, NO, THE SPARROWS AREN'T THE PROBLEM! THEY FLEW IN THE WINDOW A FEW WEEKS AGO AND HAVE BEEN PERFECT GUESTS.
BOOKS
IT'S MY CAT, MR. ALEXANDER. HE'S BEEN KIDNAPPED! BUT WITHOUT A RANSOM NOTE, OR ANYTHING...
CATNAPPED? I DON'T UNDERSTAND. WHAT WOULD SOMEONE WANT WITH A CAT? I CAN'T BELIEVE I'M EVEN GOING TO ASK THIS, BUT... DID HE HAVE ANY ENEMIES?
YES, OF COURSE. HE WAS A GOOD MOUSER... BUT NOW IT SEEMS THE MICE HAVE POUNCED AND TAKEN HIM AWAY! THOSE HORRIBLE MICE JUST GANGED UP AND DRAGGED HIM INTO THAT HOLE!
WOW, NO KIDDING, HUH?
THAT'S WHY WE WANTED TO GET OUT OF HERE. I CAN'T TAKE ALL THE MAYHEM THAT'S BEEN GOING AROUND THESE PAST FEW DAYS, WHAT WITH THOSE HOODLUMS SHOWING UP ON THE NEWS, CALLING THEMSELVES WIZARDS, CAUSING TROUBLE. BUT I CAN'T POSSIBLY MOVE TO FLORIDA WITHOUT MY MR. ALEXANDER.
OH, HERE'S YOUR CAKE, DEARY.

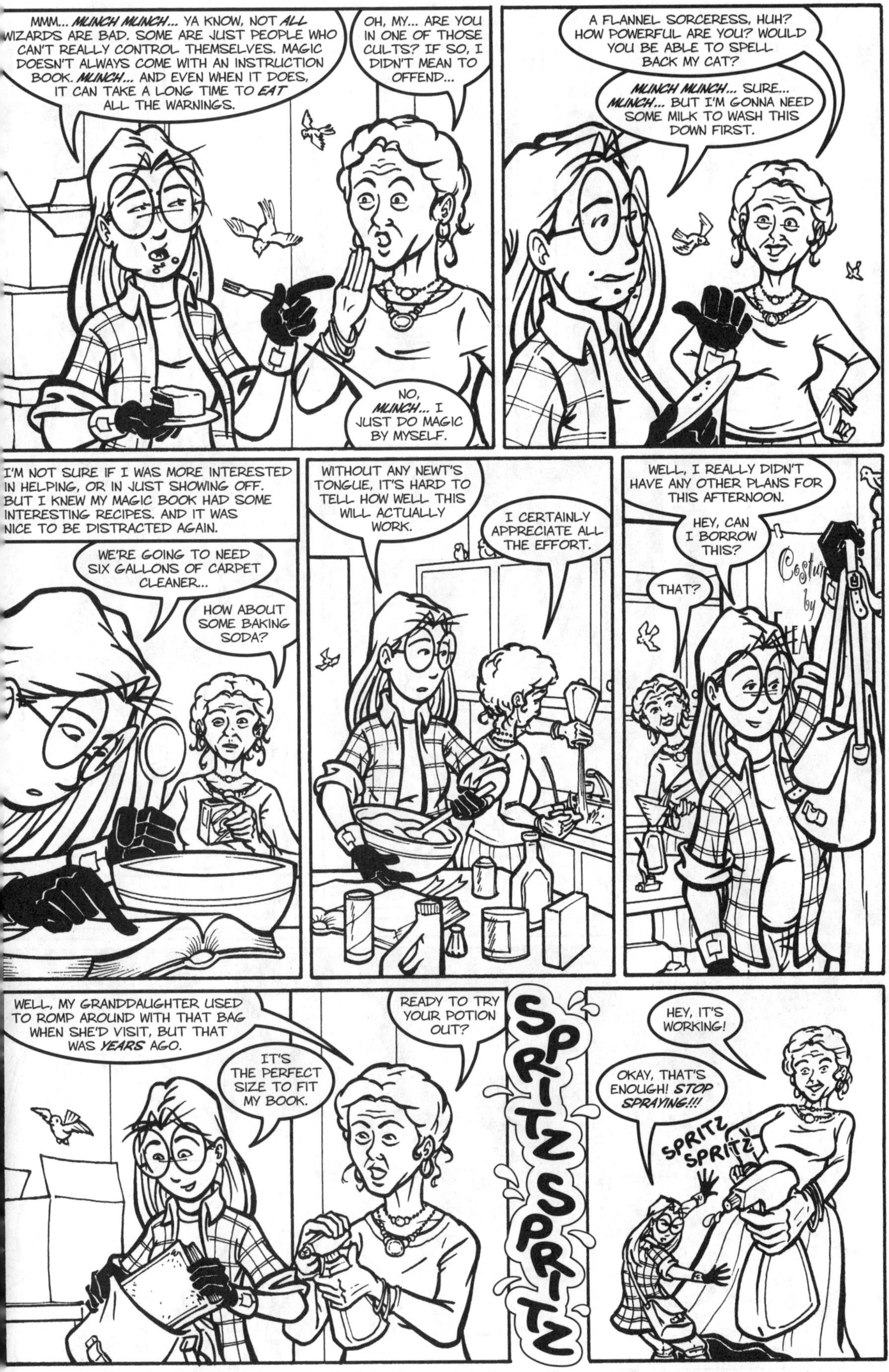
MMM... MUNCH MUNCH... YA KNOW, NOT ALL WIZARDS ARE BAD. SOME ARE JUST PEOPLE WHO CAN'T REALLY CONTROL THEMSELVES. MAGIC DOESN'T ALWAYS COME WITH AN INSTRUCTION BOOK. MUNCH... AND EVEN WHEN IT DOES, IT CAN TAKE A LONG TIME TO EAT ALL THE WARNINGS.
OH, MY... ARE YOU IN ONE OF THOSE CULTS? IF SO, I DIDN'T MEAN TO OFFEND...
NO, MUNCH... I JUST DO MAGIC BY MYSELF.
A FLANNEL SORCERESS, HUH? HOW POWERFUL ARE YOU? WOULD YOU BE ABLE TO SPELL BACK MY CAT?
MUNCH MUNCH... SURE... MUNCH... BUT I'M GONNA NEED SOME MILK TO WASH THIS DOWN FIRST.
I'M NOT SURE IF I WAS MORE INTERESTED IN HELPING, OR IN JUST SHOWING OFF. BUT I KNEW MY MAGIC BOOK HAD SOME INTERESTING RECIPES. AND IT WAS NICE TO BE DISTRACTED AGAIN.
WE'RE GOING TO NEED SIX GALLONS OF CARPET CLEANER...
HOW ABOUT SOME BAKING SODA?
WITHOUT ANY NEWT'S TONGUE, IT'S HARD TO TELL HOW WELL THIS WILL ACTUALLY WORK.
I CERTAINLY APPRECIATE ALL THE EFFORT.
WELL, I REALLY DIDN'T HAVE ANY OTHER PLANS FOR THIS AFTERNOON.
HEY, CAN I BORROW THIS?
THAT?
WELL, MY GRANDDAUGHTER USED TO ROMP AROUND WITH THAT BAG WHEN SHE'D VISIT, BUT THAT WAS YEARS AGO.
IT'S THE PERFECT SIZE TO FIT MY BOOK.
READY TO TRY YOUR POTION OUT?
SPRITZ SPRITZ
HEY, IT'S WORKING!
OKAY, THAT'S ENOUGH! STOP SPRAYING!!!
SPRITZ SPRITZ

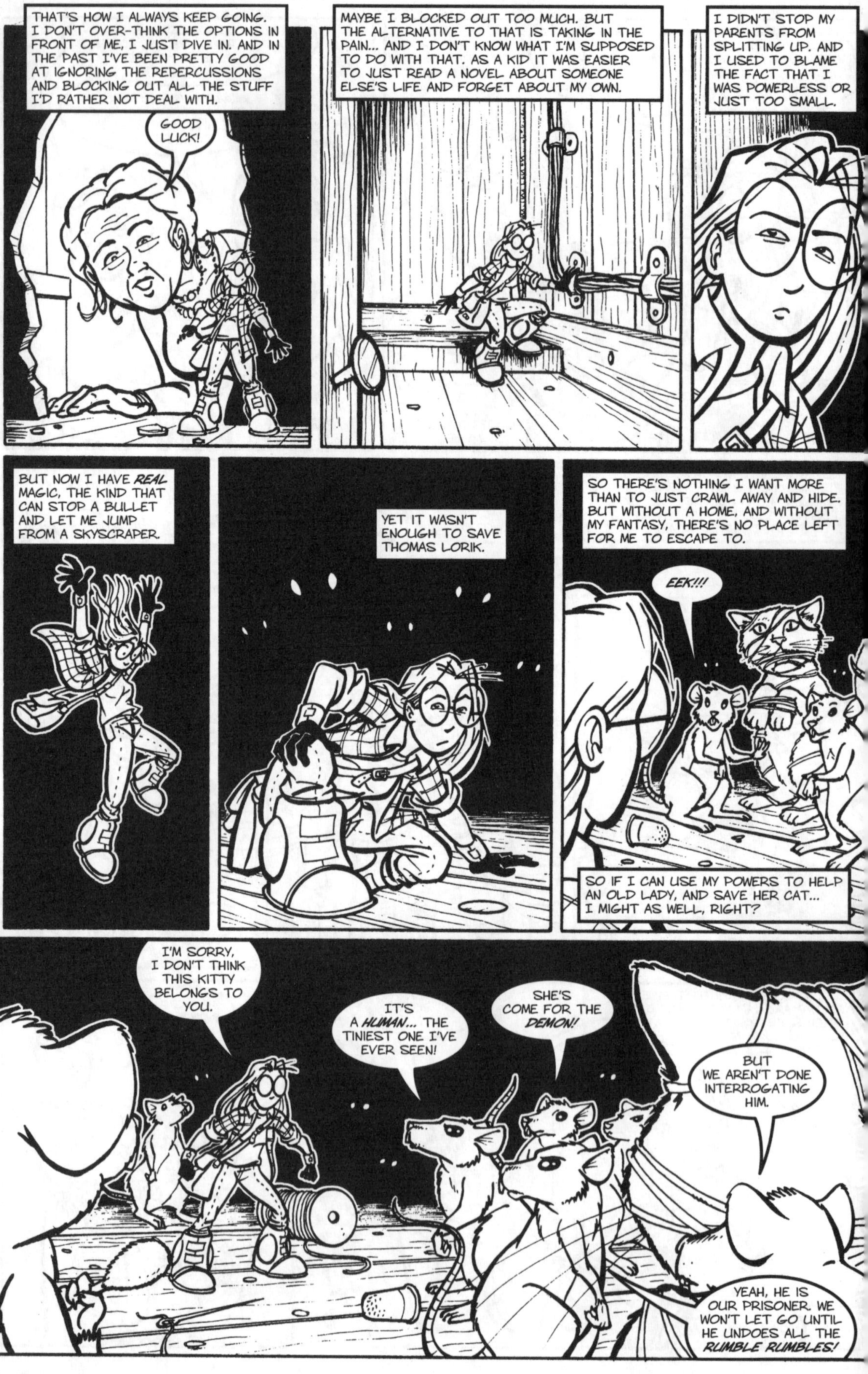
THAT'S HOW I ALWAYS KEEP GOING. I DON'T OVER-THINK THE OPTIONS IN FRONT OF ME, I JUST DIVE IN. AND IN THE PAST I'VE BEEN PRETTY GOOD AT IGNORING THE REPERCUSSIONS AND BLOCKING OUT ALL THE STUFF I'D RATHER NOT DEAL WITH.
GOOD LUCK!
MAYBE I BLOCKED OUT TOO MUCH. BUT THE ALTERNATIVE TO THAT IS TAKING IN THE PAIN... AND I DON'T KNOW WHAT I'M SUPPOSED TO DO WITH THAT. AS A KID IT WAS EASIER TO JUST READ A NOVEL ABOUT SOMEONE ELSE'S LIFE AND FORGET ABOUT MY OWN.
I DIDN'T STOP MY PARENTS FROM SPLITTING UP. AND I USED TO BLAME THE FACT THAT I WAS POWERLESS OR JUST TOO SMALL.
BUT NOW I HAVE *REAL* MAGIC, THE KIND THAT CAN STOP A BULLET AND LET ME JUMP FROM A SKYSCRAPER.
YET IT WASN'T ENOUGH TO SAVE THOMAS LORIK.
SO THERE'S NOTHING I WANT MORE THAN TO JUST CRAWL AWAY AND HIDE. BUT WITHOUT A HOME, AND WITHOUT MY FANTASY, THERE'S NO PLACE LEFT FOR ME TO ESCAPE TO.
EEK!!!
SO IF I CAN USE MY POWERS TO HELP AN OLD LADY, AND SAVE HER CAT... I MIGHT AS WELL, RIGHT?
I'M SORRY, I DON'T THINK THIS KITTY BELONGS TO YOU.
IT'S A *HUMAN*... THE TINIEST ONE I'VE EVER SEEN!
SHE'S COME FOR THE *DEMON!*
BUT WE AREN'T DONE INTERROGATING HIM.
YEAH, HE IS OUR PRISONER. WE WON'T LET GO UNTIL HE UNDOES ALL THE *RUMBLE RUMBLES!*

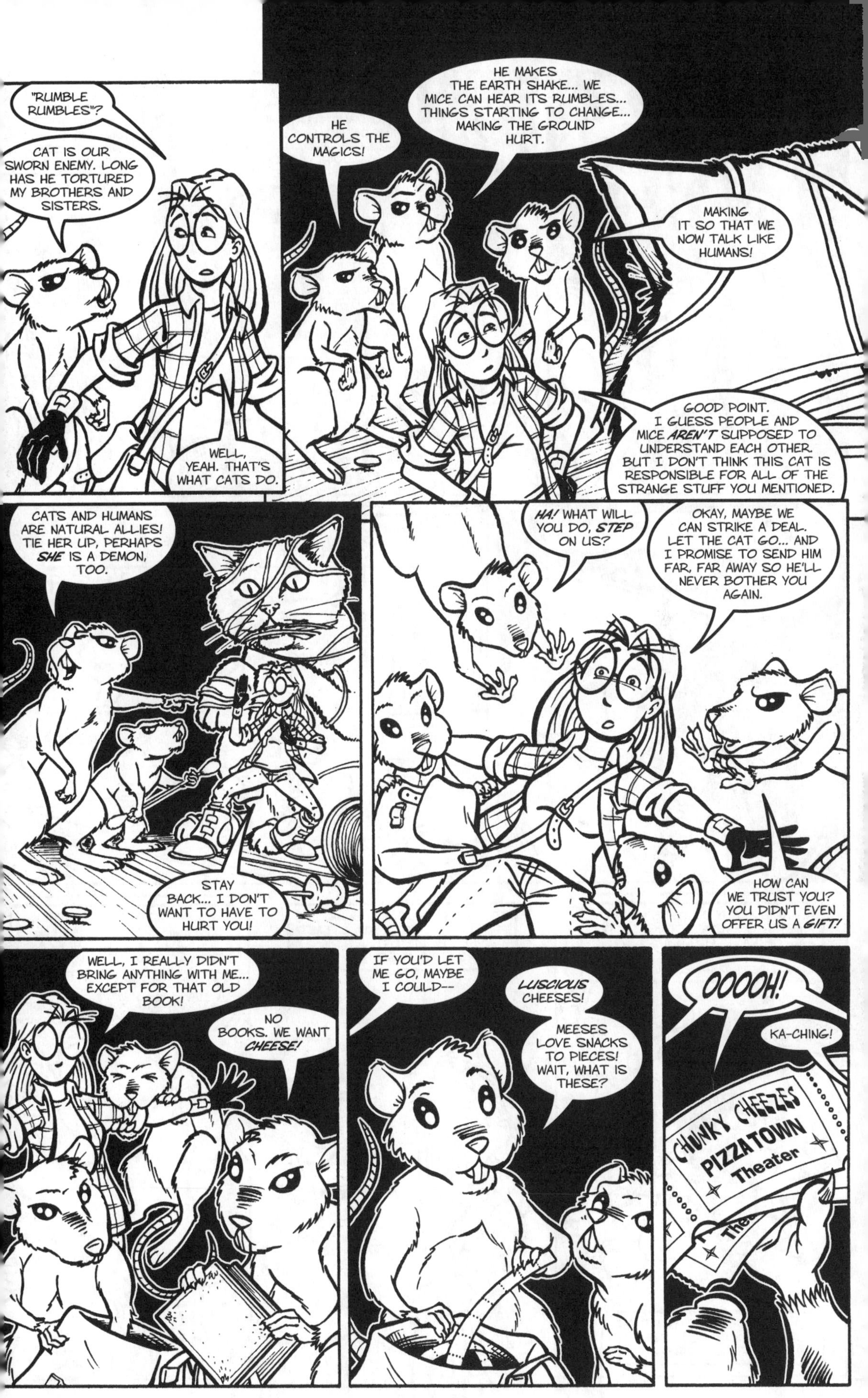
"RUMBLE RUMBLES"?
CAT IS OUR SWORN ENEMY. LONG HAS HE TORTURED MY BROTHERS AND SISTERS.
WELL, YEAH. THAT'S WHAT CATS DO.
HE CONTROLS THE MAGICS!
HE MAKES THE EARTH SHAKE... WE MICE CAN HEAR ITS RUMBLES... THINGS STARTING TO CHANGE... MAKING THE GROUND HURT.
MAKING IT SO THAT WE NOW TALK LIKE HUMANS!
GOOD POINT. I GUESS PEOPLE AND MICE AREN'T SUPPOSED TO UNDERSTAND EACH OTHER. BUT I DON'T THINK THIS CAT IS RESPONSIBLE FOR ALL OF THE STRANGE STUFF YOU MENTIONED.
CATS AND HUMANS ARE NATURAL ALLIES! TIE HER UP, PERHAPS SHE IS A DEMON, TOO.
STAY BACK... I DON'T WANT TO HAVE TO HURT YOU!
HA! WHAT WILL YOU DO, STEP ON US?
OKAY, MAYBE WE CAN STRIKE A DEAL. LET THE CAT GO... AND I PROMISE TO SEND HIM FAR, FAR AWAY SO HE'LL NEVER BOTHER YOU AGAIN.
HOW CAN WE TRUST YOU? YOU DIDN'T EVEN OFFER US A GIFT!
WELL, I REALLY DIDN'T BRING ANYTHING WITH ME... EXCEPT FOR THAT OLD BOOK!
NO BOOKS. WE WANT CHEESE!
IF YOU'D LET ME GO, MAYBE I COULD--
LUSCIOUS CHEESES!
MEESES LOVE SNACKS TO PIECES! WAIT, WHAT IS THESE?
OOOOH!
KA-CHING!
CHUNKY CHEEZES
PIZZATOWN
Theater

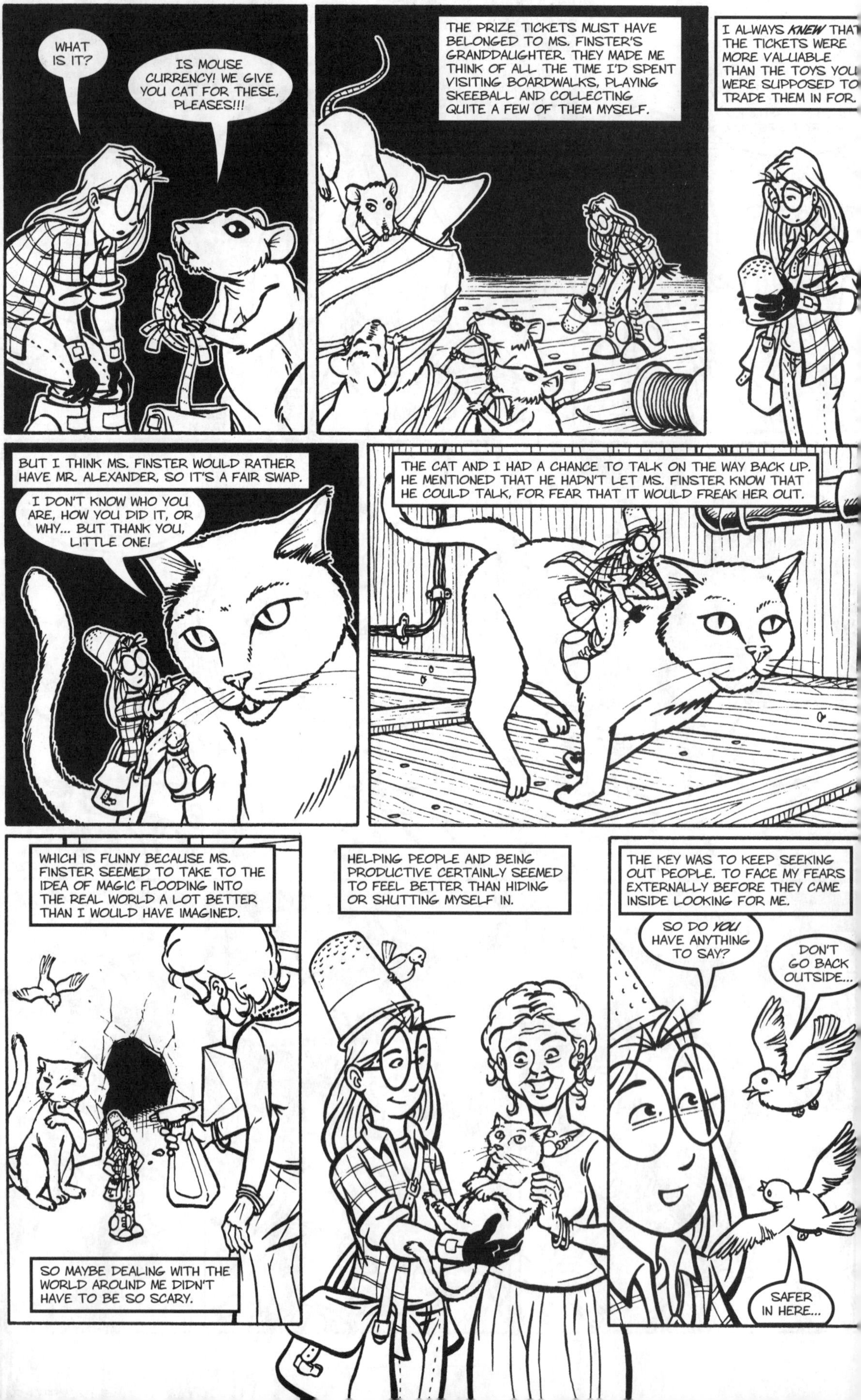
WHAT IS IT?
IS MOUSE CURRENCY! WE GIVE YOU CAT FOR THESE, PLEASES!!!
THE PRIZE TICKETS MUST HAVE BELONGED TO MS. FINSTER'S GRANDDAUGHTER. THEY MADE ME THINK OF ALL THE TIME I'D SPENT VISITING BOARDWALKS, PLAYING SKEEBALL AND COLLECTING QUITE A FEW OF THEM MYSELF.
I ALWAYS *KNEW* THAT THE TICKETS WERE MORE VALUABLE THAN THE TOYS YOU WERE SUPPOSED TO TRADE THEM IN FOR.
BUT I THINK MS. FINSTER WOULD RATHER HAVE MR. ALEXANDER, SO IT'S A FAIR SWAP.
I DON'T KNOW WHO YOU ARE, HOW YOU DID IT, OR WHY... BUT THANK YOU, LITTLE ONE!
THE CAT AND I HAD A CHANCE TO TALK ON THE WAY BACK UP. HE MENTIONED THAT HE HADN'T LET MS. FINSTER KNOW THAT HE COULD TALK, FOR FEAR THAT IT WOULD FREAK HER OUT.
WHICH IS FUNNY BECAUSE MS. FINSTER SEEMED TO TAKE TO THE IDEA OF MAGIC FLOODING INTO THE REAL WORLD A LOT BETTER THAN I WOULD HAVE IMAGINED.
SO MAYBE DEALING WITH THE WORLD AROUND ME DIDN'T HAVE TO BE SO SCARY.
HELPING PEOPLE AND BEING PRODUCTIVE CERTAINLY SEEMED TO FEEL BETTER THAN HIDING OR SHUTTING MYSELF IN.
THE KEY WAS TO KEEP SEEKING OUT PEOPLE. TO FACE MY FEARS EXTERNALLY BEFORE THEY CAME INSIDE LOOKING FOR ME.
SO DO *YOU* HAVE ANYTHING TO SAY?
DON'T GO BACK OUTSIDE...
SAFER IN HERE...

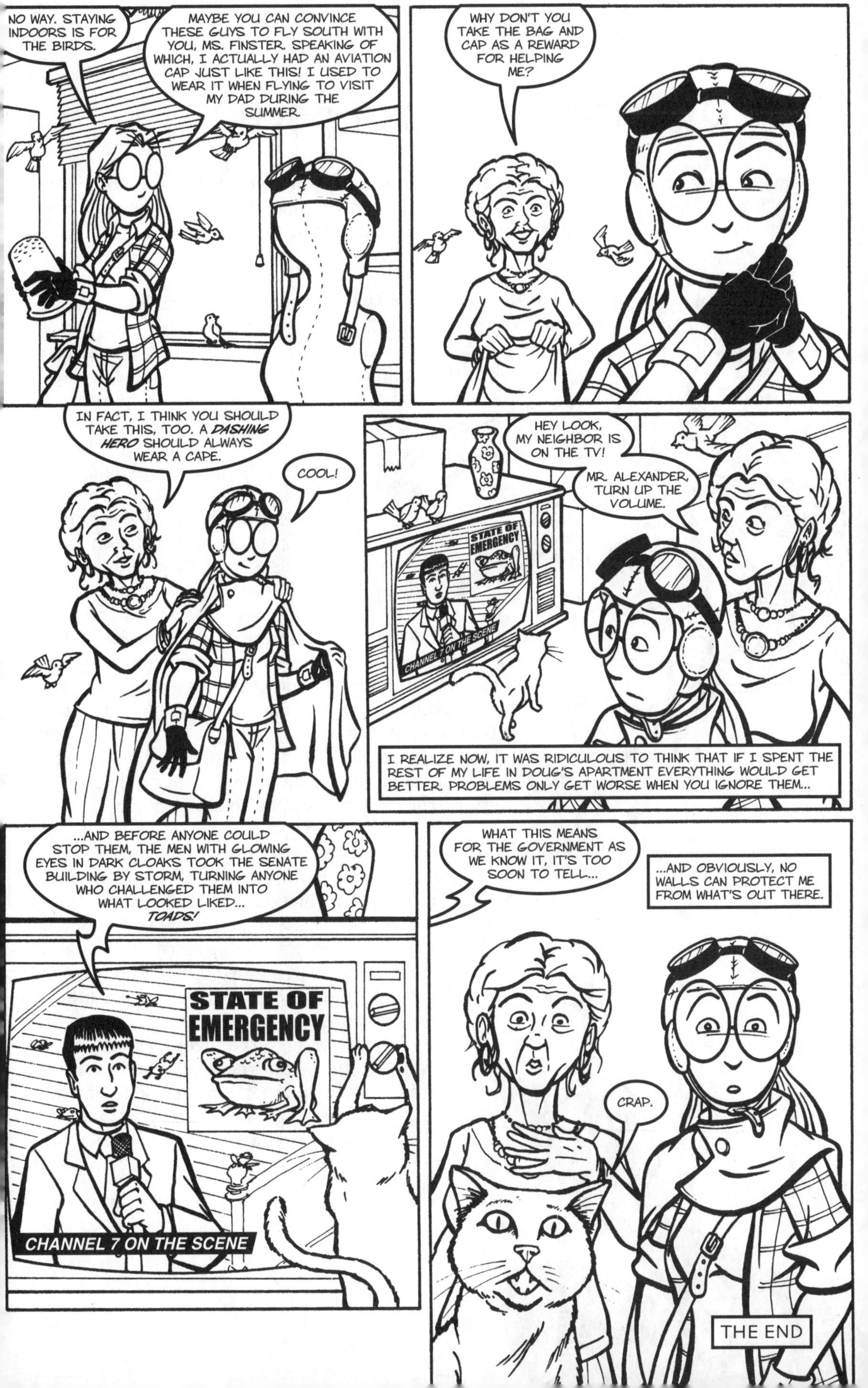
NO WAY. STAYING INDOORS IS FOR THE BIRDS.
MAYBE YOU CAN CONVINCE THESE GUYS TO FLY SOUTH WITH YOU, MS. FINSTER. SPEAKING OF WHICH, I ACTUALLY HAD AN AVIATION CAP JUST LIKE THIS! I USED TO WEAR IT WHEN FLYING TO VISIT MY DAD DURING THE SUMMER.
WHY DON'T YOU TAKE THE BAG AND CAP AS A REWARD FOR HELPING ME?
IN FACT, I THINK YOU SHOULD TAKE THIS, TOO. A *DASHING HERO* SHOULD ALWAYS WEAR A CAPE.
COOL!
HEY LOOK, MY NEIGHBOR IS ON THE TV!
MR. ALEXANDER, TURN UP THE VOLUME.
STATE OF EMERGENCY
CHANNEL 7 ON THE SCENE
I REALIZE NOW, IT WAS RIDICULOUS TO THINK THAT IF I SPENT THE REST OF MY LIFE IN DOUG'S APARTMENT EVERYTHING WOULD GET BETTER. PROBLEMS ONLY GET WORSE WHEN YOU IGNORE THEM...
...AND BEFORE ANYONE COULD STOP THEM, THE MEN WITH GLOWING EYES IN DARK CLOAKS TOOK THE SENATE BUILDING BY STORM, TURNING ANYONE WHO CHALLENGED THEM INTO WHAT LOOKED LIKED... *TOADS!*
STATE OF EMERGENCY
CHANNEL 7 ON THE SCENE
WHAT THIS MEANS FOR THE GOVERNMENT AS WE KNOW IT, IT'S TOO SOON TO TELL...
...AND OBVIOUSLY, NO WALLS CAN PROTECT ME FROM WHAT'S OUT THERE.
CRAP.
THE END

The Dynamism of Jax Epoch

I wonder if any Foreword, Afterword, or bit of explanatory prose could possibly provide an adequate description of Jax Epoch's magnetism, and the liberation she provides for all readers, not just women and girls. The content of Volume One of *Jax Epoch and the Quicken Forbidden* speaks to this issue much more eloquently.

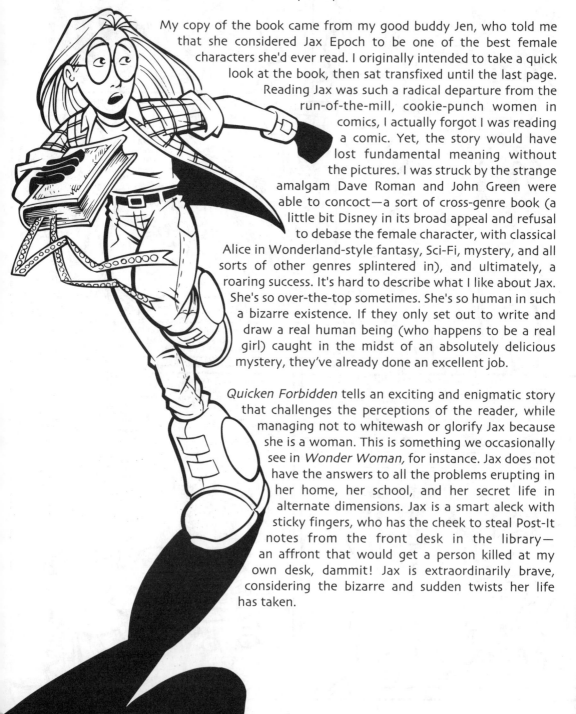

My copy of the book came from my good buddy Jen, who told me that she considered Jax Epoch to be one of the best female characters she'd ever read. I originally intended to take a quick look at the book, then sat transfixed until the last page. Reading Jax was such a radical departure from the run-of-the-mill, cookie-punch women in comics, I actually forgot I was reading a comic. Yet, the story would have lost fundamental meaning without the pictures. I was struck by the strange amalgam Dave Roman and John Green were able to concoct—a sort of cross-genre book (a little bit Disney in its broad appeal and refusal to debase the female character, with classical Alice in Wonderland-style fantasy, Sci-Fi, mystery, and all sorts of other genres splintered in), and ultimately, a roaring success. It's hard to describe what I like about Jax. She's so over-the-top sometimes. She's so human in such a bizarre existence. If they only set out to write and draw a real human being (who happens to be a real girl) caught in the midst of an absolutely delicious mystery, they've already done an excellent job.

Quicken Forbidden tells an exciting and enigmatic story that challenges the perceptions of the reader, while managing not to whitewash or glorify Jax because she is a woman. This is something we occasionally see in *Wonder Woman,* for instance. Jax does not have the answers to all the problems erupting in her home, her school, and her secret life in alternate dimensions. Jax is a smart aleck with sticky fingers, who has the cheek to steal Post-It notes from the front desk in the library— an affront that would get a person killed at my own desk, dammit! Jax is extraordinarily brave, considering the bizarre and sudden twists her life has taken.

The book is rife with action scenes that standard comic storytellers might instead give to a male character. Not only is Jax on a physical adventure, her mind is being twisted by her experiences in the Realmsend. In fact, mere moments spent in the Realmsend can last for days in mundane reality. While demanding, there are such amazing things to be learned in those other places. These competing forces become an omnipresent question: are the miracles worth the downside? Jax is nowhere near answering. Then again, if, in spite of it all, Ms. Epoch is logical enough to use Post-It notes to track her return path through an inter-dimensional maze, you know she's a survivor. The important thing is that Jax's physical departures to these other realms are not philosophical matters. She may dwell on what she has seen after the fact, but at the time, she is simply trying to get a feel for the terrain. There is nothing worse than a book that asks questions, makes convolutions, then never gives the reader a moment to find answers.

Quicken Forbidden, though, is a good balance. In Volume One, Dave Roman has dug deep into a fertile imagination to dream up a world wherein water tastes like meat, residents wear masks and sell replacement limbs in market, and people really have everything written all over their faces.

Finally, I have to comment on the artwork, if you'll allow—Ohmigod. Yes, indeed: Ohmigod. John Green makes it look easy, but his range really left me shaking my head. Take a look at the street scenes. Some streets could pass for anywhere, some look straight off a *Star Wars* lot, and some are the kinds of places Dalí might dream up. Still, some character designs are wonderfully understated: Nosteiries, the Realmsend's spear-wielding guardian, is evidence of that: this intimidating but intriguing character is almost always inked completely but for the whites of his eyes. In fact, finally seeing his face is less informative than interpreting the body language of his shadowy silhouette, as in the sequence where Jax, on her hands and knees, reading on the floor, is watched by the guardian. His posture so well mirrors his curious interest, while conveying a jarringly alien mannerism; it's just as well we don't see his face.

Together, Dave Roman and John Green have created an insightful, daring, and intelligent character, with sticky fingers, and all the good intentions in the world. And she can do her own stunts. Jax Epoch breaks with the repetitive status quo that has brought comics low and killed many readers with ennui. Now...if only we'd all run out and buy *Jax Epoch and the Quicken Forbidden* for our friends, and our friends' kids, and our English Profs—particularly our English Profs—the industry would look a lot brighter.

-Tracy Paddock
www.*SequentialTart.com*

forbidden TREATS

Page

125   Pin-up by John Green

126   Painting by Megan Weber

127   Pin-up by John Peters

128   Sketch by Mike Mignola

129   Pin-up by Craig Thompson

130   Pin-up by Gerard Way

131   Pin-up by Kirsten Petersen

132   Pin-up by Amy Kim Ganter

133   Pin-ups by Scott Roberts

134   Pin-up by Andi Watson

135   Back cover of issue
       nine by Andi Watson

136   Back cover of issue seven
       by Dave Roman

137   Back cover of issue six
       by Mark Crilley

138   Back cover of issue eight
       by James Jean

139   Back cover of issue ten
       by Stuart Immonen

140   Front covers of issues six
       through ten by John Green

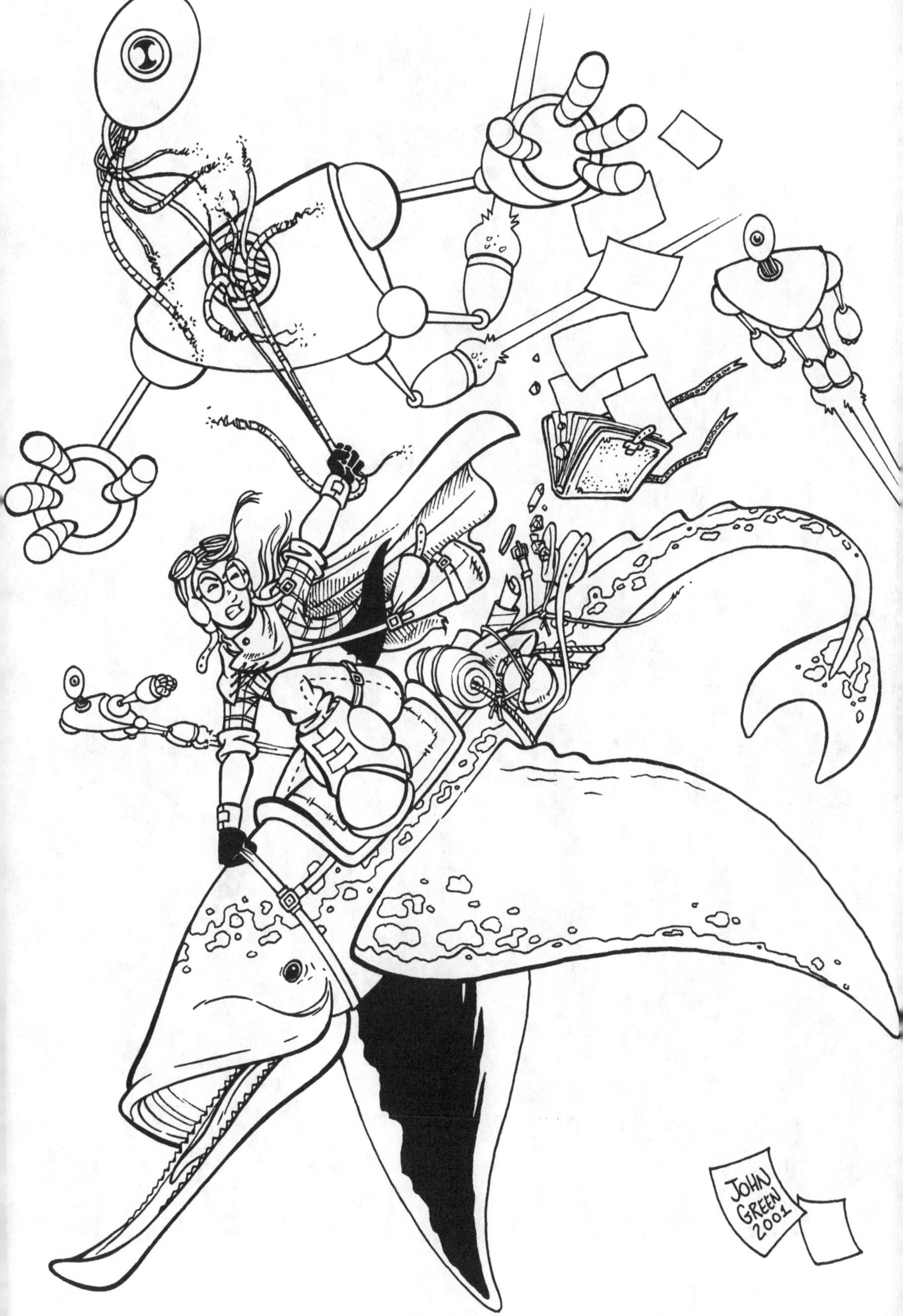
JOHN GREEN 2001

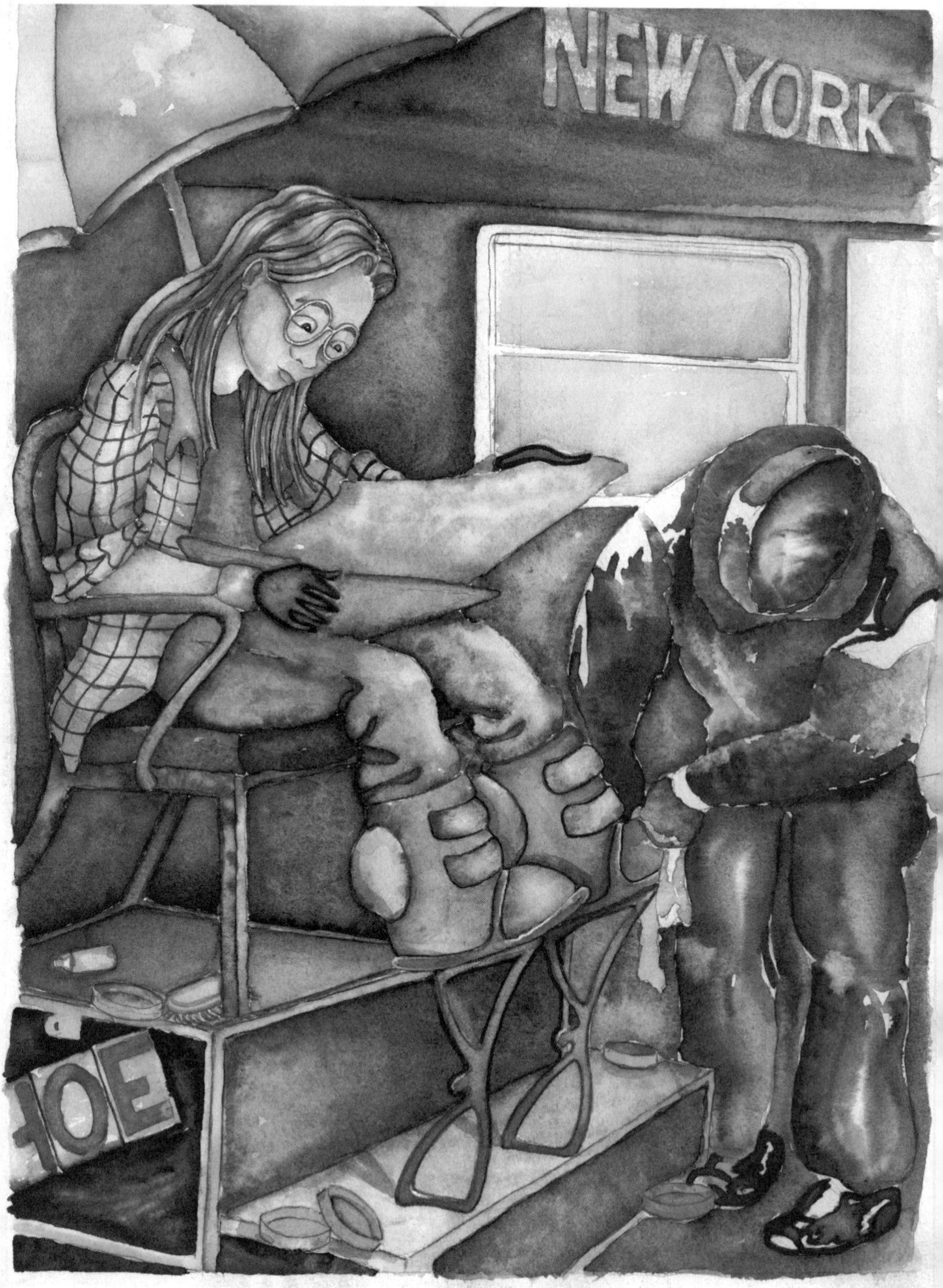
NEW YORK
HOE

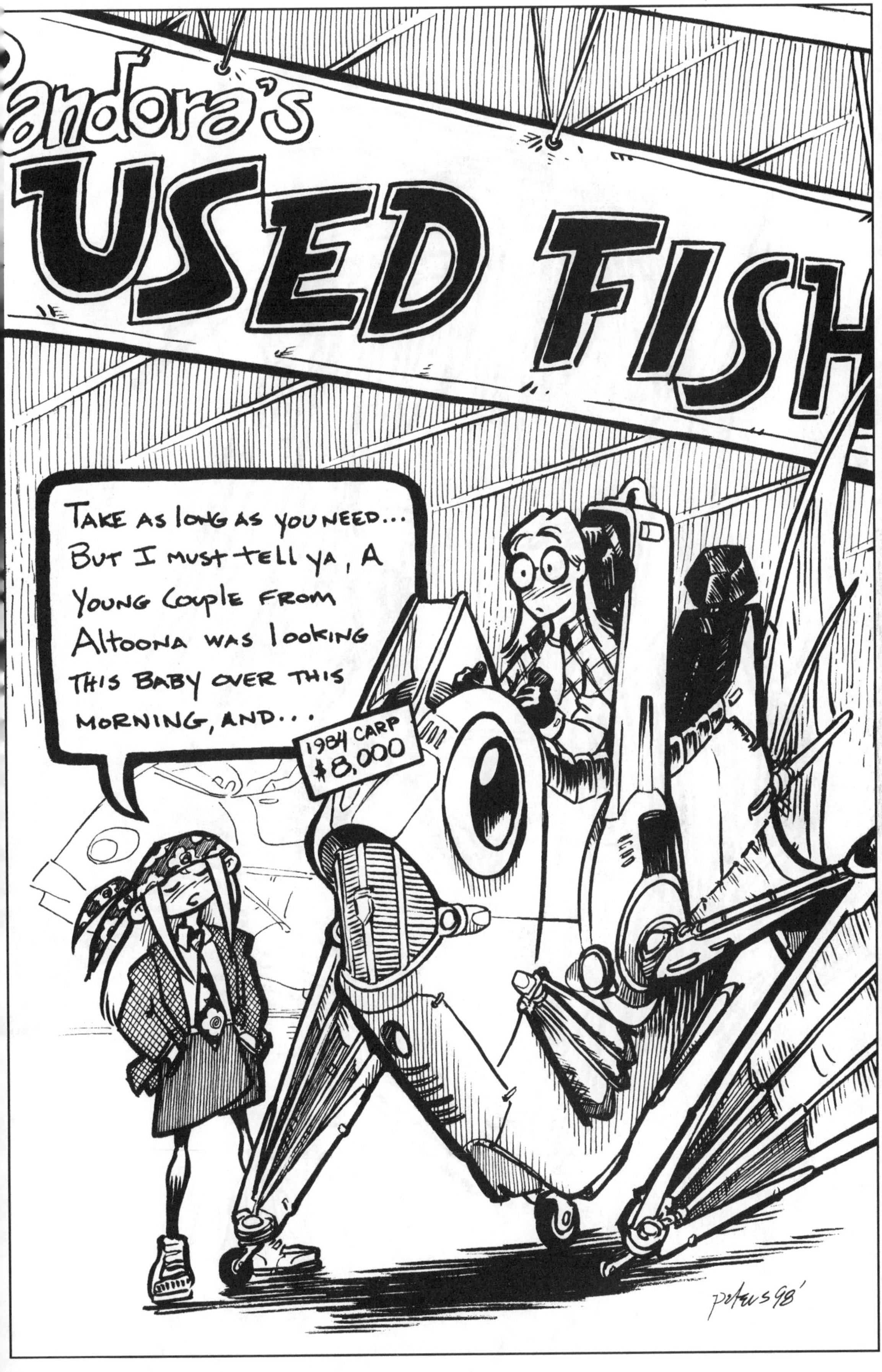
Pandora's
USED FISH
TAKE AS LONG AS YOU NEED... BUT I MUST TELL YA, A YOUNG COUPLE FROM ALTOONA WAS LOOKING THIS BABY OVER THIS MORNING, AND...
1984 CARP
$8,000
peters 98'

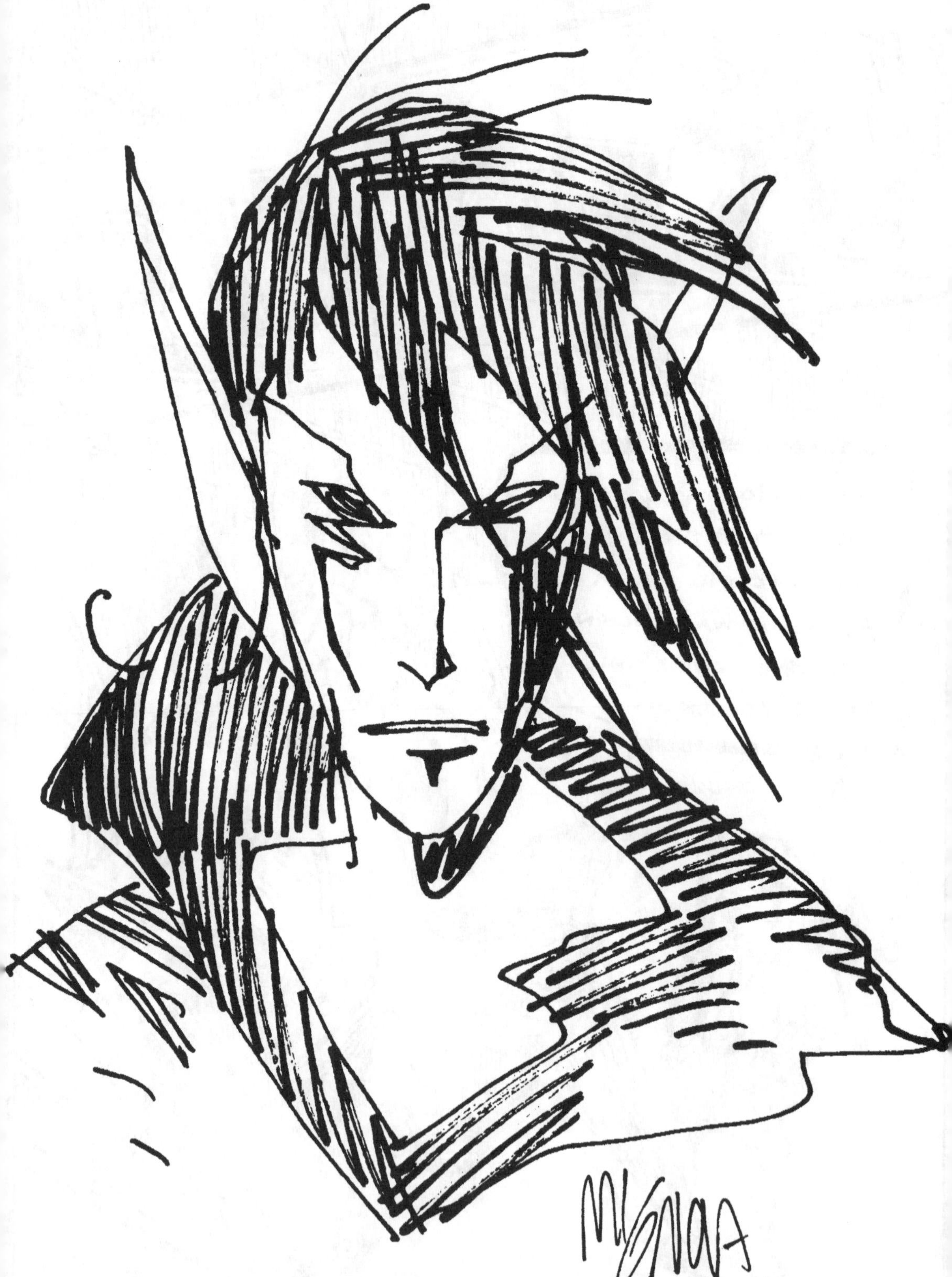
MIGNOLA

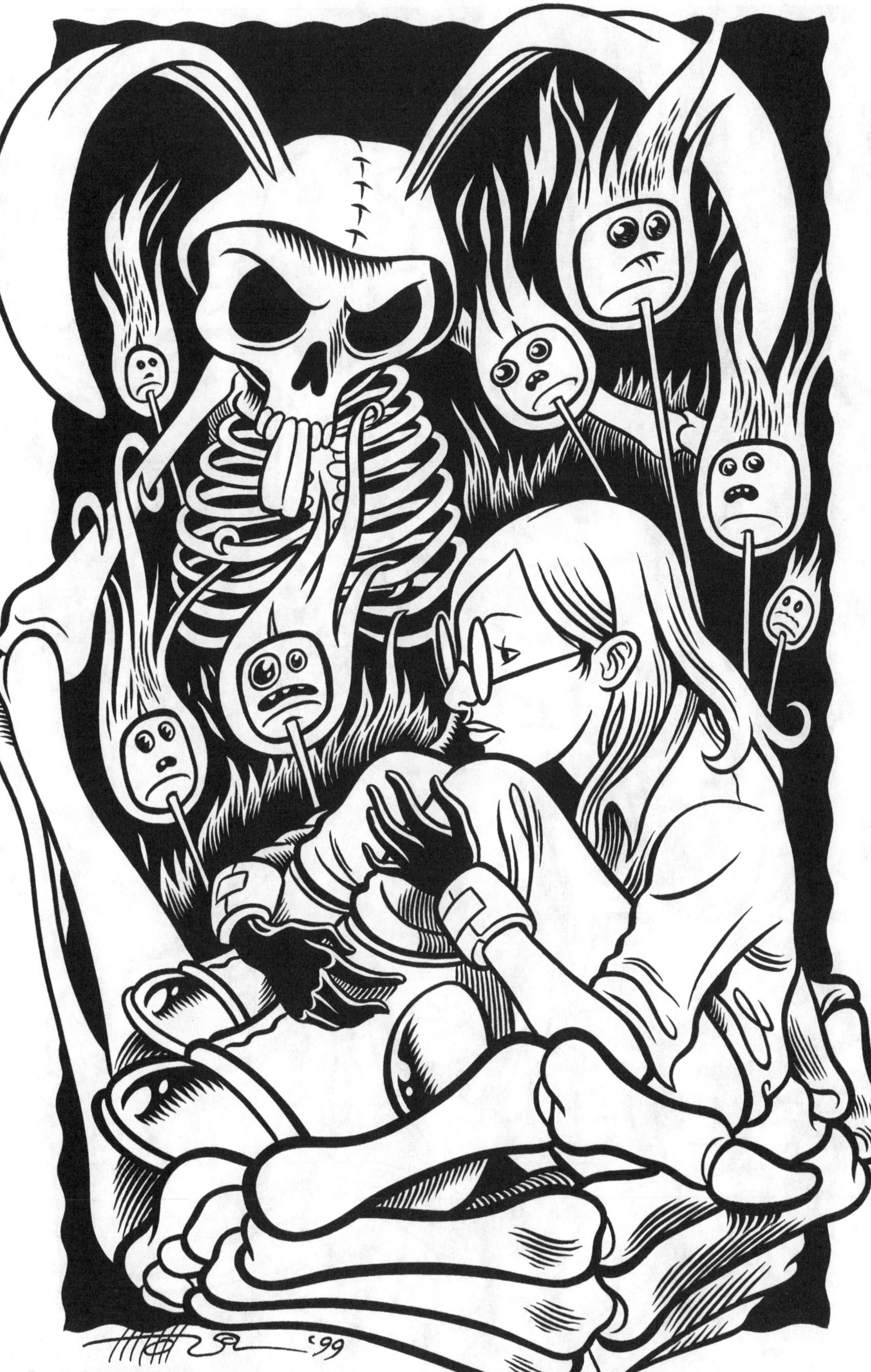

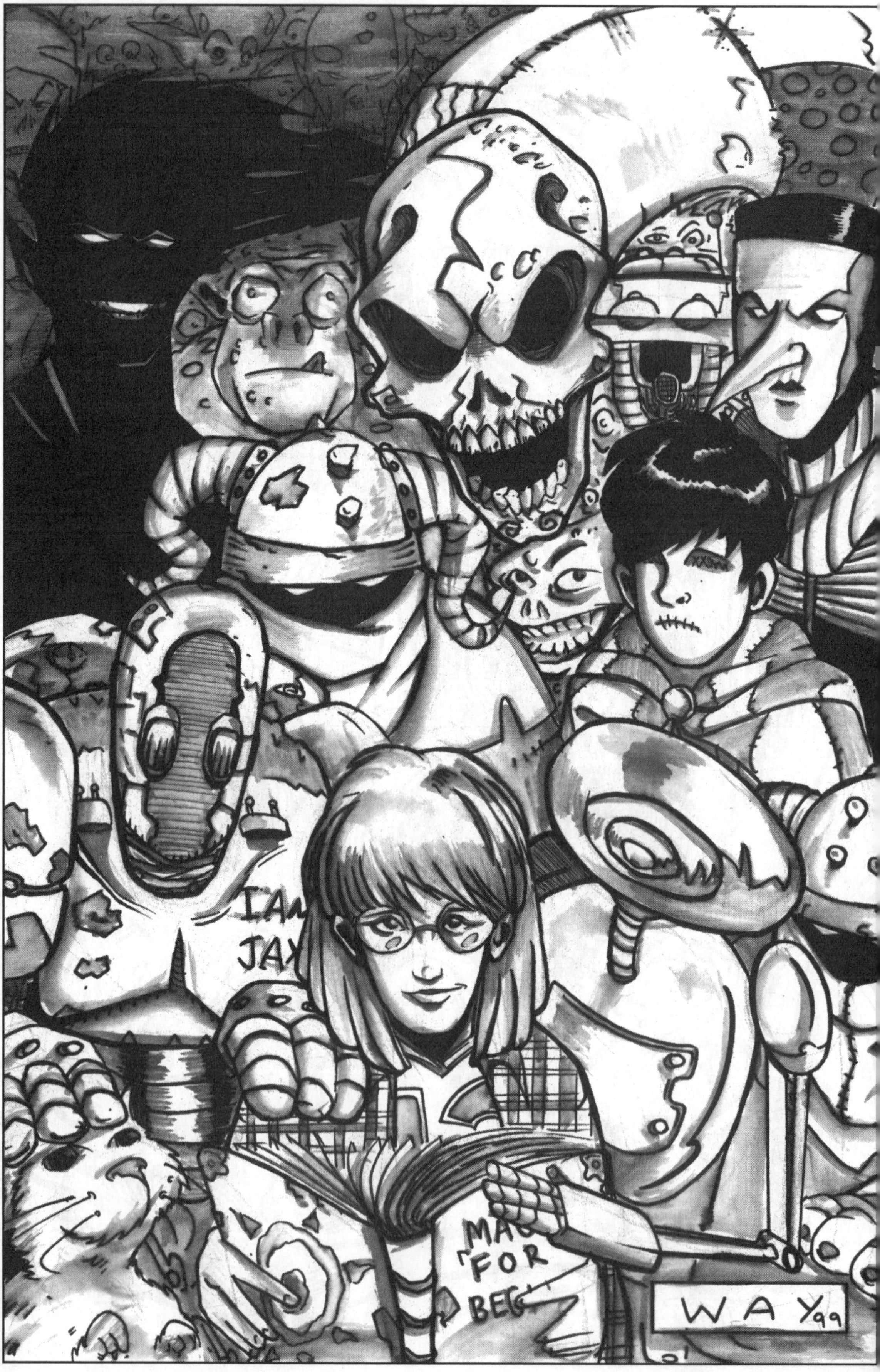
W A Y99

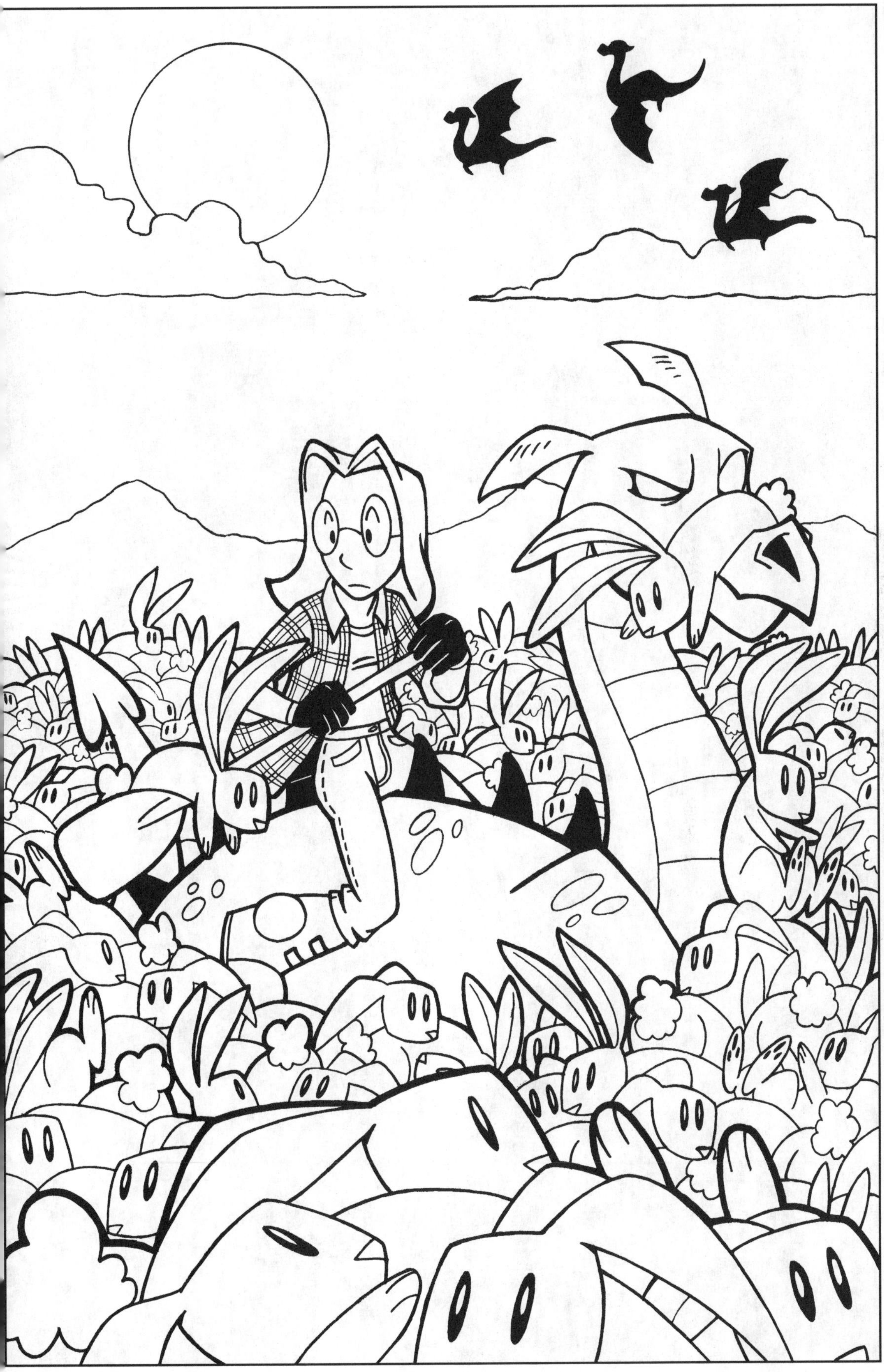

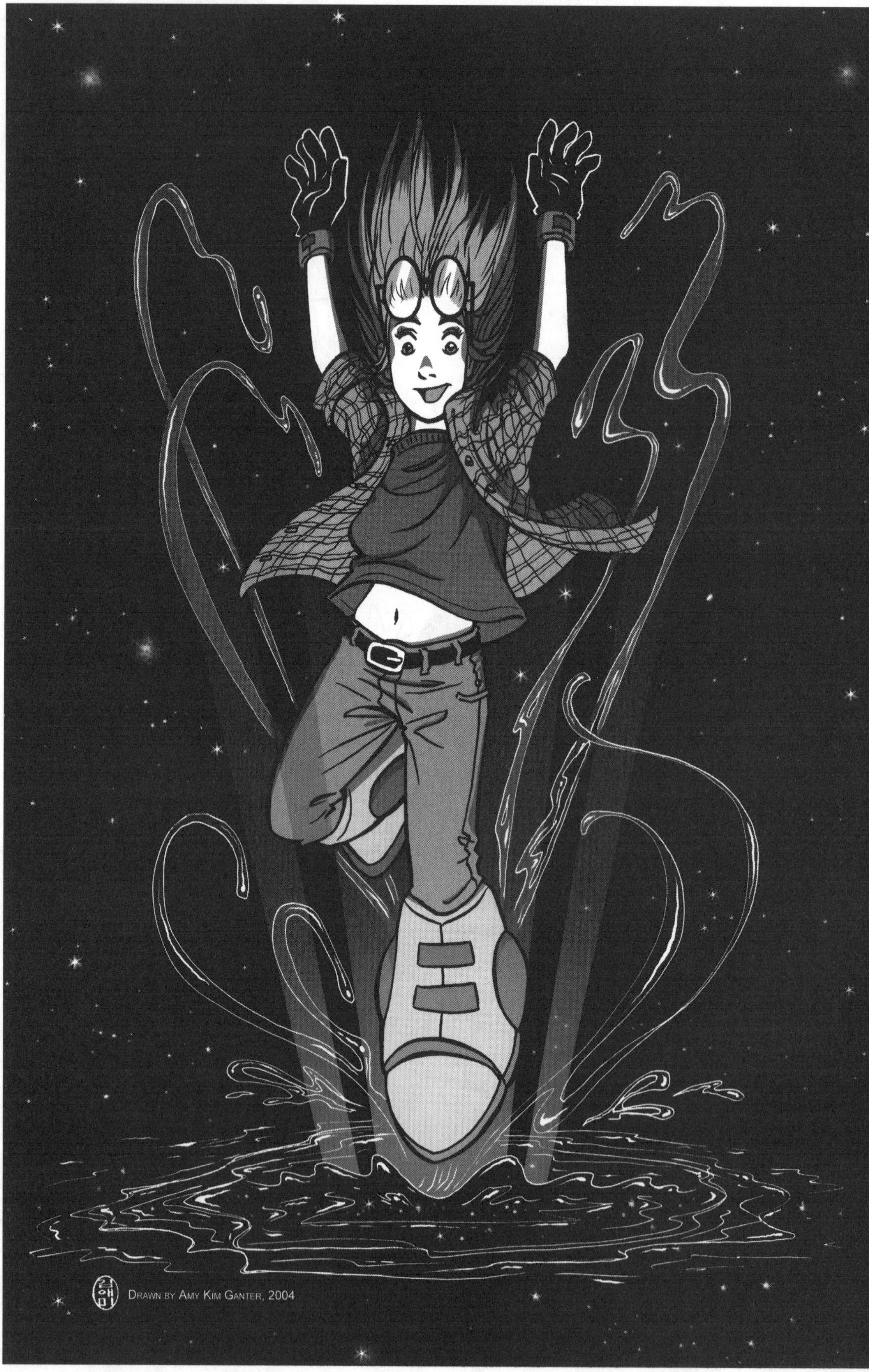

Drawn by Amy Kim Ganter, 2004

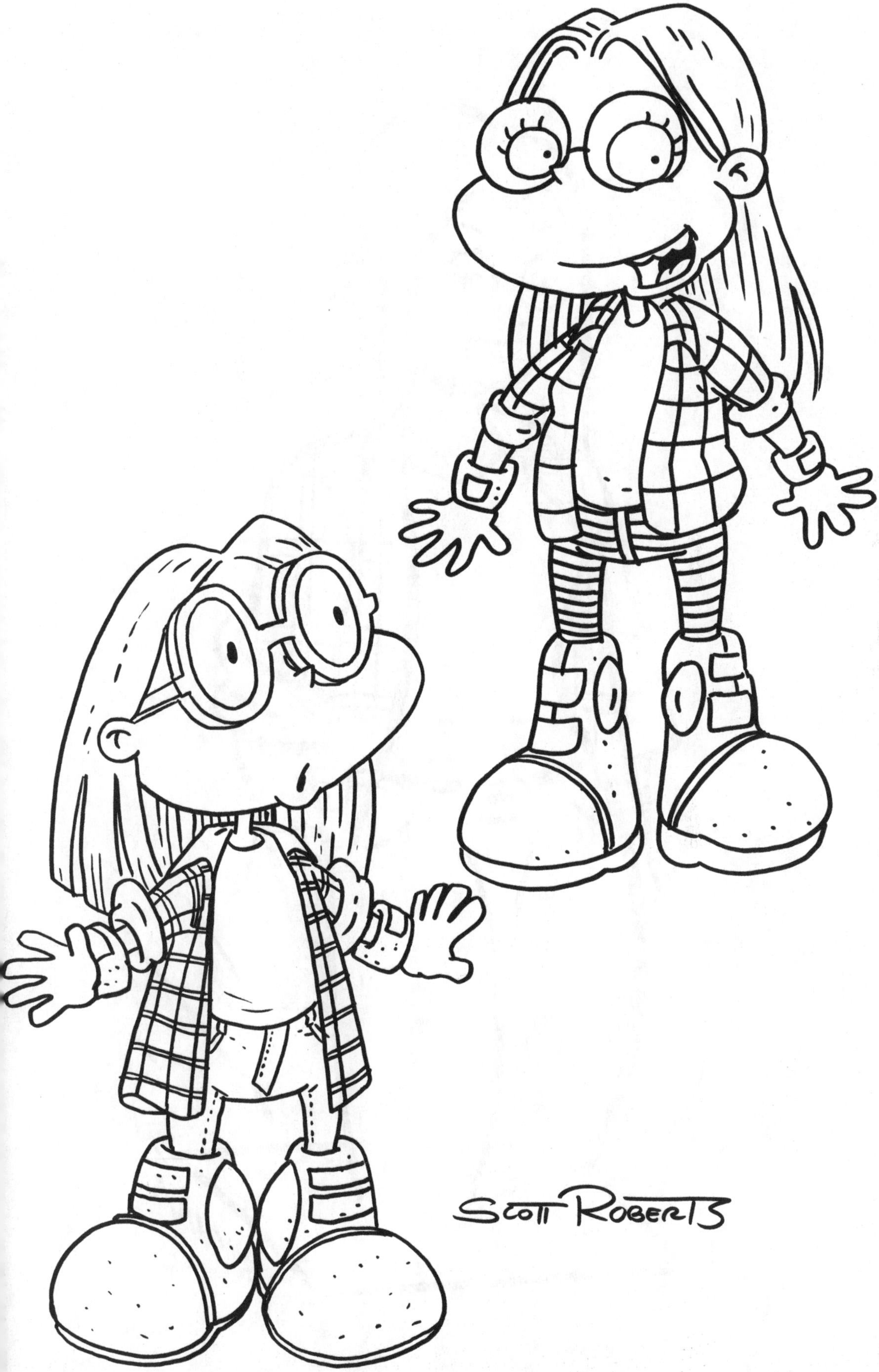
SCOTT ROBERTS

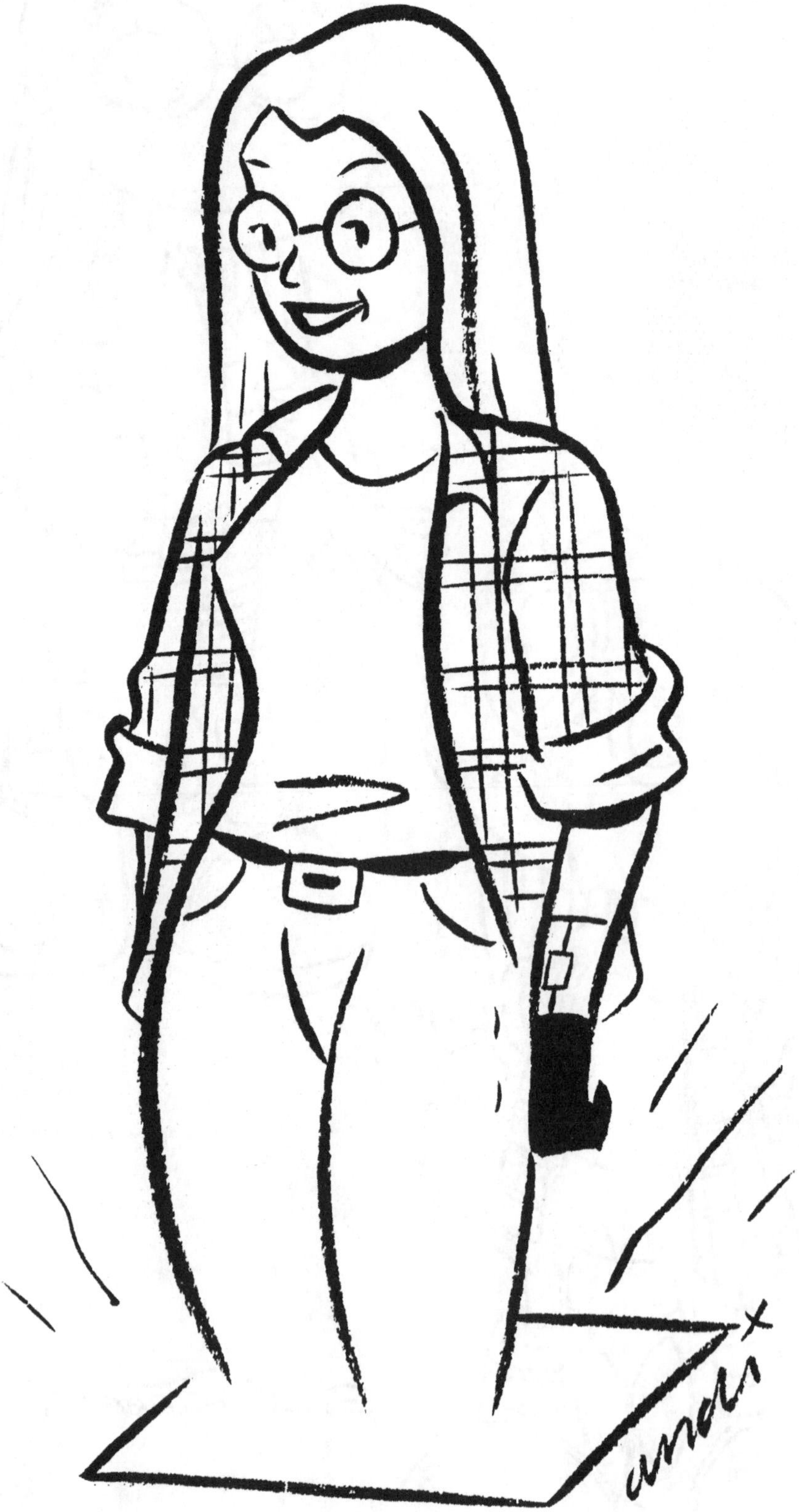

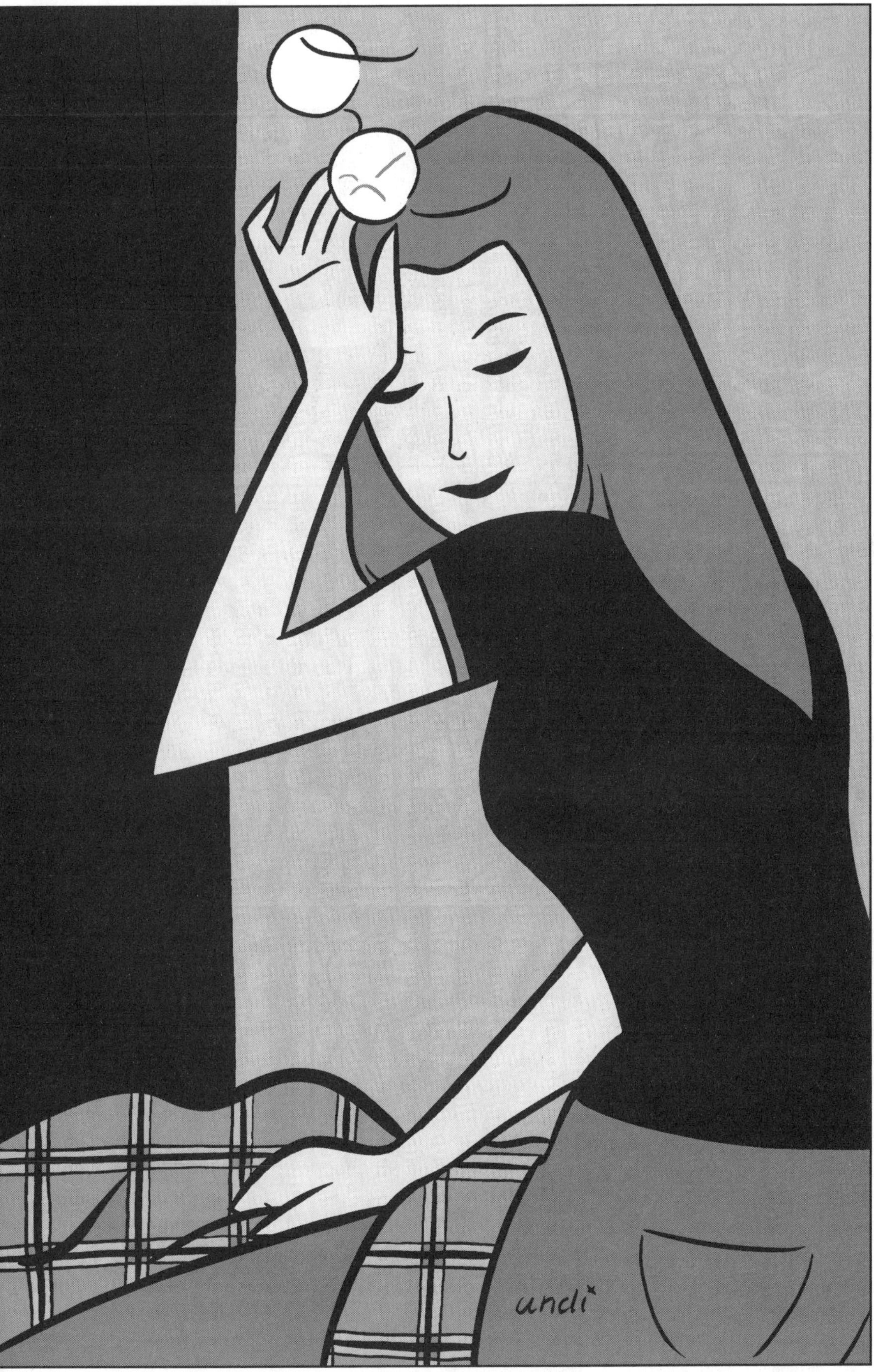

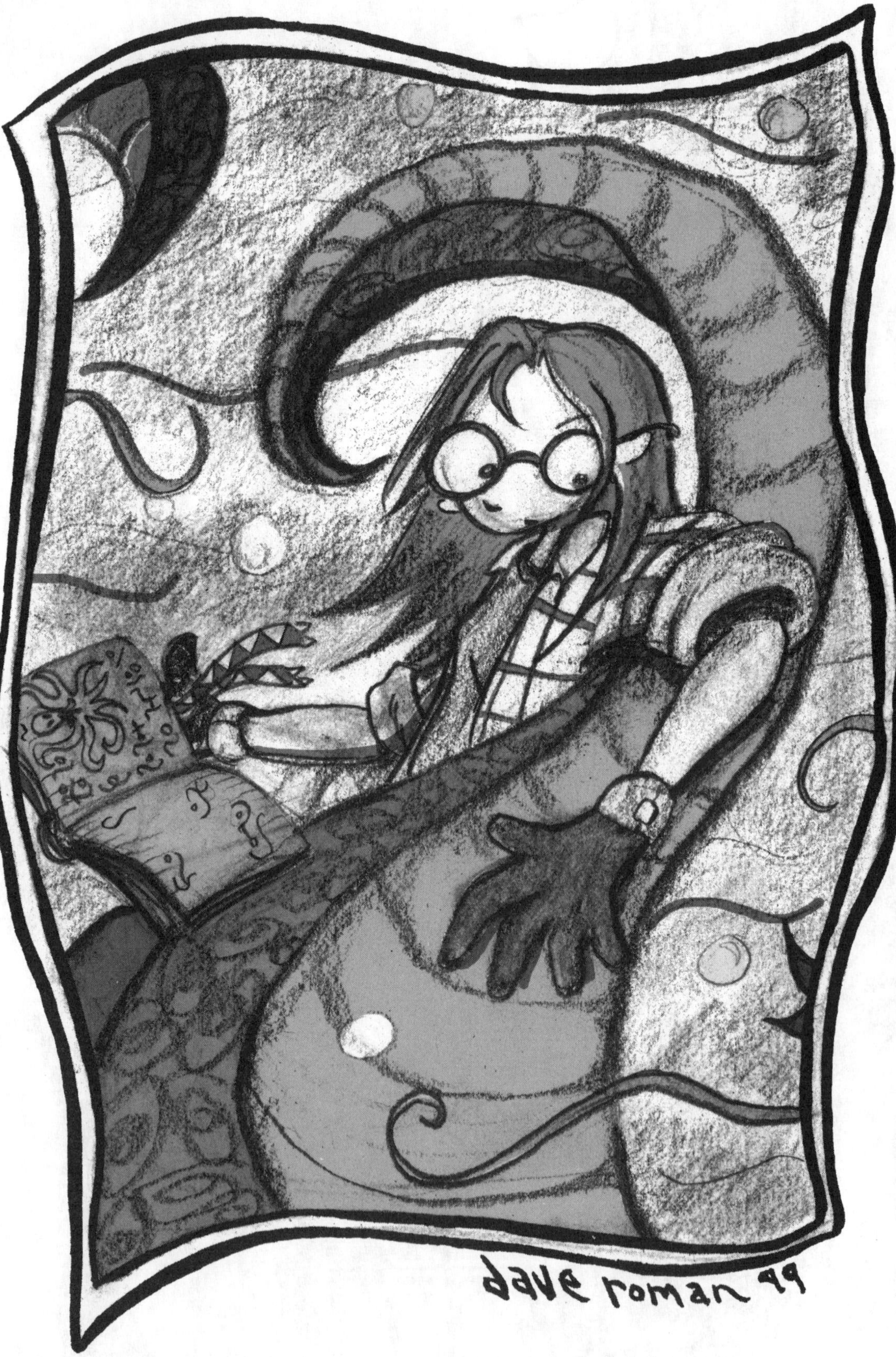
dave roman 99

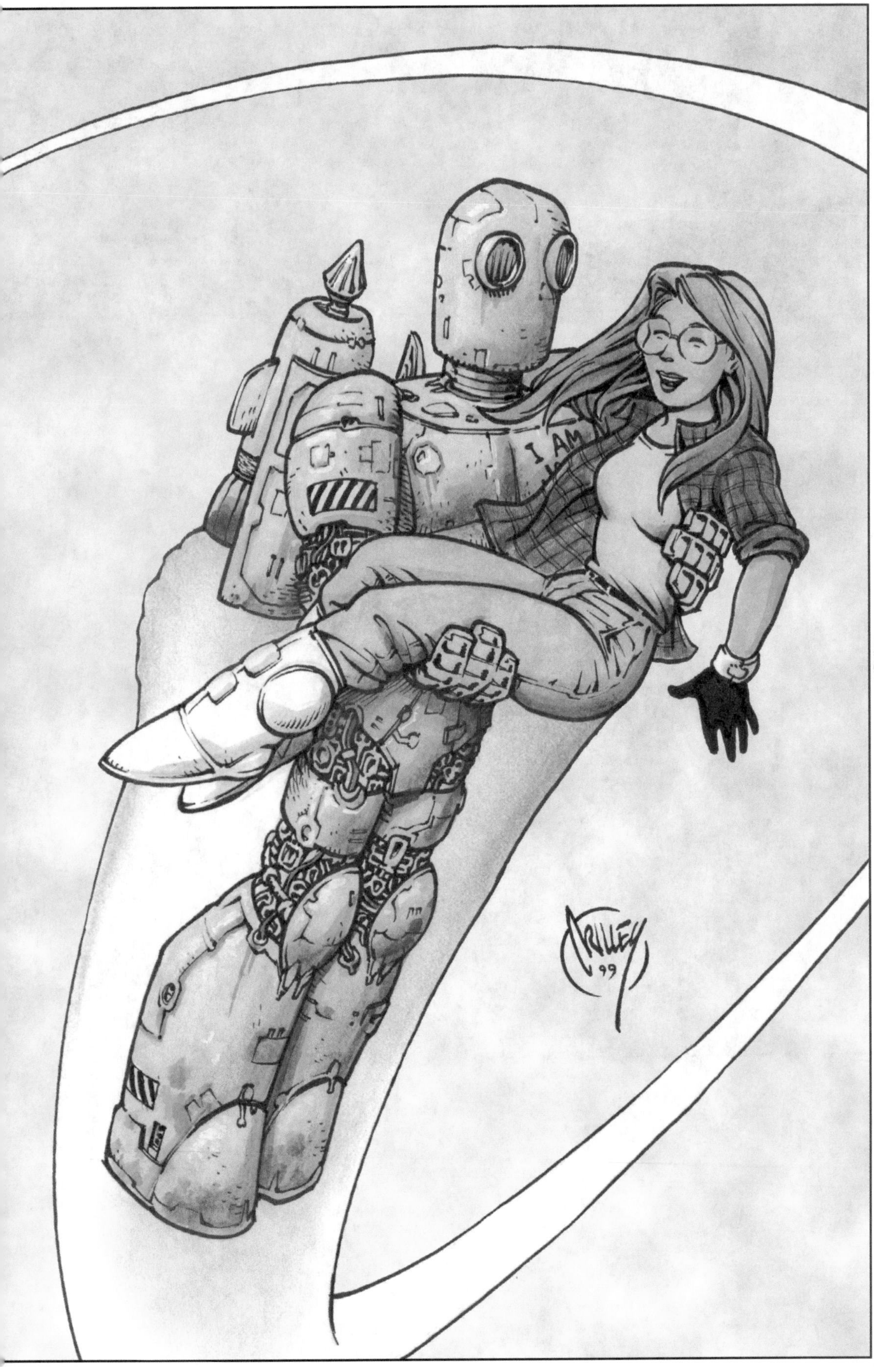
I AM

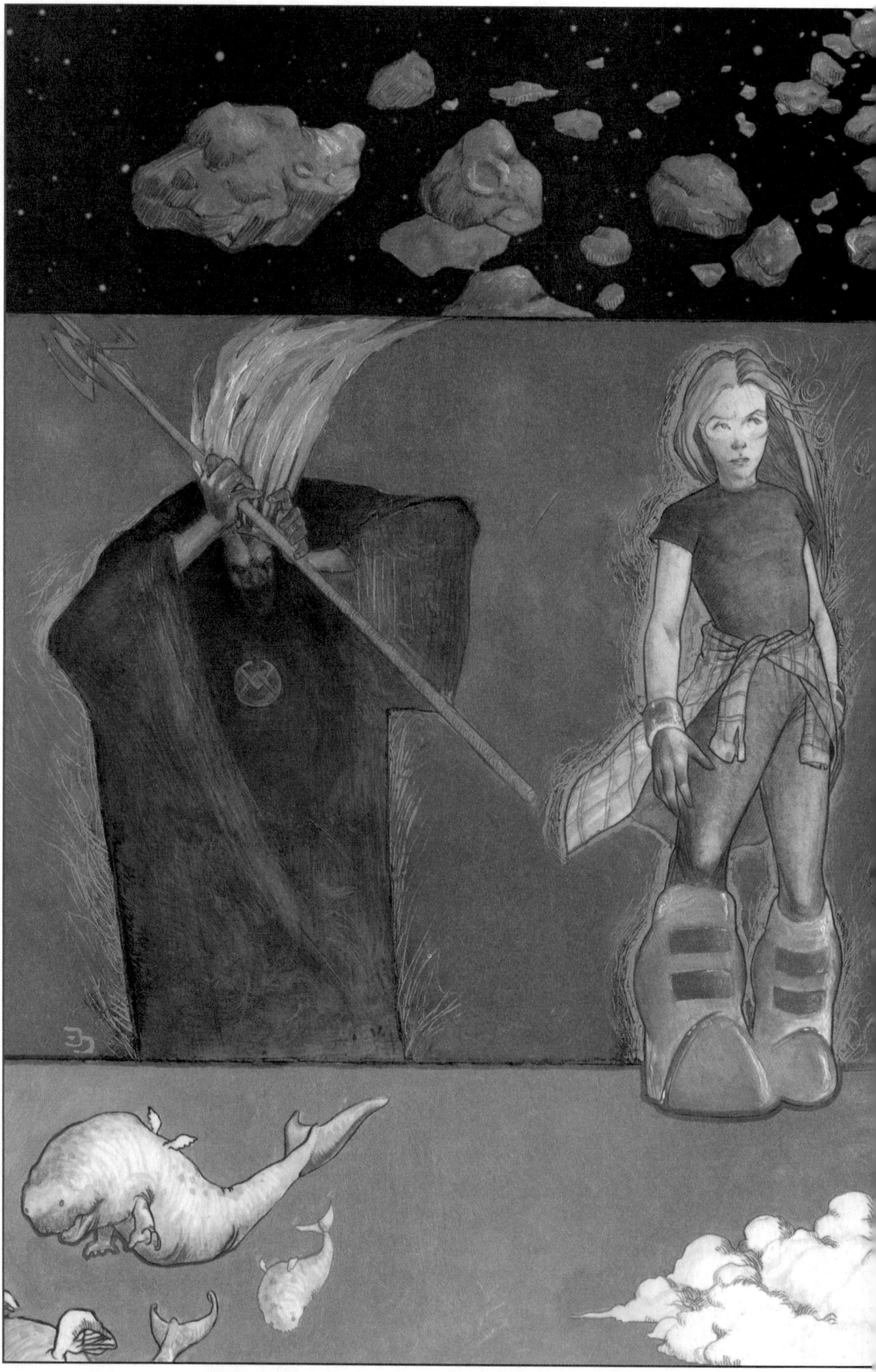

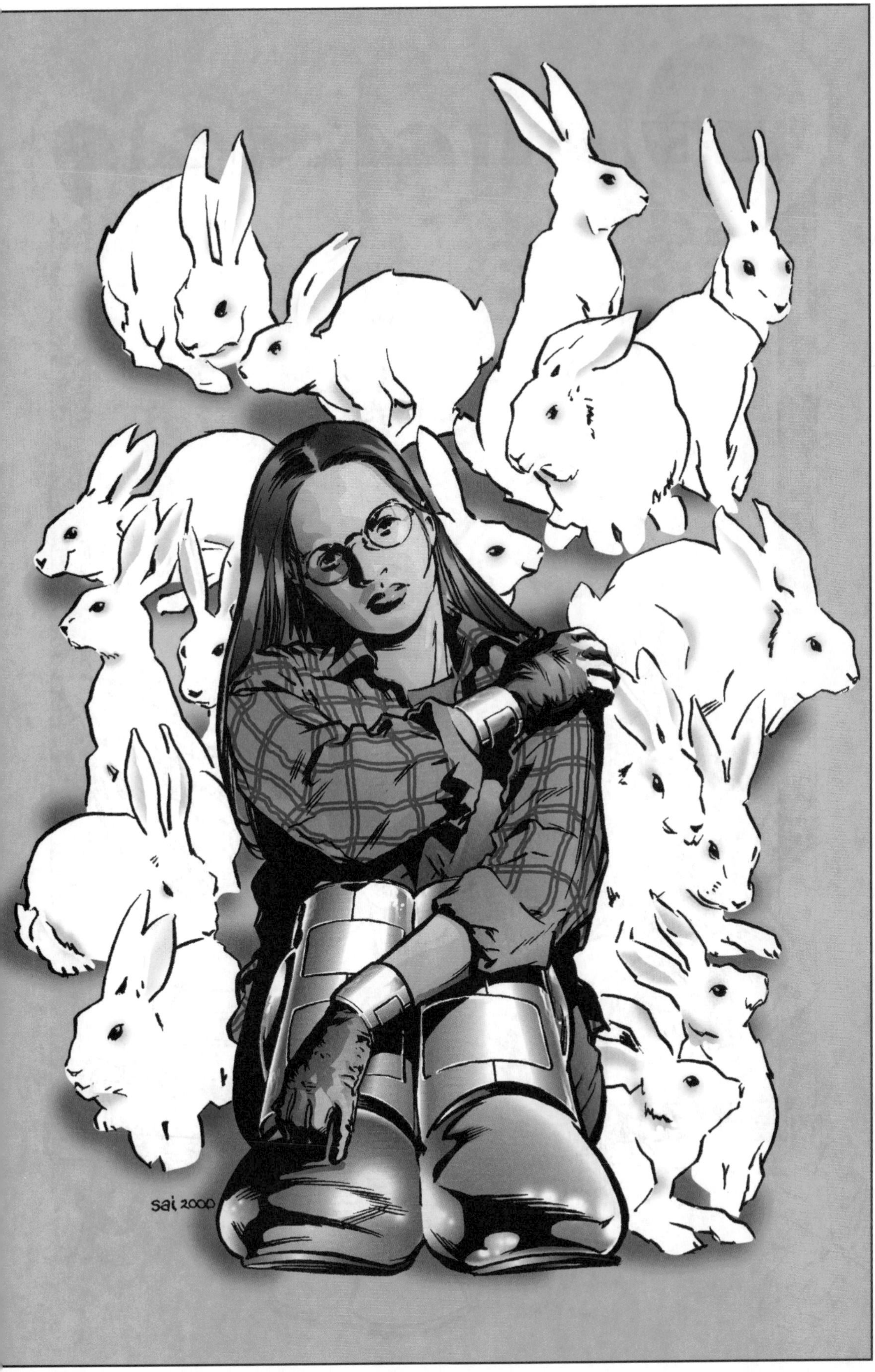
sai 2000

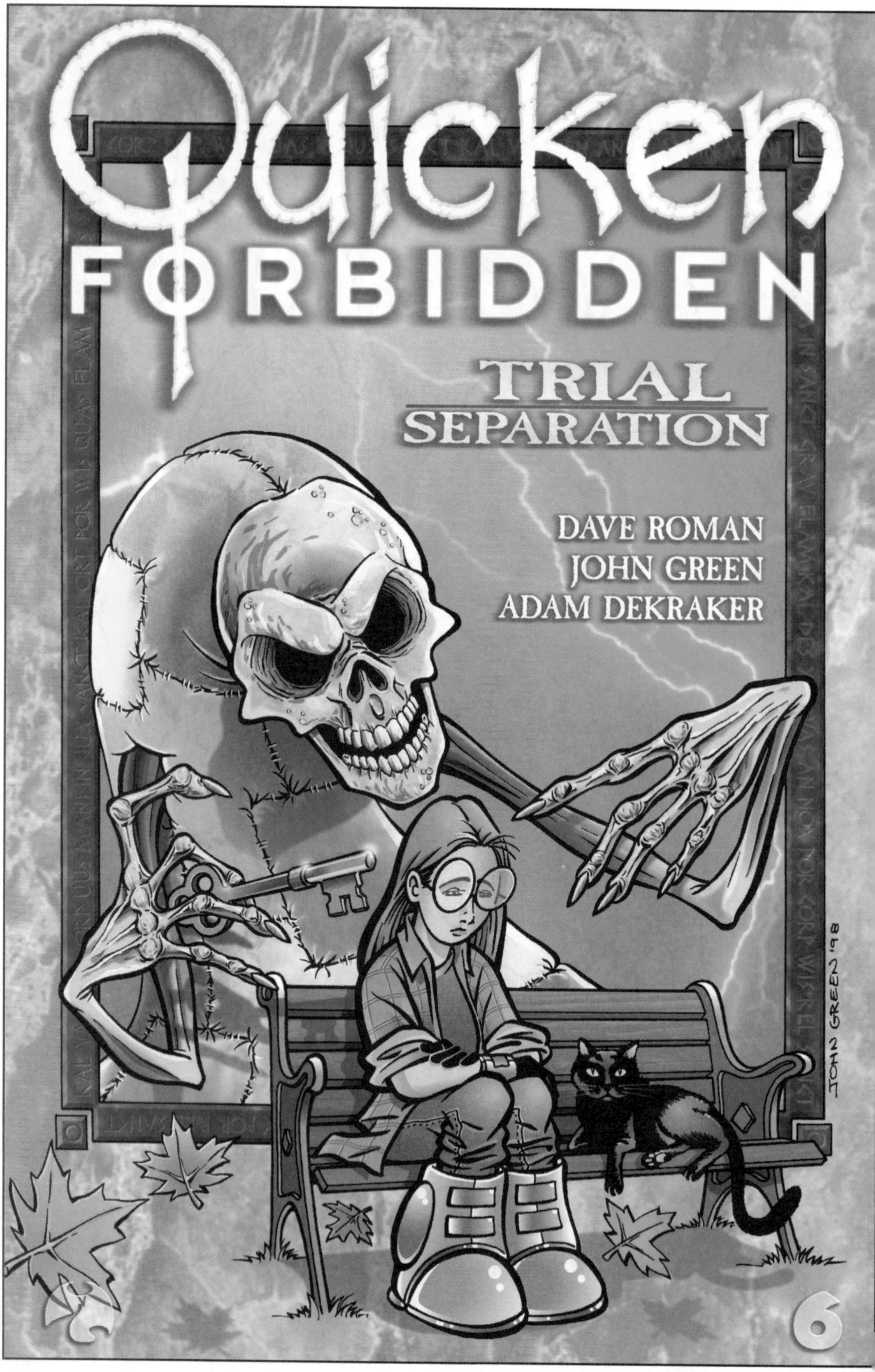
Quicken
FORBIDDEN
TRIAL
SEPARATION
DAVE ROMAN
JOHN GREEN
ADAM DEKRAKER
JOHN GREEN '98
6

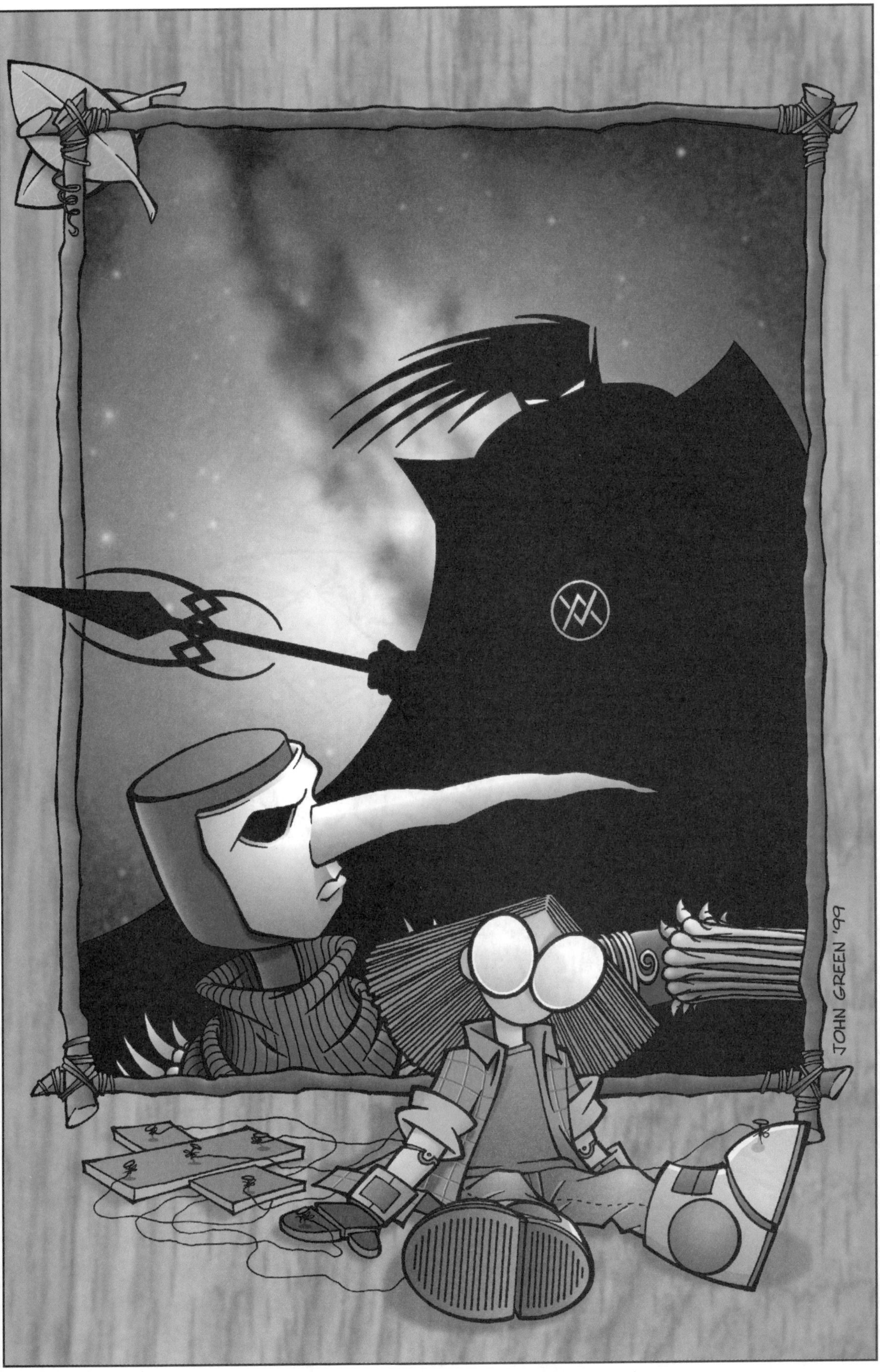
JOHN GREEN '99

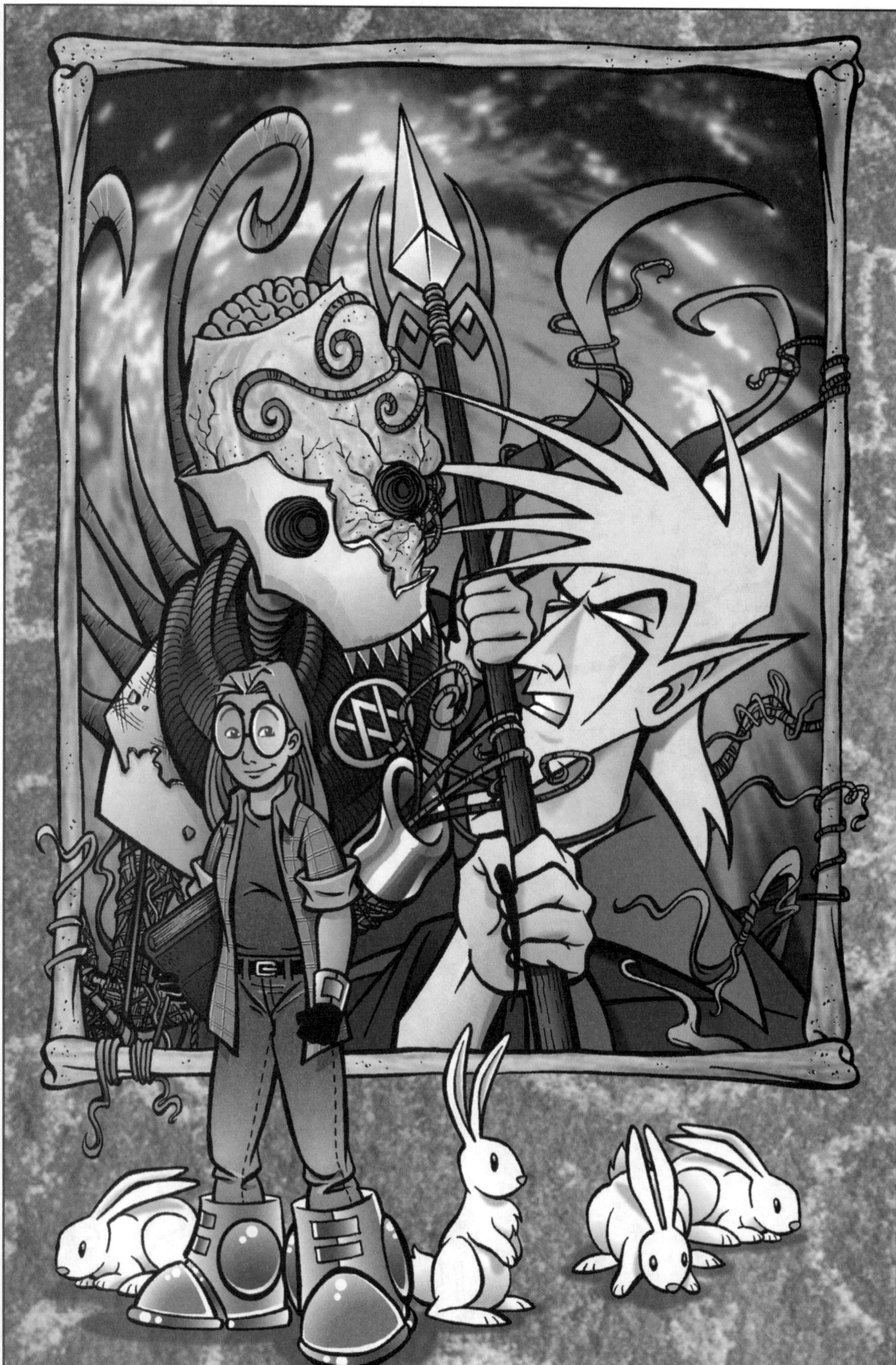

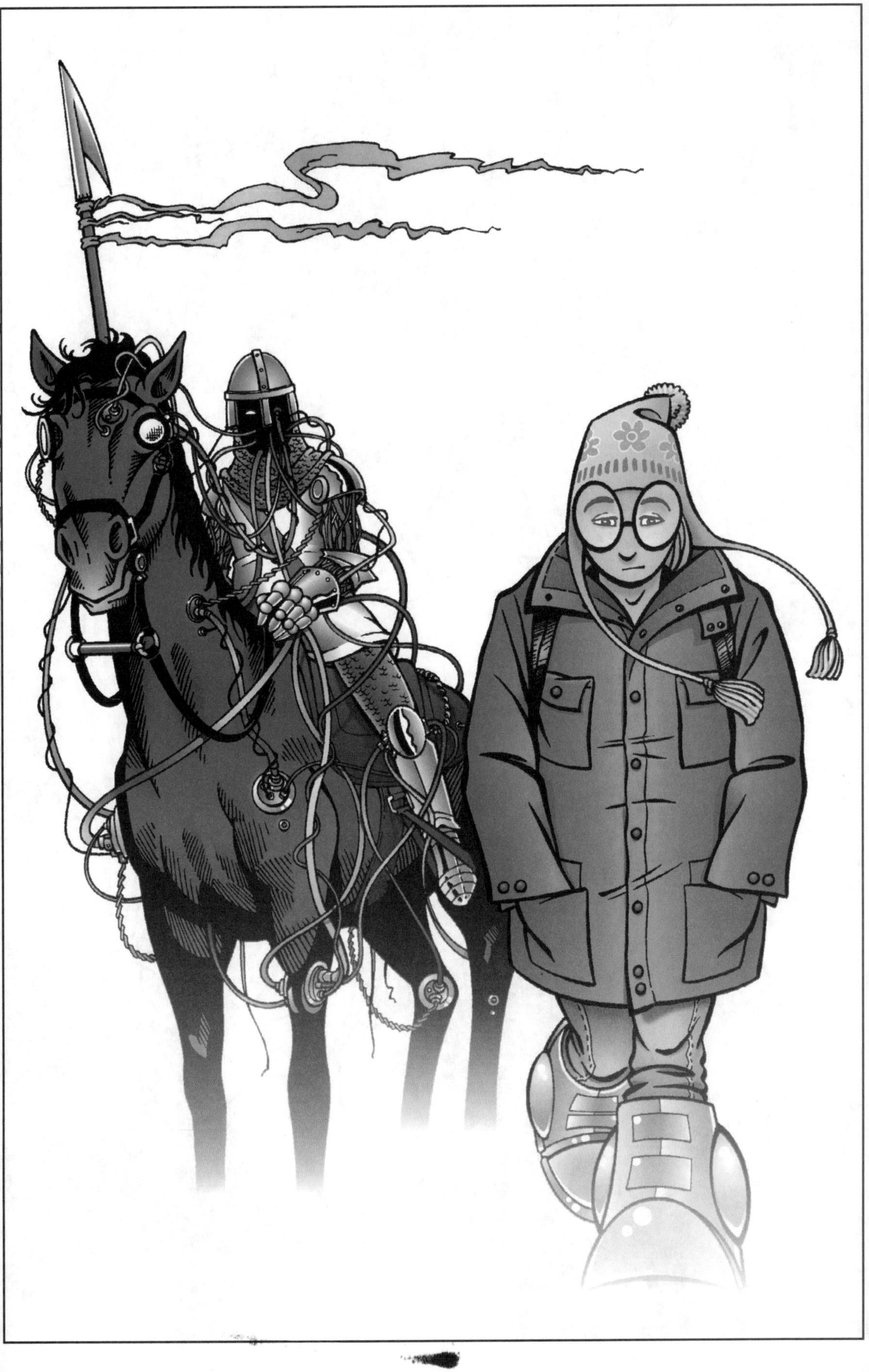

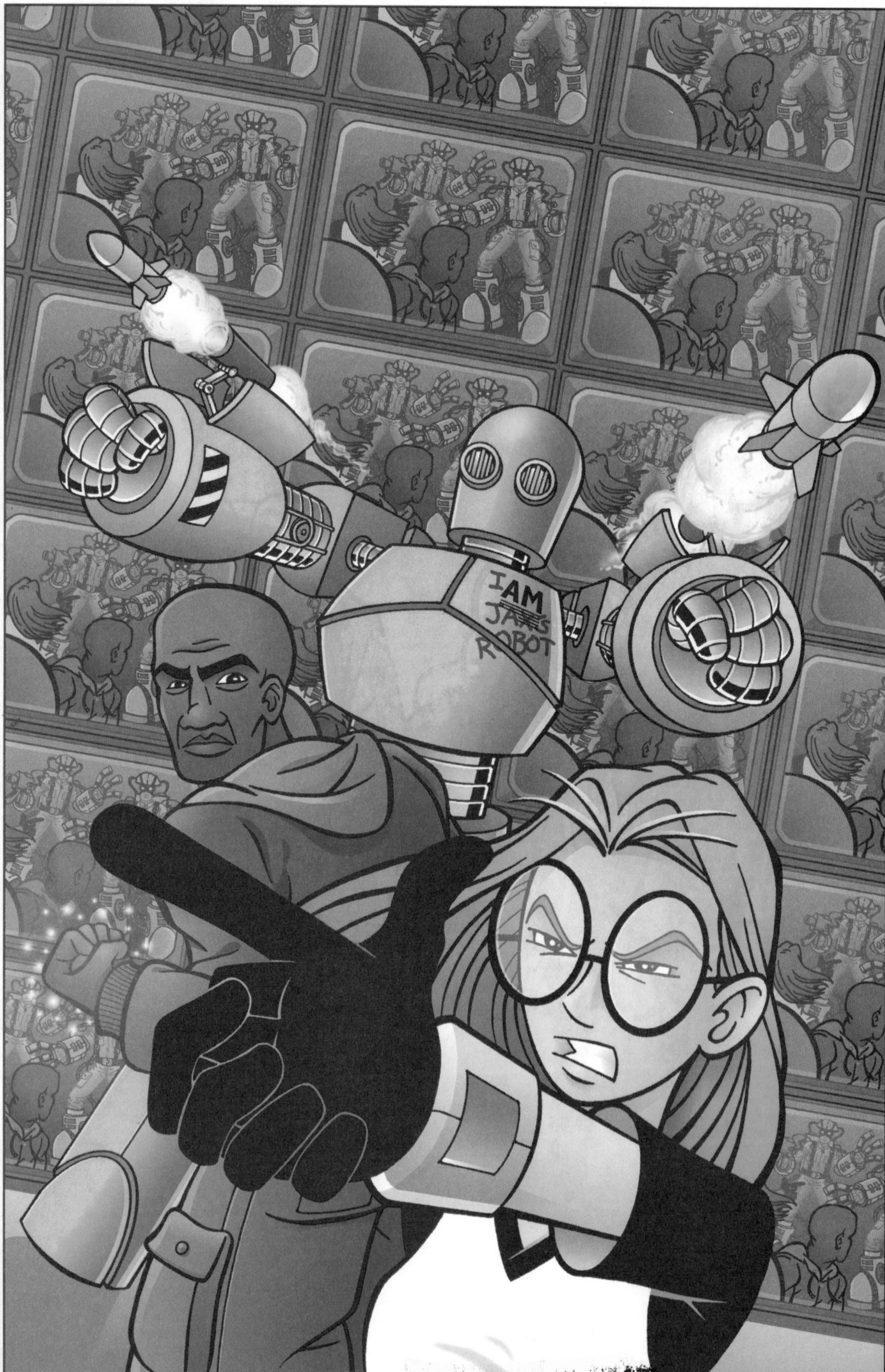
I AM
JAX'S
ROBOT